W9-AHA-649

Leaving South Carolina

RICHARD PAWLEY

Bloomington, IN Milton Keynes, UK

authorHOUSE™

AuthorHouse™
1663 Liberty Drive, Suite 200
Bloomington, IN 47403
www.authorhouse.com
Phone: 1-800-839-8640

AuthorHouse™ UK Ltd.
500 Avebury Boulevard
Central Milton Keynes, MK9 2BE
www.authorhouse.co.uk
Phone: 08001974150

This book is a work of non-fiction. Unless otherwise noted, the author and the publisher make no explicit guarantees as to the accuracy of the information contained in this book and in some cases, names of people and places have been altered to protect their privacy.

© 2006 Richard Pawley. All rights reserved.

No part of this book may be reproduced, stored in a retrieval system, or transmitted by any means without the written permission of the author.

First published by AuthorHouse 8/31/2006

ISBN: 1-4259-3871-X (sc)
ISBN: 1-4259-3872-8 (dj)

Library of Congress Control Number: 2006904425

Printed in the United States of America
Bloomington, Indiana

This book is printed on acid-free paper.

Disclaimer

This is the story of my life, some of the interesting experiences I have had, and some of the wonderful people I've met and known. I have been free with my opinions on a number of topics in this book. Consequently, just to be sure, and not to unintentionally break any laws, I must say that I am not a registered investment counselor or financial advisor nor am I a doctor. If any of the things I share in this book seem reasonable or good to you please check with your minister or rabbi, doctor or lawyer, investment counselor, or anyone else you feel is smarter than you to make sure you are not making a mistake or being misled. This book, while as accurate as I know how to make it, contains my own opinions, understandings, conclusions, and the way I see things. It is some of what I remember, have experienced, and what I believe. Others may well see things differently and that is still their right. I believe that many of the rights we take for granted in this country may change in the near future, unless, as Goldie Hawn said in the movie Protocol, words to the effect that we had better be watching very carefully what is going on in Washington. When even the President of the United States has not been told what the bureaucracy is doing (I'm thinking of the planned take-over of our ports by a company owned by a foreign government, which almost happened) then our government is simply too big. I have read that one out of every seven employed people in the United States works for government at some level or in some capacity. Look at the recent passing of HR4167 in the House of Representatives, a law that would eliminate all the protections that many states have passed to protect their citizens from contaminants in our food supply, in lieu of an all encompassing generic watered-down "Federal Law" that would assure we don't know what is in our food or how it is processed or what eating it might do to us. More than two thirds of the State Attorney Generals in all 50 states have opposed this law which was passed without hearings from the public who are starting to catch on that the quality of our food, while some of the cheapest in the world, is not the quality it could be and may, over time, be a contributing factor in many diseases and illnesses. The House did pass an amendment allowing states to continue to warn about mercury in some farm raised fish but DEFEATED A PROPOSAL THAT WOULD LET STATES KEEP LAWS THAT WARN CONSUMERS ABOUT EXPOSURES TO SUBSTANCES THAT MIGHT CAUSE BIRTH DEFECTS, REPRODUCTIVE HEALTH PROBLEMS OR EVEN CANCER! The Food Industry has contributed over $30 million dollars to Congress in the last few years. Let us hope and pray they do not get their way and that HR4167 does not pass the Senate. There is a reason why people live longer in many other countries than they do in the USA and why many industrialized countries will not allow us to sell them our meats and grains. It is more than just politics. This book has only a tiny bit about nutrition in it but this law is so dangerous I had to mention it here. It is not unlike the 55 mph speed limit that Congress passed years ago and then had to rescind except that this law is much more dangerous. My hope is that you will continue to become informed on what is happening all around you and what is going to happen as a result of that which has already taken place. If this law fails to pass this year, watch out for next year or the year after that! If we could see just ten years into the future we would all be astounded. In any event you are still responsible for your own decisions if you take any of the suggestions I have written about here. That said, I hope you enjoy reading this book and that you get something out of it other than just a couple of hours of entertainment. It could change your life, financially, spiritually, or both.

Dedicated to all those who have helped make this journey worthwhile. To my mother who taught me much of what I know and who instilled in me the determination to never give up, no matter what. To my wife, Sharon, who put up with revision after revision (this is the first book I ever actually finished). To all my friends, for what would life be with out friends? Special thanks to Peter George for sharing his knowledge of pebble bed technology. Dum Spiro Spero.

Table of Contents

1. Arriving in South Carolina

Maybe it was the roar of the engines or perhaps the sharp bullet-like sound of an engine backfiring but for some reason I turned around to look at the gleaming silver aircraft in which I had just arrived. It was a huge Douglas DC-6, Eastern Airlines, if I remember correctly. Just moments before, I had stepped off the craft and set foot, for the very first time in my life, in sunny South Carolina. It was December 1950 and I was seven years old. It would be three years before I would leave South Carolina, the first time, and I would leave many times.

I had arrived just a few months after the first Southern 500 stock car race was held in Darlington on September 4, 1950, and for more than half a century it was a Labor Day tradition until the race itself left South Carolina and moved out west for a new televised nighttime showcase. For many South Carolinians Labor Day will never be the same, as this sport, which originated in the Carolinas with bootlegger's transporting their moonshine and outrunning (or trying to) the revenuers of the day, moved on to greener pastures, bigger crowds, and more money.

Moving to a new place can be exciting for adults. For children it can be a wondrous experience akin to fantasy games of exploration. Columbia, the capital of South Carolina, was about as bustling a city as a laidback southern city could be at mid-century before shopping malls and Inter-state highways. The widest street in Columbia was not Main Street, but one block west of Main, Assembly Street.Here the farmers assembled to sell their produce though not long after I arrived in Columbia they moved to a new "farmer's market" a few miles south of the capitol. I remember an old ornate water fountain in the center of the north end of the widest part of Assembly Street where horses could stop for a drink as they carried their owner's produce to the stalls for the daily sale of fresh fruits and vegetables. Of course, by the time I arrived, most of the farmers had old Ford or Chevy pick-up trucks and I cannot say for sure if I ever saw any of the horse drawn wagons.

My dad had rented a house for us to stay in but he had not actually seen the house and it was not ready when we arrived. The owner of the house lived in Charleston where dad eventually became the Art Superintendent for the Charleston County Public School System (he was responsible for some ninety schools and art teachers). Dad had not met the owner either as she handled the renting of her small building through a local real estate agency. Dad was told that the house had three bedrooms but the agency was counting a screened-in back porch as a bedroom. The landlady in Charleston was told that the house had been rented to a nice couple with one child. The truth was that the nice couple did have one child (on the way) but they also had four other children, including me. I was the oldest.

My dad, Hans Anton Pawley, grew up in Iowa where the winters are laden with so much snow that cross-country skiing has become a major sport. In South Carolina, however, in the Midlands section, and even more so in the Piedmont, a good snow of several inches is a once-in-a-decade phenomenon. The winter dad spent in training at the beginning of WWII at Camp Jackson east of Columbia was apparently one in which no snow fell and dad made up his mind that if he survived the war that South Carolina would become his permanent home. Then he was single. Now, less than a decade later he had a wife and four boys. Dad had one younger brother, Eddie, who settled in Seattle, Washington, after the Great War and we never saw him again after that although the family wrote occasionally, almost a lost art in today's world of instant messaging and truly inexpensive long distance telephone rates (I remember placing a ten minute call to my friend Sabine in France in the 1960's and it cost me more than 5 hours pay to do so at the time). Uncle Eddie used his grandfather's name of Pawlak and worked for more than 40 years for the Boeing Aircraft Company in Seattle. Many years later when my nephew Jason Pawley graduated from the Navy Academy in Annapolis, Maryland, his roommate at the time was dating a girl from the west coast, Washington State in fact. He later married her. That girl was my uncle's granddaughter.

For my immediate families first two weeks in South Carolina we actually lived in one of the gallery rooms in the Columbia Museum of Art at 1501 Senate Street. I can remember, somewhat in awe, the large paintings and sculptures, and playing on the grounds of the museum. The beds were aligned, army style, in a row, in the Chinese Room. For our first two weeks in Columbia that darkened room (or so it seemed to me) was home. The building, a huge mansion, is still there, but now it is part of the University of South Carolina, Division of Law Enforcement and Safety. I vaguely remember a kitchen somewhere in the back of the museum, which had undoubtedly once been a fine estate in an earlier era. That red brick building was the museum for over half a century until a new modern multistory building was built in the late 1990's.

Our rented home on Pickens Street was finally ready, not quite adequate for our needs but better than the room at the museum.Our little house was not on the prairie like the popular books and TV series but on the left side of one of the steepest hills in Columbia. It was a single story white house long since torn down to make room for the ever-growing University of South Carolina, over a 165 buildings at last count. Across the street from out little cabin-like home was a vacant wooded property that, even then, belonged to the university and today is a little park.

The house was a rather ordinary house. Nothing in particular set it apart from any other small wood frame house except for the concrete porch and that only stood out because a driver lost control of his automobile on the steep hill and crashed into our porch. Since most cabin-like wooden houses don't have solid concrete porches I can only surmise that the owner had had to replace the porch at least once previously and chose concrete as a more durable solution. It was good for us that she had done so or more than one of us could have been killed or seriously injured. The solid concrete kept the vehicle from flying into our living room. Quite a few other accidents happened on that steep hill but most of those vehicles crashed into the fence surrounding the university's property across the street.

Dad's title at the museum was that of Art Director. He was not the Director. That position belonged to Dr. John Richard Craft. How my dad met Dr. Craft, "Jack" to his friends, and how he met my mother, was all tied together in what some might call a cosmic coincidence. Some might say it was fate. I see it as Divine Providence.

It was in the beginning of WWII and dad had been on maneuvers in central Florida and had been involved in a march of some thirty miles. Most of the soldiers were from cooler northern climates and were collapsing under the weight of their backpacks and the relentless Florida sunshine. My dad was no exception. The heat was unbearable and apparently, everyone's water supply was exhausted. Few soldiers were left in the march when dad spotted a chained gang of convicts working on a road, which the men had just crossed. Quickly breaking rank dad ran to a large wooded wagon that car-

ried a huge barrel of water for the convicts. Dad filled his canteen
and the rest of the soldiers quickly followed suit. Consequently,
dad was one of the few who completed the march and he and the
others who had succeeded in the grueling undertaking were given a
three-day pass. When it came time to use the pass the first bus dad
saw was going to St. Augustine, and although he had no idea where
that was, he just "knew" that it had to be better than where he was
in tiny Ocala.

St. Augustine! He even liked the sound of the name. Arriving
there after a few hours dad just happened to meet an artist who
was impressed with dad's enthusiasm and this artist let dad use his
studio for the weekend. Clay, plaster, and tools were all available
and dad enjoyed creating a piece of artwork. Some time later one
of the officers in dad's unit was transferred to New York and when
he went, he took with him that piece of artwork and delivered it to
the museum, the Metropolitan I think, that was sponsoring a national contest for artwork created by members of the armed forces.
Four weeks later dad was notified that he had won first prize and he
received a check for $50.Since his monthly income was only $20,
this was a hefty sum. At the time dad was recovering from food
poisoning having purchased a loaf of bread and a can of apparently
"very old" sardines from an even older country store. The store had
looked as if it had dated back to the Civil War (known affectionately
as The War Between The States to all South Carolinians and other
southerners). Dad's illness was so intense that he concluded that
the sardines must have been that old too, although he did not notice
anything unusual about their taste or smell when he ate them. In
the same Florida hospital in which my future dad was recovering,
my future mom was visiting her brother Bert who was not recovering very well from an appendicitis operation. Although dad felt
well enough to return to duty, the army insisted that he recuperate
fully and to pass the time (two weeks) dad painted murals on the
walls of the recreation room in the hospital. When dad received
the notification that he had won first prize in a national contest and
along with the notification a check for two and a half months salary
dad practically ran to the recreation hall to tell the director. The
hall director was talking with the pretty young woman who was to
become my future mom and he introduced her to my future dad.
Something clicked and after a couple of hours of conversation, addresses were exchanged. Soon thereafter mom returned to Rhode
Island. The two of them corresponded frequently and during that

time dad received a "permanent" assignment to North Carolina at an underground clearinghouse for coastal defense. Together with a member of the air corps, the navy, and a civilian defense person, all movements, on, under, and above the ocean were tracked. It was a plush duty assignment and dad lived in a nice hotel and ate his meals there. He invited my future mom to come and visit him there in Wilmington, N.C. It was their first date. She did and they were married the weekend she arrived. The following Monday dad learned how "permanent" his assignment was when he received orders transferring him to Texas. They were both tremendously disappointed. Mom returned temporarily to Rhode Island and dad shipped out to Texas. Today such trips are only a few hours by jet but commercial jets had not yet been invented so the journey for both of them was measured in days by railroad travel. Commercial airlines existed using propeller-driven aircraft and carried passengers to major cities but the cost was prohibitive to ordinary people.

Before dad's assignment in coastal defense at Wilmington, he had applied for every interesting position that had come along but he had received no response on any of his applications. Now, when he was newly married and quite content to stay where he was, at least for a while, he was being moved, alone, to Texas. When dad complained of the irony of it to his commanding officer, the colonel pointed to a large brown envelope containing all of dad's applications, none of which had been forwarded. "We have something that was tailor made for you," dad was told but the colonel was quite secretive and would say no more.

Dad had first come under the eye of the regimental colonel on maneuvers in or near a large southern swamp. Dad had spotted a huge cypress tree that had fallen long ago, perhaps the victim of a tornado. It had been quite a tree but now what was left of it was covered in moss. Dad began hacking away at it and after removing an inch or two of decaying matter found good solid wood underneath. Ever the artist he was busy hacking away when the colonel drove by, saw him working, and ordered his driver to stop the jeep. "What in Sam hill are you doing?" the colonel asked. "Sir, I understand that we have a regimental insignia but I have never seen a copy of it or even a photograph so I finally decided to carve a phoenix bird myself." "With an axe?" the colonel asked somewhat incredulously. "It's the only tool I have," dad replied. "Come with me," the colonel commanded. Dad got into the jeep and they drove out of the swamp to the first farm they came across. The colonel asked the farmer if he knew anyone who had some carving tools. "My neighbor has a lathe and all kinds of chisels," the farmer replied. They drove to the next farm, explained the problem to the farmer, and dad said that a one inch chisel would be ideal. The farmer went and got a one-inch lathe chisel which was thicker than a carving chisel and dad volunteered that he could grind it down to where it could be used for carving. "I've got a grinder right over there," the farmer replied as he pointed in the direction of a foot-powered grinder. Dad took the chisel and ground it down on the grinder until it was suitable for artistic carving. The colonel offered to pay the farmer for the chisel but the farmer refused, saying, "let it be my contribution to a good cause."

For the next several weeks dad used that chisel and all his spare time to carve a phoenix bird. The regimental insignia arose not from the burning ashes but from dad's creative hand and a decaying log. When the colonel next saw the bird, it was complete. Forgetting all about the scheduled inspection (probably as an intentional reward) the colonel exclaimed, "That must go in my office. I'll have a glass cage built for it."That was the end of dad's phoenix bird. It was this colonel, however, who recommended dad for the special assignment in Texas.

In Texas, dad's commanding officer was a general and dad told me once that the general had a cousin by the same name who was also a general but in the Nazi army of Germany. "He was not a Hitler man," dad said. Although I did not have the time nor the inclination to verify what dad had told me I accepted it at face value because I had often heard of the two brothers who came to America and wined and dined the major bankers of America in 1912 and in the year that dad was born in Germany (1913) and while most con-gressmen were home on their Christmas vacation, congress abdi-cated it's congressional duty to oversea the issuance of money and voted into existence a new privately owned corporation called the Federal Reserve Bank to do that for them. One brother helped establish the Federal Reserve Bank in the United States while the other brother headed its German counterpart. Soon both brothers were getting richer while the two Federal Reserve banks were loan-ing money to their two respective countries, which were soon at war with each other in World War 1. Of course, since we were no longer issuing our own United States Notes, which were interest free, the government had to pay interest to the new mostly European owned Federal Reserve Bank and to do that the Internal Revenue Service was established to collect income tax to pay that interest. Life is filled with such irony's or coincidences. United States Notes continued to be issued sporadically along with silver certificates. Once when I was in high school I had three $5 bills in my wallet and I remember noticing that one was a blue certificate (silver certificate), one was a red certificate (U.S. note) and one was the typically green Federal Reserve Note, although that too has been eliminated on all but the one dollar bill and replaced with an all-encompassing black seal of the Federal Reserve. I even heard one conspiracy theorist claim that the real reason that President John F. Kennedy was assassinated was because he dared to issue over two billion dollars in U.S. notes, the last president to do so, and this was money on which the owners of the Federal Reserve could not collect interest. A good novelist could make quite a story out this and couple it with the aircraft accident that the late president's son had after saying that with his money and prestige he would find out the truth of what really happened to his father. "The truth is out there," as Fox Mulder of the hit TV show "The X-Files" would say.

In any event, when the general in Texas told those assembled of a new cooking school that had just been established and then called dad's name as one of those chosen to attend, dad was sure there was some mistake. "There is no mistake," the general told him. "You have been chosen because of your unique qualifications. We are starting a top-notch baking and cooking school." Dad was astounded. "Sir," he replied, "I don't know a thing about cooking and baking." "That's why we selected you," the general replied half facetiously, and then he whispered into dad's ear, "It's a camouflage for a military intelligence school." Dad had been selected to attend the first class in a new school for the army. He may not have had any experience with cooking but he did have one unique talent. Although he had been born in Hamburg, Germany, he had moved to the United States before he was 8 years old and spoke English like an American and German like a German with no trace of accent in either language. After completing the school dad was chosen as an instructor. Mom rejoined him and for their first month in Texas they survived on dad's meager salary of $20. Their apartment cost them $15 per month and that left just $5 for food. The water was undrinkable where they lived so all of that $5 along with some of their meager savings went for red wine and popcorn, two of the cheapest things that could keep one alive.Dad was soon promoted and with promotions go raises so they did not have to "rough it" for to long. The school was eventually moved to a secret underground location near the Maryland Pennsylvania border. Although they lived in Maryland, the nearest hospital was across the border in Pennsylvania and so I was born in a northern state and therefore I am technically a "Yankee" although I have always considered myself a South Carolinian, having been raised there from the age of seven.

It was while stationed in Maryland that dad heard of an art exhibit in the Hagerstown Museum and he made up his mind to check it out. The museum's director was Dr. John Richard Craft, who upon meeting dad told him that his name sounded familiar. It turned out that "Jack" Craft had been the judge that selected dad's artwork in the national contest that had been held in New York City almost two years previously.

A few years after the war "Jack" Craft offered dad the position of Art Director at the Columbia Museum of Art and that is why we left Virginia and moved to South Carolina. This reminds me of a joke I once heard in South Carolina. It seems that there was once a Godly gentleman who was born and raised in Virginia and then attended college and seminary in North Carolina where he served his first pastorium. Later he was transferred to South Carolina where he had a long and distinguished career serving in several towns and cities. Finally he died and after he was in "the third Heaven" (see St. Paul in the New Testament) he ran into St. Peter who asked this former minister of the Gospel if Heaven met with his expectations. "Well, to tell you the truth (and that's all you can do in Heaven) the change was so gradual that I hardly noticed."

Both my dad and Dr. Craft were strong willed and independent men and their relationship did not last long. Dad and Dr. Craft parted ways but Dr. Craft's wife, Marjorie Craft, always "Bunny" to me, remained my mother's friend and was sort of a lifelong Godmother to me. She paid my way to summer camp when I was eight years old although I did not know this until many years later.

Bunny came from an aristocratic Long Island, New York, family. Once when Bunny's mother was down from New York visiting she took my mother to see a movie. No such thing as a shopping mall yet existed in South Carolina and all the theaters were located on Main Street. My first job other than baby-sitter and paperboy was as an usher at one of those Main Street theaters. There may still be theaters in this country that have ushers who help patrons find seats but I have not been in one in decades.

Bunny's mom had taken my mom to see the latest blockbuster, "The Ten Commandments," with Charlton Heston as Moses. The line of people waiting to purchase tickets stretched around the block, and that, I have always supposed, was why such movies were called "blockbusters." Mom expressed some words of dismay at how long they would have to wait in line and Bunny's mom said something to the effect of, "Don't worry, just follow me." They walked past hundreds of movie patrons to the head of the line.Getting the attention of the person selling tickets this not very tall lady who was perhaps seventy said, "I demand to see the manager. Would you please get him for me?" The firmness in her voice commanded action and the manager soon appeared. "How may I help you?" he asked. "I'm a little old lady and I'm over sixty years old and I don't think I should have to wait in this very long line for tickets." "No, mame" the much younger manager agreed, whereupon he had the ticket seller sell them two tickets and he personally escorted them into the theater ahead of hundreds of others still waiting in line. While they were walking into the theater Bunny's mom leaned over and whispered into my mom's ear, "this works every time."

I do not have many memories from my days on Pickens Street: Bunny visiting us was one and mom making sandwiches for the hobo's who road the trains more for adventure than for necessity was another. Our home then was the second house up from Blossom Street in the good section. The railroad tracks were well over 500 feet away and Maxcy Gregg Park and Pool, a park with a public swimming pool that was for whites only, was between the tracks and our small house. That park was closed for a while when integration became the law of the land years later. Of course, it later reopened when integration did not cause the world to end.

We had a private nurse for a while, a black woman name Leola, and once a week a handyman named Henry who helped with various tasks around the house and who always said grace before eating his lunch.I remember that we paid Leola $40 per week and that seemed like a fortune to me. My allowance was not yet a quarter. I had a severe case of measles and I remember the hallucinations I had because of the disease. I've never studied measles and I have not read that they can affect the brain as well as the skin but I know from experience that they can. My younger brothers had the disease as well. Perhaps that is why we had the nurse. Of course, at the time, mom was pregnant with my sister Mary, still a Columbia resident.

My dad had always wanted a daughter. I was the first born so when he was told that mom was going to have a second child he figured that he had a 50-50 chance of getting a girl. I do not remember much from the biology course I took in high school where we studied Mendel's work on genetics but I don't think it quite works like that. My brother Bill, also a lifelong Columbia resident, except for the years he served in Vietnam, was born while mom was visiting her parents in Rhode Island. When Mike, another Columbia resident, was born in West Virginia, dad was still hoping for a girl. I remember hearing that when dad found out he was going to be the father of four he said something like, "It will probably be another boy." The statement was prophetic because number four, Francis, was born in Hampton, Virginia.

I started elementary school in Hampton and can remember going with my dad, a bushel basket and a rake, and gathering our supper from Hampton Roads, where the James River flows into the Chesapeake Bay. The waterfront was just two blocks away from our home on Greenbriar Avenue. We would watch the sandy bottom carefully, as the tide went out, for the telltale sign of clams, a little spurt of water into the air and then the quickly disappearing hole from whence it came. We would rake them up as fast as we could from their hiding places and soon we had as many clams as we could carry. With melted butter and some of mom's freshly baked homemade bread, this was supper on more than one occasion. It was delicious.

Actually, we never used butter. What we did use consumers today would find very strange. Of course, the term "consumers" would have sounded quite strange back then, to similar to what Hitler called retired people, "useless eaters."

What we used, of course, was margarine, but it was not anything similar to the convenient yellow margarine that comes four quarters to the pound and can be purchased in any grocery store today. In fact, it was illegal to sell yellow margarine. When I was a kid margarine came in one pound plastic pouches and it was white as pure snow. The dairy industry said that they were "afraid" that people would "confuse" yellow margarine with butter so a law was passed that prohibited yellow margarine from being sold (sort of like the laws they tried to pass prohibiting Soy Milk from being called milk). There was no objection to margarine being colored after it was purchased so at one corner of the pouch of the very unappetizing but inexpensive white margarine was a yellow "button" about the size of one of today's M&M candies. This contained the food coloring. It was a hands-on experience to pop the "button" within the bag and to mash and squeeze and move the color around until there was one pound of somewhat normal looking yellow looking margarine. I don't remember when this nonsense ended but as a five or six year old, it was one of my responsibilities to make the margarine yellow. Of course, at five or six, it was a fun thing to do.

I was seven years old when I left Hampton, Virginia, for Columbia, and in my thirties when I saw Greenbriar Avenue again. The stately mansions along the shore had fallen into disarray and badly needed upkeep but there were a few other things that really stood out on that visit. The large two-story house that I thought I had lived in turned out to be the smallest two-story house I had ever seen. The other surprise was the scull and crossbones signs in the water where we used to clam. By the time I was in my thirties, the waters had become so polluted that the clams had become poisonous. Gone were the large ferryboats that took cars and trucks and buses across the James River to Norfolk. I had ridden on them occasionally. The ferryboats had been replaced by a more modern bridge and tunnel.

I don't know if it was the weather in South Carolina, mild winters and hot summers, something in the water, or perhaps something not in the water (minerals) but after we moved to South Carolina, my dad finally got his wish. Mom had four more children. They were all girls.

While living on Pickens Street I was enrolled in the second grade at St. Peter's Grammar School where I continued through the fifth grade, spent two years at St. Joseph's Grammar School and then returned to graduate from St. Peters in the eighth grade. One of my classmates at both schools was Jean Hoefer (Toal), South Carolina's Chief Justice of the State Supreme Court. Jean was also the first woman to sit as a justice on the State Supreme Court. She was an excellent student, always first academically. I was usually second in the class and never learned how to study properly. I can remember the nuns telling me that if I studied I could be like Jean but since I could read and write before I even started the first grade and with no accelerated classes of any kind, I was so bored for so many years that school itself became just another chore. I was not challenged until I hit subjects like algebra and Latin, and because I had never developed any study habits, much less good ones, I had a difficult time and barely passed some of the courses. When Jean was gradu-

ated from law school in 1968, South Carolina had less than a dozen
lawyers who were women. Today there are well over 2,500. One of
those (and a friend of Jeans), Barbara Pearce O'Hanesian, has been
a dear friend of mine for more than 35 years.

In 1999, I was reading in the USA TODAY that Jean had been selected to be chief justice so I wrote a letter to South Carolina's largest
newspaper, THE STATE, about a favorite memory of mine from the
seventh grade. That letter appeared in THE STATE on Thursday,
April 8, 1999. In it, I wrote of something that always impressed me
about Jean and which I thought she might have forgotten. I also
thought that others might find it interesting too. Even today I can
hardly believe that it was half a century ago when we were students
in the same class at St. Joseph's Elementary School in Columbia. I
can remember it like it was last year.

We were both in the seventh grade and Sister Phillips who was
not only our teacher but also the principal had left the room on a
short errand. She had not been gone long when one of the boys held
up a live snake about a foot and a half long and when everyone had
seen it he let it loose on the floor. Well, you can imagine what happened. Girls were shrieking and boys were running around. Then I
noticed that one of the students, a girl in front of me, got up and quietly walked up to the where the snake was slithering across the floor.
After picking it up and looking at it for a few seconds she said, "It's
only a snake!" and then she tossed it outside. That student became
the new chief justice of the South Carolina Supreme Court.

Jean had not forgotten this incident and not long after the letter
appeared in print, Jean wrote me a very gracious letter thanking me
for reminding her and others around the state of those simpler by
gone days.Of course, when you are growing up, it never occurs to
you that these will someday be the "good old days."

One of my mother's favorite stories is how I complained to her
when I was in the seventh grade that Jean was the teachers pet.
Concerned that perhaps I was not being treated fairly she questioned me on just why I thought that Jean was the teachers pet. "I
just can't figure it out," I told her. "Jean always does twice as much
work as she's asked to do and she always turns in her assignments
before everyone else but other than that I just don't know."

Ah, youth!

We didn't stay on Pickens Street very long. Dad had signed a
lease and the agency was making him stick to it although he had
found a bigger place and a better opportunity. However, the owner

of the house was in Columbia one day and she dropped by to meet her tenants. I was the first to greet her and then my mom who was obviously pregnant came to the door. That was OK, but when Bill, Mike and Francis followed, the poor woman almost had a stroke. When mom told her of the opportunity that had been presented to my dad and how we had a bigger place waiting for us but the agency wouldn't let us out of the lease, well the woman must have still been a bit stunned at the size of our family when she had been expecting a "nice couple with one child." As the details of what mom had said sank through to her consciousness the woman finally said, "Oh, you want to move?" "Yes," mom answered. "Well, that won't be a problem. I'll talk to the rental agency you can be sure." We had no problem moving after that.

A new life in the country awaited me.

I was eight years old when the family moved from Pickens Street but I wasn't even there at the time. I was attending summer camp for two weeks at Camp St. Mary's near Ridgeland, S.C. This was a camp primarily for Catholic kids who went to public schools and got very little spiritual education (today, of course, they get none in the public schools so fearful are we of offending the Muslims or the Atheists or the Hottentots). Campers at Camp St. Mary would attend religion classes for part of the day and the rest of the day was devoted to typical camp activities. For two weeks, the camp was open, for a fee, to those who attended Catholic schools, and who supposedly did not need the religion classes.

The ocean was supposed to be just a ways down the river and although I never got as far as the bend in the river in one of the rowboats, we all knew it to be true because the water was salty and frequented by porpoises and blue-shell crabs and other typical salt-water creatures. I distinctly remember being stunned to see my first live shrimp swimming in the water. To me it looked like a miniature alien from one of my science fiction comic books, not at all like the shrimp I enjoyed eating. Someone must have told me what it was because I had no idea.

While at camp, I received a letter from my mom telling me that the family would be moving before I returned to Columbia. I was somewhat between surprised and astounded. Although mom told me that she would meet me at the bus station when I returned I wondered what would happen if she did not. Mom did not drive and we did not even own a car. All sorts of possibilities entered my mind. Although it would be a good walk for an eight year old I figured I could find my way to the house on Pickens Street if mom didn't meet me, but what good would that be if we didn't live there anymore?

I arrived back in Columbia with some trepidation, got off the bus, and walked into the bus station. I looked around at all the people coming and going and was greatly relieved to see mom in the crowd, that is until I walked over towards her. I was looking up at her and was about to say something when she looked down at me and then turned away to look in another direction as she walked on past me. It was the strangest look I had ever seen on her face. It was as if I was as invisible as the map on the back of the Declaration of Independence in the Walt Disney movie "NATIONAL TREASURE"."Mom!" I cried out. Although she did not recognize me at first, she instantly recognized my voice. I was greatly relieved to see a smile appear on her face. Two weeks in the coastal South Carolina summer sun had bleached my hair blond beyond her recognition.

My dad's new opportunity was at the Opportunity School in West Columbia. I had never lived in the country before and in 1951, this was definitely the country. The school itself was within walking distance of the Columbia airport where I had first set foot in South Carolina the previous year. Dad was an art teacher for three years at this most unusual school. The Opportunity School had been founded by Dr. Wil Lou Gray as a school for adults who never finished high school. She had begun teaching even before my dad was born in 1913. In 1947, the school acquired a former WWII Army hospital and converted that into a high school campus for adult students. In the days before GED (General Educational Development) tests adults would come and live there as they worked towards completing the requirements for a high school diploma. Their most famous student did not come until years after dad had left. Glenn W. Turner, a former sharecropper with a cleft pallet and a third grade education, attended for a while but left to seek his fortune elsewhere. He once earned $100 million dollars in twenty four months and in the late 1960's that was worth a great deal more than a $100 million is today (back then a brand new 3 bedroom brick house only cost about $20,000). Even earlier than that Glenn W. Turner had donated a trust fund to the Opportunity School to update the antiquated buildings that by that time had begun to look a little frazzled around the edges. Most military buildings during WWII were built on a temporary basis and some across the country saw decades of use beyond their intended life span.

The Opportunity School was a new experience for me in another way because for the first time my parents purchased a large freezer and dad planted a huge garden. This meant chores after school like weeding and picking beans and corn and squash. We had strawberries, cucumbers, cantaloupes, watermelons, and probably a few things I have forgotten. Okra just came to mind. We grew a good portion of our own food supply and what we didn't grow we purchased from a well known wholesaler, Pearce, Young, and Angel, Inc. in such large quantities that they never caught on that Pawley and Company was really the Pawley family and whatever company we had visiting.I especially remember 100-pound barrels of Tide soap but we purchased foodstuffs as well.

Considering how little money my folks had to work with they did amazingly well.

I raised a few rabbits although I don't remember why. I never ate one but I did have a number of chickens that I had raised from chicks and we did get a few fresh eggs from them. I was always fascinated at the crushed granite or "grit" as it was called that we bought to feed the chickens along with their food. This crushed stone was their supply of calcium from which the eggshells were constructed. Dad occasionally dispatched one of the older hens or a rooster for our Sunday dinner. I didn't mind eating it but I never had any desire to learn how to butcher the chickens myself. If I had to kill all my own meat, I would probably be a vegetarian. Actually, I am pretty close to being one already. Don't get me wrong. I like a top-notch steak once in a while but a few times a year is enough for me.

In any event, one of the chickens was sort of a pet and when it died of old age, I took it out into a large field in front of our house (across the street) and buried it. Some days later, I was upset to discover that some vultures had located my chicken and had dug it up. It was early in the year and the fields were still barren from the previous winter so it was easy to see what was going on from the height of the front porch even though it was quite some distance to where I had buried my pet hen. Mom explained that I probably didn't bury it deep enough. I ran out into the field and chased the vultures away but the damage had already been done. Vultures still live in the isolated lowlands of South Carolina and I saw one as recently as Thanksgiving, Y2K, on the edge of the Pee Dee Swamp. They also live in Dutchess County in New York where I now live and

I have seen them cleaning the road kill in Pleasant Valley along side the Taconic Parkway in 2006.

Shopping centers have become a way of life for the past 35 years although the internet may change that somewhat. Now-a-days even towns with 10 or 12 thousand residents often have something that can be called a shopping center and Wal-Mart super centers are almost a shopping center unto themselves. In the mid-1950's we did our shopping at Belks or Tapps or more likely Sears and Roebucks and J.C. Penny's. Most of these stores were located on Main Street in Columbia or close to it. In addition to P.Y. & A. Inc., we purchased some grocery items from Winn-Dixie and Piggly-Wiggly, names that still sound a little strange to "Yankees".

Mom had a job outside the home, unusual for a mother of five at any time but especially half a century ago. She was a jewelry buyer for the post exchanges at Fort Jackson, S.C. Mom told me once that if a GI purchased a ring his down payment covered the wholesale cost of the item. If he was shipped overseas or skipped his payments or was killed in the Korean War, (which without a television I was only dimly aware of), or for some other reason did not complete paying for the ring the only money that was lost was profit. Credit cards had not been invented yet and credit purchases were relatively rare for anything other than a house. Thirty two year old Lee Iacocca, who worked for Ford Motors at the time, more or less invented monthly financing for automobiles in 1956. It was something like $56 dollars down and $56 dollars a month to buy a new 1956 Ford. Before that, if you wanted something, you saved your money until you had enough to buy it. Today that sounds almost un-American but then it was a way of life. Of course, the government had very little debt by today's standards and a paper dollar or a silver dollar or a dollars worth of gold all had the same value. Today a silver dollar even in run of the mill condition is worth seven or eight times what a paper dollar is worth and a dollars worth of gold purchased then is worth about 16 dollars today. Of course, since our paper dollars are no longer backed by anything but faith and credit in our government it is hard to say what they are really worth. I remember as a pre-school child watching my uncle buy gasoline for his car at 16.9 cents per gallon and I filled up my own car outside Shaw Air Force Base in Sumter, S.C., in the 1960's, for 23.9 cents per gallon. In the 1970's I had to pay 32.9 cents per gallon in Poughkeepsie, N.Y. and today I had to pay over eight times that much for a gallon. When I graduated from McClenaghan High School in Florence, S.C. a new

Ford or Chevy cost around $1850 unless you wanted air condition-
ing and then you had to pay an extra $70. I remember buying three
pounds of ground beef for a dollar in 1957 on the way home from
school. A loaf of bread cost twenty cents.

Before the 1950's ended, Sears and Roebucks, and a few others began offering something called revolving credit to customers
who wanted to purchase items like freezers and refrigerators and
washing machines, and so began an economic revolution of deficit
spending that continues to this day. Of course the result of this
spending what you don't yet have by both the government and the
private sector is such that more than one and a half million people
have been filing for bankruptcy each and every year, and to top it
all off, we Americans now pay well over one THOUSAND MILLION
DOLLARS each and every day in interest to those mostly Europeans
and Chinese and Japanese who loan us the money to run the country. A day of reckoning is coming and Americans are going to be
shocked to see over four hundred percent inflation when it finally arrives but too many believe that it cannot happen here thereby guaranteeing that it someday will. The secret code discovered hidden
in the Bible by Israeli scientists using super-computers (see THE
BIBLE CODE by Michael Drosnin) seems to hint at a devastating
earthquake destroying much of Tokyo and triggering a world wide
economic collapse. We can't do anything about that but Americans
who come up with a viable solution (for us any way) like a 10 cent
per gallon per year tax on gasoline for five years, gradual so it doesn't
disrupt the economy, to be used EXCLUSIVELY for paying off the
national debt, are laughed out of town or at least off the airways.
We Americans have become a stubborn lot much like the ancient
Israelites. We want to do things our way even if it kills us. It is
likely to kill the savings of many. Of course, those who oppose a 50
cent per gallon tax over 5 years and who say that congress and the
president would probably just spend the money on other things are
probably right too. I don't know the answer. Since Ross Perot first
proposed that tax to pay off the national debt the cost of gasoline has
gone up far more than 50 cents per gallon and the national debt has
doubled. While President Reagan was in office the deficit increased
several trillion dollars. Under the current administration the deficit
has increased two trillion dollars and continues to grow. Still, the
spending is in the hands of congress much more than it is in the
hands of the president. Thirty years ago, no economist could imagine that we could owe as much as we do and not have our economy

come crashing down around us. Since it's only paper and cotton, we can print it with abandon. I read once that Saddam Hussein was counterfeiting our hundred dollar bills in such high quality that they were indistinguishable from the real thing and that the crooks had to put a tiny mark on one of the "L's" of the word "Independence Hall" on the back so they could tell the difference. Of course, since one of the engraving plates used to make $100 bills disappeared from the Bureau of Engraving and Printing a number of years ago he may have been printing one side of the bill with a genuine plate. In the investigation following the disappearance of that plate, the FBI was even searching the municipal dumps in the hopes of finding the steel engraving plate but it was finally written off as a clerical error. A couple of years ago two teenagers less than 30 miles from here were copying $20 bills on a color copier until they were caught.Hey! It's only paper! The Bureau of Engraving and Printing has been manufacturing U.S. currency since 1877 and at any given moment, they have 30 high-speed presses printing 200 million dollars worth of currency. The 25 acres of floor space they occupy in Washington has not been enough for years and since 1991, the presses have been spitting out paper money in Fort Worth, Texas, 24 hours a day and seven days a week as well. That printing facility covers the area of four football fields. The amazing thing is that all this paper is only three percent of our money. The other 97 percent is just numbers in a computer (well, actually, lots of computers).

Of course, in the early 1950's I did not think about such things. My biggest financial concern was whether I should spend my silver dime allowance at the Strand theater on Main Street just a few doors north of the capital in Columbia where a kid could get in on Saturday for nine cents (I purchased a penny tootsie roll with the change) or perhaps a Superman or Captain Marvel comic book that took the whole dime. Sometimes I purchased a full quarter-pound Baby Ruth candy bar, also a dime, which was my favorite. The movies often won out because in addition to the feature film there was usually a serial film that lasted perhaps ten or fifteen minutes.The film always left the viewer wanting more because one had to go back the following week to see how the hero had escaped whatever predicament he was in only to discover that he had gotten into another one, which meant, of course, that another trip to the movies was necessary. My favorite films starred Roy Rogers, Randolph Scott, and John Wayne, though later I added James Stewart, Glenn Ford and Audrey Hepburn. When I was 13 I had a crush on Grace Kelly who was twice my age. I never joined any fan clubs or wrote to any of these people but I did go to see their movies much as I go to see movies starring Harrison Ford, Nicolas Cage and Jennifer Love Hewitt today.

One big event for me was going to the steps of the South Carolina State House to see General Dwight David Eisenhower who was running for president as a Republican. Truman was still president but I do not remember anything about him except what I have read. Like Eisenhower, I am rather apolitical (he had to decide whether to run as a Democrat or a Republican) and I usually felt that the man was more important than the party was. If a person is truly objective then he can see the good and the bad that both the Democrats and the Republicans do and it is difficult for some one like me to identify completely with either party.

I was not able to get very close to where Eisenhower was speaking that day because of the crowd and I do not remember anything he said. My biggest recollection is that of marveling at how someone had gotten a roll of toilet paper to unravel from the fourteenth floor of the Wade Hampton Hotel almost all the way to the ground. I thought that I would like to try that someday but I never did.

In 1953, my sister Anne was born and with so many younger brothers and sisters, I became quite adept at mixing pabulum, heating bottles of milk, even changing dirty diapers, which was my least favorite. I felt quite grown-up to be helping in this way but it was also necessary because mom had her hands full at home as well as at Fort Jackson.

Teachers salaries have never been great in this country and in the South they are even less. Of course taxes, especially property taxes, are less in the South as well (compared to New York State where I now live). I remember a plantation that was for sale once in South Carolina, probably around 35 years ago. I do not remember the price, which was fair, but I do remember the taxes because of the numbers involved. This plantation had a modern six bedroom home and it had seven MILES of river frontage. The total acreage was 3,700 acres and the annual tax was $3,700. A South Carolina millionaire once told me that more people had become millionaires through real estate than through any other medium. Sometimes I have wished I had listened to him.

I suspect that teachers back then earned even less at the Opportunity School than regular teachers earned. I know that money was always tight but mom had the frugality of her Scottish ancestors. Her father was of pure Scottish descent. He was born Charles William Dunbar in Stellarton, Nova Scotia, on the Northumberland Strait in 1888 but he moved to Rhode Island when he was but a child. Mom inherited or learned his frugal ways. Thus, I was actually able to take two vacations in the summer of 1953. One was my second and final visit to summer camp for two weeks at Camp Saint Mary's. The other was my last visit to my grandparents at their home in the country in the tiny state of Rhode Island.

Compared to South Carolina Rhode Island is about the size of any two typical counties. Alaska, then just a territory, has a least one state park that is six times the size of the State of Rhode Island, but Rhode Island is big in other ways. Historians have often called Rhode Island the South Carolina of the North because of its independent people who think for themselves and go their own way.

My grandfather had been a skilled craftsman, a ship builder who lost his fine city home on Sackett Street in Providence during the Great Depression of the 1930's. It was a large city home, formerly owned by a sea captain, in an older but well to do neighborhood. Sadly, the huge bronze doors were practically falling down when mom visited the area in the 1970's. The taxi driver at first refused to take her to see her former home. "Lady, even the cops don't go there alone," he told her. Finally, he agreed to take her as long as they did not stop and did not go slower than 20 miles per hour. Today all the old homes are gone, replaced with modern housing in an attempt to reduce crime, and I am told that downtown Providence has actually experienced a renaissance of sorts.

Fortunately, my grandparents owned several acres of land and a summer place out in what then was the country. At the age of ten it was quite an adventure for me to travel all the way from South Carolina, alone on a train, to Pennsylvania Station in New York City where I had to get to Grand Central a mile or so across town (or was it the other way around?) in order to catch another train to Rhode Island. An organization called Travelers Aid was supposed to assist me but our schedules were off by an hour because at that time South Carolina had not yet chosen to participate in Daylight Savings Time. When I finally got to the other station, the train had just started to pull out and I had to run to catch it.No person in their right mind would let a ten-year-old travel to and through New York City or any major city alone today but it was a different world back then. No one could have imagined a USA where there would be an actual court case on whether the Ten Commandments would or would not be posted on public property. Majority rule was still the rule half a century ago and the government was not ruled by the special interests of the few as it is today.

It fascinates me how far we have fallen from the ideals of our founding fathers, not one of whom was an atheist, and all of whom believed in the God of the Bible. Every single state constitution from those written in 1776 to that of Alaska in 1956 and Hawaii in 1959 gives thanks or reverence to "Almighty God," "The Supreme Ruler of the Universe," or "The Sovereign Ruler of Nations." If the atheists of the 21st Century can force us to change our national motto ("In God We Trust") or to eliminate that terrible phrase, "one nation under God" from the Pledge of Allegiance, can all 50 state constitutions be far behind? William Penn for whom the State of Pennsylvania was named said it best, "Those who will not be ruled by God will be ruled by tyrants." Thirty-seven years ago a professor at the University of South Carolina posed a question to a class of political science students. He asked, "Should the states be abolished? Have they served their usefulness?" It was a question that had never occurred to me. I was so surprised by it that I could not think of a suitable answer. For well over a quarter of a century now over a hundred colleges and universities in the United States of America have been teaching courses in One World Government. Should the USA be abolished as well or relegated to the status of a county in the new world order? I do not think so but then I do not try to persuade college students that this is what is best for our future. Perhaps "The Supreme Ruler of the Universe" will see that we get what we have been asking for, demanding now for decades, that He leave us alone and take His commandments and laws and leave us to our own wisdom. I do not believe that a free society can remain a free society and win a war against terrorists who are guided by the Chief Ruler of the Underworld unless they also fight with spiritual weapons and righteousness. Nuclear weapons and laser guided missiles alone cannot stop those who are dedicated to the false belief that they will be rewarded in the next life if they destroy themselves killing "the enemy" in this one. "As you sow, so shall you reap," is one of the foundational principles of the Universe, like gravity.

In any event visiting my grandparents was like something out of the Walton's, the TV series in the 1970's in which Richard Thomas played the role of John Boy near Walton Mountain in rural Virginia. My grandparent's summer place had become their permanent home after the depression. It was situated by the side of a lake on a small bluff overlooking the water in the town of Coventry.

My grandmother had been born in Coventry, Connecticut, and her final home was in Coventry, Rhode Island, both named I presume, for Coventry in England. Of course, my grandmother did not have a drop of English blood in her veins but was of pure Irish descent all the way back to the American Revolution. Her full name was Elizabeth Moriority Hogan. Her uncle, Rear Admiral Bartholomew William Hogan, was once the Navy Surgeon General. When I was nineteen and in the United States Air Force I looked him up once in a book of Admirals and Generals. This book looked a lot like a high school or college annual.As I turned the pages looking at dozens of look-alike photos, suddenly one picture jumped out at me. The photograph looked like a Hollywood press photo, different from all the others. It did not look at all like the typical staid "official" photos. It was Adm. B.W. Hogan!

Although my grandparents had been living in their country cabin for more than a decade before I was born and it was their permanent place of residence (or "home" as we used to say) it did not have electricity. Their lighting was by kerosene lamp and they kept their food in an old-fashioned icebox, which had to be replenished with ice once or twice a week. I think they could have had electricity if they had really wanted it but they would have had to bring the cabin up to certain standards and they had lived that way so long that they were accustomed to it. I had never seen anything like it and I thought it was great!

My grandfather was a kind and decent person of Methodist heritage. He planted and grew most of his vegetables although the garden was of considerable distance from the cabin. Often he would find vegetables missing, not eaten by wild animals but harvested. I was amazed to see a wildcat or bobcat once as I walked to the garden one day in 1953. It was not the wildcat, however, but two neighboring boys who were stealing my grandfather's vegetables. When "Pa" as we always called him, investigated, he discovered that the boys' father would beat them if they did not steal the vegetables when he told them to do so. My grandfathers' solution in the days before child abuse laws was to plant enough extra vegetables so that he would have enough for his family after the others had been taken. I wish I had known him better.

"Pa" died two years later in 1955. Following my grandfathers death his faithful dog would go down to the mailbox and wait for him to return around 5 p.m., the accustomed time of his arrival. The dog would wait for him until it grew dark and then trot back to the cabin. Maybe tomorrow...and the next day around 5 p.m. the ritual would begin all over again. How do you explain to a dog that a person is not ever coming back? That dog went down to the mailbox on Harkney Hill Road to await my grandfather's return every day for five years until it could wait no longer and it too died. Not long after that my grandmother died, the result of a doctor's mistake. My Uncle Bert who suffered for 50 years from another doctor's mistake still lived in the ramshackle cabin and he decided it was time to move on. Like some Viking warrior from long ago the last thing he did when he left was to torch the place, burning away a thousand dreams and memories. Today, only the lake remains and that too, seemed to be disappearing, filling in with silt, the last time I saw it.

2. The Kidnapping and the Lightning Storm

I have been blessed over the course of my lifetime in many ways. The biggest blessing of all has been that there was never a time in my memory when I did not believe in a personal God who was watching over me, concerned with my welfare, and receptive to my prayers. Like all believers, there have been times when God certainly did not seem very close or interested and other times when I knew my life was in His hands and His Presence was unquestionable. Having been raised in the Catholic tradition of Christianity I believed that God had many friends with Him in heaven (saints) and that some of them specialized in certain kinds of entreaties. One of these was St. Anthony, patron saint of lost objects.

My first encounter with answered pray was when I was about three years old. Certain objects were forbidden to me at that tender age and one of these objects was scissors. Of course, that made them all the more desirable and enticing. For some reason I took a very large (to me anyway) pair of scissors out of their drawer and out of the house entirely. Whatever I used them for is long forgotten and so were the scissors until I heard my mom returning from somewhere. I had to find them and quickly get them back where they belonged. Desperately I searched with no success and then I remembered the saint who was supposed to help with finding lost things. I knew little of theology, the Bible, religion, only that I would soon be in big trouble, likely to get a spanking, if I didn't find those scissors and return them. In desperation, I prayed that St. Anthony would help me. What I remember is very clear, probably because of the intensity of the situation. I searched for those scissors as best as I could, was unsuccessful, prayed in all earnestness to St. Anthony to please help me, and then, suddenly, there they were in front of me resting on a dandelion plant, a location that I was absolutely positively certain that I had checked before. I was too young to doubt that my prayer would be answered. It just had to be answered. I do not remember if I got the scissors back in the drawer in time. I don't even remember if I got a spanking for playing with something that was forbidden or any other details except my great relief at finding the scissors and my great surprise at finding them where I found them.

Those scissors, resting on that dandelion plant, are as clear to me today as they were more than half a century ago. Of course, with the logic of adulthood it has crossed my mind that as a three year old I could have been mistaken and found them on another dandelion plant. Dandelion plants are, after all, rather common.

Other memories are not so clear. I was kidnapped even before this and I have no memory of it at all. I can only surmise that for me the kidnapping was not in any way traumatic and therefore did not imbue itself upon my mind or spirit. Considering what I have been told about what happened I must have thought that it was all in a day's fun. I am sure that many prayers were said for me at the time but not by any human beings because not even my mother knew I was missing. Those prayers, by angels and saints, were answered and I am alive today to write these words. What might have happened to me had I not experienced one of the biggest "coincidences" of my life is to frightening to speculate upon. Skeptics will say that this was all just "luck" but as Obi-Wan Kenobi said to Han Solo as they flew through space aboard the Millennium Falcon in the very first STAR WARS movie, "In my experience, there's no such thing as luck".

I was about two at the time and my dad was still overseas fighting the Nazi's in Europe. My Uncle Bert had received a medical discharge as the result of a blotched operation from which he never fully recovered. We know today that more people die in hospitals from accidents and mistakes each year than all the Americans who were killed during the entire Vietnam War but this knowledge was seldom known by even the victims 60 years ago. Of course since the number of "accidents" is in the neighborhood of 120,000 a year there are those who do not believe these accidents are all accidents.

Uncle Bert was back in Rhode Island and mom had plenty of vacation time accumulated so the two of them decided to take a trip, along with me of course. First they drove to Florida where my earliest memory was formed, that of oranges floating on the water of a swimming pool. It fascinated me that the oranges did not sink. Why I thought they should, I do not know.

From Florida, Mom and Uncle Bert drove north to the Thousand Islands area of north- western New York State. They crossed over into Canada just to mail postcards (I did that once myself). Then they stopped for a few days at something like a bed-and-board. Motels as such were almost non-existent and when they could be found consisted of little cabins all in a row. It wasn't to long before someone thought of placing the cabins right next to each other, eliminating the extra walls, and creating what we today would recognize as a motel. I remember the little cabins though and for some reason I liked them.

On the second day of our residence a woman who lived next door dropped by for a chat. Mom told her that we were vacationing and when the woman asked if we had any relatives in the area mom told her that we did not. At the time, I was an only child and mom dressed me up in some sharp outfits. I have seen photos of myself from those days, and in one of them, I was wearing a complete replica of an army uniform right down to the insignias and campaign ribbons. I also had a similar outfit that was a miniature replica of a navy uniform. Apparently, I was, most of the time, a well-dressed kid or baby. Perhaps that is why the woman dropped by to introduce herself. It was fortunate that she did so. That short visit and her memory for details undoubtedly helped to save my life.

We had only been staying in this small upstate New York town for a few days when a white male with gray hair, unshaven, about 55-60 years of age, took me. The neighbor who had stopped in the day before was shopping in a nearby town about two miles away. As she walked down the street, she recognized me and asked me where I was going. "To my grandfather's," I answered. The woman thought that was a little odd. Hadn't she just been told that we had no relatives in the area? How then could I be walking to my grandfather's house? She undoubtedly had a puzzled look on her face. Suddenly the man dropped my hand and took off running down the street. The neighbor was somewhat stunned and unsure of what to do so she packed me into her automobile along with her groceries and took me back to my mother. We had been staying on the second floor so when the woman took me upstairs and said to mom as she handed me over, "I brought your son back," mom naturally thought she meant from downstairs in the fenced in yard. The yard I had been playing in was completely fenced in and had a gate that was necessary to unlatch in order to open. It was beyond my reach. Mom who was 26 or 27 at the time was quite surprised to find that I had not been in the yard at all but that the helpful neighbor had found me in the next town, a couple of miles away, being led away by an unknown person of questionable appearance. The probability of that woman doing her shopping on the very same street and at the very same time as I came walking along with a total stranger is too awesome to contemplate. Thousands of children disappear each year in this country. Practically everyone has heard of the kidnapping and horrible death of 6 year old Adam Walsh in Florida or 7 year old Danielle van Dam in California but no one might ever have heard of me if that next door neighbor who had only been a neighbor for a day or two had not recognized me and stopped and asked where I was going. Luck? I don't think so. Providence is a much better word if you don't like miracle.

Miracles happen all the time. It is one of the tragedies of mankind that we have not been trained to see them. Most are ordinary miracles: the birth of a baby, the sound of spring in a contented bird's song or the beauty of a spectacular sunset. Even the complexity of the human brain, the most complicated "thing" in the known universe, is a miracle of sorts. The other kind of miracles happen too, the extra-ordinary kind, but we are conditioned to think of them as coincidences. I like the word "coincidence". It was the name of a yacht in the best book on motivation and success that I have ever read, "A Rich Man's Secret" and it has been said that "coincidence" is when God elects to remain anonymous.

Coincidence? The cancer just happened to disappear after three churches full of people prayed for the patient. The down-on-his-luck financially depressed person buys his first lottery ticket and wins big. The young girl is fired from her job at the World Trade Center the day before the evildoers attack. The father decides to take his child to school and is late getting to work thereby missing the destruction on the day of the attack. All just coincidences? Not in my experience! I worked with someone who told me that her brother was slightly injured (burned) in the 1993 attack on the WTC and he quit his job, telling her that these people were fanatics, people who hated freedom and democracy, and that they would not stop until they succeeded. He was out of work for six months but he wasn't there eight years later when the powers of Darkness succeeded. There are those who have moved out of NYC believing that it isn't over yet. "Better to be years too early, than one day to late," they say. Each person is entitled to his own beliefs and I do not criticize those who have moved or those who believe it will be years before anything more happens. They might both be right. I do recall, however, that in one of the many odd predictions that were written in Old French by Dr. Nostradamus over 450 years ago (and may have been accurately translated) was this one, "Nothing can save New City!" All just coincidences? I have no idea. It doesn't keep me from going to NYC on the rare occasions when there is a reason to do so but I have learned to always pray before going on any trip of consequence. Of course I believe it was the same Nostradamus who said that World War Three would begin around the year 2000, be fought between the Muslim nations and the west, and last 27 years! Of course he was only a mystic and not a prophet.

One 20th Century theologian, a man who had studied about God all his life but who had never, apparently, experienced God in any meaningful way, even wrote an article for Newsweek Magazine in the spring of Y2K on why he didn't believe in miracles. How terribly sad, to believe that God exists, but that He is so weak he cannot, or so uncaring He will not, do anything outside the laws of nature which He created. Why bother with a God like that?

This theologian was bothered by the fact that a person was warned of an impending disaster in which several people were killed. The survivor gave credit to God for the warning that had saved her life. "Why didn't God warn everybody?" was the gist of this theologian's complaint. My thought was "I wonder how many were listening" but I didn't want to let that one go by so I decided to write a letter to the editor which I do every few years (or at least once or twice a decade). I knew of many situations in which people were saved from an untimely death by Divine Intervention but I couldn't report them all or it would be to long a letter to be published. As it was, even my very short letter was rejected.

One case, if I may call it that, comes to mind. A woman had her ticket in her hand and she was waiting in line to board Pan Am Flight 103 in 1988. I saw the television inter- view in which she said, "I kept hearing, 'don't get on board'." The woman was obviously excited: "DON'T GET ON BOARD!" The thought was so strong, so clear, that she got out of line and did not board the jet. All who did, 270 people, perished over Lockerbie, Scotland. "It was God who warned me," The woman exclaimed, "who else could it have been?" The woman had no doubt as to who had warned her and she was obviously open to the possibility. Many are not. I might have been in serious trouble when I was a student at the University of South Carolina because I heard a warning that I did not recognize as a warning. My guardian angel must have been working over-time that day (as always) because although it turned out OK for me it could have been a disaster. I had just pulled my Volkswagen Beetle up in front of my apartment at 1804 Green Street. It was a tight squeeze but I got the car in the small space. Suddenly in my mind, I heard a distinct voice that said, "Drive around the block!" The voice was gentle but urgent. "Drive around the block?" I repeated aloud, "What for?" I said to myself. The four men leaning against the automobile two cars in front of mine were talking among themselves. There was nothing unusual in that. My apartment was just three blocks east of the University and finding a parking space in front of it was a rare occurrence. In fact finding a space within a block of the huge white columns of the old building was often difficult as parking spaces near the University were always at a premium. I was fortunate to find one right there. "Besides," I rationalized to myself, "if I drive around the block the space will undoubtedly be gone." I got out of my VW and locked the door. As I turned around to go into my apartment, I was surrounded by what at first appeared to be fellow students. They looked young and the newspaper the next day listed the ages of three of them, two were 18, the third was 19.

"We're soldiers out at Fort Jackson," the leader of the group began. "We're broke and we're trying to get back to the Fort." At this point, I cannot take credit for the words that flowed out of my mouth. Somewhere in the Bible God says that he will give us what to say when we need it and it has been my experience that this is so. The interesting thing here was that I did not even know that I needed the right words or actions.

"Gee! I'm just about busted myself!" I said as I reached into my pocket pulling out all my change, two quarters, a dime, a nickel, and some pennies. "Here," I said, handing the leader the two quarters, "you ought to be able to get some tokens with these."

"You're not from around here, are you?" the leader asked. Now my family moved to South Carolina before I was eight years old but following cue I immediately answered, in the most northern accent I could muster, "No, I'm from Pennsylvania." I had been born there but never actually lived in Pennsylvania as our home at the time was south of the Mason-Dixon Line in Maryland.I discerned from their accent that they were not Southerners themselves. "You're not from here either," I said, and then asked, "Where are you from?" "We're from Joisey!" (New Jersey) someone else answered, a note of pride evident in his voice.

"Well, I've got to go," I said, turning away. The whole episode lasted less than a minute and a half. I walked straight into the building and upstairs to my apartment. From my other pocket, I removed

$76, my bi-monthly pay from my part-time job. Unknown to me at the time three of the four soldiers walked up the street and at knife-point robbed the next three persons they came upon. It was on the radio and in the newspapers. Who knows what might have happened it they had tried to take my hard-earned money away from me. I now believe that the same Spirit that warned the woman in 1988 had warned me two decades earlier though I pretty much took it for granted at the time. Just a coincidence I guess.

Of course, similar to the theologians thinking, I too, was somewhat upset when I learned of a family (a husband, wife and young child) who were on Flight 103. What bothered me was that although I didn't know this family personally I had heard that they were devoted praying Christians who would have been open to being warned, who would have known what to do if they had received such a thought. Of course, not all such thoughts come from God, only the good and true ones. I was once in miles and miles of traffic on I-95 and I heard a voice say that it was all right to pull over and pass some of the cars on the side. I did not pray to make sure it was God but pulled right over and quickly got a ticket for my efforts - the enemies of man like nothing better than to pretend that they are God and lead men astray. Look at all the cults in the USA (over 3,000 last I heard). "Test the spirits and see if they are of God," it says in the New Testament.

I could understand how ordinary, non-spiritual persons with little or no understanding of God's love for His creation (us) could reject or not even be aware that they were being warned. People who refuse to believe that God exists put a barrier around themselves that even God has a difficult time (but not an impossible one) bridging. Still I wondered why this family had not been warned. Fortunately, a relative of the deceased family had the same concern and thought to pray about it. "Why, God?" she asked.

Now I will be the first to admit that God does not always answer that question or at least not right away. Sometimes the answer takes decades. However, this relative wanted to know and when she prayed she asked the Lord why her dearly beloved relatives had not been warned and this woman received an answer while she was praying. The answer she received was one that had not occurred to her or to me either. Why had these seemingly wonderful people not been warned? Why had they all died aboard Pan Am Flight 103? The astounding answer that their relative heard in her spirit or in her inner thoughts when she prayed was a clear and concise, "because I had need of them over here."

Of course, there are those who will argue that this woman's subconscious mind simply manufactured the answer, that God had nothing to do with it, even that there is no God. I try to avoid discussions with people like that. A South Carolina millionaire one told me that there has never been a statue raised to a critic but many statues have been raised to those who were being criticized. I have wondered if that is true but at least it sounds true. Perhaps it is simply an old saying from long ago. You are on dangerous ground, however, if you believe all old sayings just because they are old sayings.

One old saying that sounds true is most definitely not true: Lightning never strikes the same place twice! Don't you believe it! Whoever authored that saying is long dead. Whether lightning killed him or her, I do not know but by the age of ten, I had heard that saying so often I believed it. I found out, rather dramatically, that you couldn't automatically believe all old sayings no matter how often they are repeated.

Our residence at the Opportunity School was in the extreme northeast corner of the school, the last building on a nice large tree filled lot where dad made a good-sized swing from one of the branches of the nearest big tree. I enjoyed many hours on that swing.

Adjoining the eat-in kitchen of our "home" in that barracks-like building was a side porch where we often ate in good weather. The porch was screened in and large enough for a big table and six chairs. Just outside the porch were several southern pine trees perhaps 40 feet tall. About 40 feet to the south of us was another barracks-like building that was used as a nursery school. The next building was only a stub of a barracks, most of it having been destroyed by a tornado. The building after that was used as a dispensary where we all went for shots and to be bandaged for the typical boys-will-be-boys cuts and scrapes. All the buildings were connected by long narrow hallways in which we occasionally rode our bicycles much to the consternation of the administrative staff. They liked it even less when we played on the roof. Since these buildings were for the most part raised on concrete pillars it was a dangerous place to play but we were relatively careful considering our age and none of us ever received any serious injuries.

Behind our porch was another screened in porch, an extension really, and stairs going down to the outside on the left. To the right was a door to a large storeroom that separated the two apartments and which was shared by our family and the one on the other end of the building, the Peters family when we first moved there and then later, a teacher from Sweden, Bror Person, his wife and a 5-year-old daughter, Marianne. Mr. Peters was a pilot. He was dying from cancer and no one talked about it above a whisper.It's hard to believe that cancer in the early 1950's was about as mysterious as AIDS was in the mid-1980s. It was something you didn't talk about openly, although it was in 1953 that two researchers at the then more politically neutral Centers for Disease Control were able to show a definite correlation between the use of cigarettes and an early death. I spent two years studying the avoidable causes of cancer for my own benefit when I was in my thirties but as a child, I knew nothing about it at all, except that it must be very scary and bad because it was killing people and adults only whispered about it.

My dad never read the whole study of what the doctors had discovered about the use of cigarettes but what he did read was enough to convince him to quit smoking the few cigarettes he did smoke. Both the researchers who had conducted the study were smokers and both of them quit.Unfortunately, one of them was up to four packs per day and subsequent research has shown that all people who smoke four packs per day will die of lung cancer. Smoking can cause brain cancer and bladder cancer and breast cancer but those who smoke four packs per day of cigarettes will never live long enough to get those other cancers because they will die first from lung cancer, even if they quit smoking entirely. The doctor who co-authored the research that convinced my dad to quit smoking forever was no exception. He eventually died from lung cancer. The other researcher smoked far less and he went on to a distinguished career in the field of public health.

It shouldn't surprise me that the general public is always about a generation behind the curve as far as knowledge of what is healthy and what isn't. A magazine article in the early months of the 21st Century told how marijuana cigarettes, or "joints" as they used to be called, did five times as much damage to the lungs as ordinary tobacco cigarettes. I read a Swiss study saying the same thing over a quarter of a century ago. I believe that in the future it will be discovered that monosodium glutamate which is now used in hundreds and hundreds of products intended to be eaten will prove to have a synergistic effort and that when eaten in significantly large amounts with other presently unknown food items or additives will prove to be detrimental to the health of human beings. I have nothing to base this assumption on except that I don't like taking drugs of any kind and having them put in my food to make it "seem" to taste better is not something I like fostered upon me by big business. I don't avoid monosodium glutamate 100 percent because that is nearly impossible to do. However, nine times out of ten when I see a can of soup or snack foods or TV dinners (do they still call them that?) that contain MSG I put the package back. If you start to do this, you will be amazed at how much of this natural chemical is put into our foodstuffs. It is a billion dollar business and even restaurants have been known to sprinkle a little of it on some dishes. I always thought that my taste buds were a little unusual because I could usually just taste and "know" that monosodium glutamate was in the food but science has now identified MSG as a distinct separate taste like sweet and sour. Use it if you like but remember you read it here and see what is being said in 20 years about the stuff. If you choose to reduce your intake of this "natural" substance be aware that it sometimes is simply called "other natural flavors" or listed under "artificial and natural flavors." I have even found it used in the bread coating of several different brands of fish fillets.

In 1953, however, dad's withdrawal from the little "cancer sticks" made him so agitated and temperamental that we all wished he would go back to smoking. Today, of course, I'm glad he did quit because we all had a good lesson on why never to start, and dad who is in his 90's as I write this, would not likely be around to enjoy his twenty-five or so grandchildren or his great-grandchildren.

I don't remember Mr. Peters that well. He had a pretty daughter named Donna Sue but I hardly saw her enough to have a crush on her. The neighbor I remember the most was Katherine Clark, a refugee from Latvia, a country just a little smaller than South Carolina in both size and population, which was taken over by the Old Soviet Union in 1940 and which again regained its independence in 1991.

Katherine Clark was a first class portrait painter and she and her daughter Violet lived in the first barracks-like building that was not adjoined to ours. Actually all the buildings were joined to one another by the long and narrow parallel hallways but since it was over a quarter of a mile walk to go all the way to the center connecting hallway and then cross over to the hallway that eventually reached the Clark residence I simply walked the 200 feet across the park-like grounds directly to their apartment. I did take the long way once when I was exploring but that was sufficient and I only did it once

in three years. A person could go to almost every building at the
Opportunity School through the long narrow hallways and never
have to go outside.

Violet was a year or two older than I was and very sophisticated.
At least she was the most sophisticated person that I knew. Once
I was visiting her and we had been talking for quite a while when
she said, "I have to take a bath," and she left the room. She quickly
returned wearing a bathing suit and we continued our conversation
as I followed her into the bathroom and she filled the tub. Then
she climbed into the tub and began using soap and a face cloth. We
continued to talk and all of a sudden, it occurred to me that I had
never seen a person take a bath while wearing a bathing suit. The
thought was so sudden that I blurted it out asking, "Do you always
take a bath with a bathing suit on?" The answer was obvious had
I given myself the time to think about it. "No silly," Violet replied,
"but you're here."

Katherine Clark became one of South Carolina's foremost
portrait painters and she painted the portraits of many of South
Carolina's leading citizens. A decade or so later I visited her home in
West Columbia. Violet was away at college so I didn't stay long. Set
up on an easel was an unfinished portrait which Mrs. Clark stopped
working on long enough to offer me some lemonade and a few minutes conversation. I believe that the portrait was of General Mark
Clark, hero of WWII and president of the Citadel. While there, I
saw the most amazing oil painting. It was a dark painting of deep
purple, blue and black and was quite obviously the night sky. Stars
and barely lit clouds filled the space of a normal portrait and then,
suddenly, there it was, out of the starry depths of space like a half
remembered dream, the face of a man. A father? A husband? God?
I never knew because I did not think to ask. I really liked it though
because I did ask if it was for sale. It was but the price was beyond
my meager means as a university student. Someone, somewhere,
has that oil painting and whatever he or she paid for it was not too
much.

LIGHTNING NEVER STRIKES THE SAME PLACE TWICE!
Don't you believe it! We were all sitting around the table eating our
lunch on the back porch when a storm approached. Now I have never disliked thunderstorms. They are part of the weather system and
for the most part necessary for our survival on this planet. Life as
we know it could not even exist on earth without the biggest storms
of all, hurricanes. Called typhoons in the Western Pacific and in the

South Pacific where my niece Jennifer was born, such storms have one vital function. They spread the heat from the equatorial regions of the earth to the more temperate zones. Without hurricanes, no one could live near the center part of the earth as it would be to hot and land to the north and the south of the equator would be much colder. Hurricanes help moderate earth's temperatures.

The reason I have never been afraid of storms is that when I was two years old I used to watch the thunder and lightning with my mom. "Wow! That's a big one!" I remember mom saying as we looked out a window amid the thunderous booms of a nearby storm with lightning flashing down. My dad was overseas helping to preserve freedom in the world, one of Tom Brokaw's "The Greatest Generation" people. When he returned my first brother was born and when a storm approached dad would quickly run and close nearby windows. Consequently, that brother grew up much more apprehensive over storms than I have ever been.

Many years later when I was living on Church Street in Poughkeepsie, N.Y., I had sort of an unusual out-of-body experience. I was thirty something at the time. Storms had been forecast for late night or early morning but it would take quite a storm to keep me awake. Sometime during the night, I got out of bed, went to the window, and knelt down to watch a glorious display of lightning and thunder. It was awesome! I watched for some time and then I returned to bed and sleep. When I awoke in the morning, I remembered the display of lightning that I had seen and how fabulous it had been. Everything outside was still wet from the downpour. Then I happened to glance over towards the window from which I had watched the storm and was amazed to discover that I had previously placed several large boxes of books and other stuff in front of the window so they would be out of the way. There was no way that I could have physically knelt anywhere near the window to see anything. If I had actually done so, it had to be in the spirit, which is not limited to space, or even time as physical bodies are. Perhaps I only dreamed the entire episode.

On this particular day, however, in the early 1950's a storm was fast approaching and mom said, "Come into the kitchen" (where we had another table and where we ate in wintertime and in bad weather). Flashes of lightning were visible rather close now and rain had begun to pelt the roof of the porch.

"We'll be OK mom," I yelled back with the conviction of my ten or eleven-year-old wisdom. "If lightning strikes it will strike the trees because they are much higher than the porch," I added, and they were much higher. Mom was unconvinced. "Get into the kitchen right now," mom said in a tone that meant to do just that. Dutifully we brought in all our plates, glasses, and dinner-ware (which we always called silverware but which never was made of real silver except for an occasional piece). Mom had worked at Gorham's Silver Company when she was just out of high school but even with a company discount the prices were still to high for her to ever buy more than a piece or two. Of course, in her pre-teen years before the Great Depression mom had undoubtedly used real silver-ware or perhaps she had picked up the term from her mother but we always called our knives, folks and spoons silverware.

In any event we had gotten everything properly arranged around the table, had sat down and had just begun to eat when a very loud, almost deafening loud, crash of thunder accompanied by a stoke of lightning that did not hit the tall southern pines but instead hit the metal table that we had been sitting around and the metal chairs that we had been sitting on not five minutes previously. The light-ning flashed around the porch not 15 feet from where I was now seated facing the porch. My brothers Bill and Mike facing me and with their backs to the porch were even closer. They could not see that the nails that held the screen to the wood of the porch were steaming and it could well have been a miracle that the porch itself did not burst into flame. It was an awesome display of the power of nature up very close.

Within seconds, I picked up my plate of food and was picking up my silverware when I heard mom's voice almost demanding to know where I was going.

"Back to the porch," I replied, "after all, lightning never strikes the same place twice."

"SIT DOWN!" I heard mom's instant reply in a voice with more firmness and resolve than I had ever heard before. I sat down and had not finished two mouthfuls of food before lightning once again filled the porch with a sizzling display as dazzling as the first one had been. There were actual burn marks on the metal chairs as if they had been singed in a fire. I never had to be told again to come in from the porch during a storm. It was years before I learned the scientific reason why it is actually easier for lightning to strike the same place twice than it is to cut a new path thorough the atmo-sphere. I now knew, for a fact, that lightning was indeed capable of striking the same place twice. I also wondered what other "old sayings" might not be true.

3. The Fire and My Native American Friend

Mom worked at Fort Jackson for several years and although I helped out at home, I was only ten and it was necessary for her to hire a maid to help with the housework and to keep an eye on all of us. When Anne came along in 1953 that made an even half dozen children to watch. Most of the women did not like having to walk the three blocks to our apartment from where the bus dropped them off and we had a succession of "helpers." One used to wash all the clothes until she discovered that some of the pants she was washing belonged to my two-year-year old sister Mary. This particular maid was an American black women but her church believed in the Old Testament and the rules that God gave to the ancient Israelites as surely as if they were a an ultra-conservative orthodox synagogue rather than a 20th Century supposedly Christian Church. She refused to wash any pants that any girl would wear or even touch them for that matter. If my baby sister's pants were hanging on the line outside where my mother had placed them to dry before she went to work, well, there they would stay. Mom would come home and find all the other clothes dry and neatly stacked but in the pouring rain, Mary's tiny pants could be seen blowing in the wind. This particular maid used to have a cup of hot tea ready for mom when she returned from work and it was much appreciated. That ended when the maid discovered that her church would not allow her to make a pot of tea! Where these "rules" came from and what cult leader made them up I do not know. I have read the entire Bible, Old and New Testaments, some 2,000 pages, and I am not aware of a single reference to coffee or tea. What I do recall is the Jesus Himself said that it was more important what came out of ones mouth than what went into it. Jesus also rebuked the religious leaders of His day for making up extra rules and regulations. He thought that the leaders or elders of the people should be doing all they could to lift men's burdens, not add to them. Of course the Bible does say that we should avoid that which is harmful but the latest scientific evidence shows that tea drinking may help prevent some cancers, and while drinking a great deal of coffee may be harmful, there is absolutely no scientific evidence that drinking a cup or two each day does anything but perk up the mental faculties a bit and there is some evidence that a cup or two per day may help prevent some diseases.

One summer day when the rain hadn't fallen in weeks I wanted to make some popcorn but the maid we had at the time would not let me "mess around in the kitchen" as she put it. Consequently, I took a pan, some popcorn and some matches and together with my younger brother Bill, we rode on our bicycles about three quarters of a mile to a back road that was paved during WWII but was seldom used after that.It was part of the property that belonged to whatever authority administered the Columbia Airport. There were no houses or buildings of any sort for at least a quarter of a mile in any direction. Even the trees were sparse, mostly scrub oak and less than ten-year-old pines. The area had been barren once and was used for something during the war but had since returned to a wild state.

We gathered some odd pieces of wood and built a small fire by the side of the road. If we had built the fire on the road itself, there would not have been a problem but the popcorn had not even begun to pop when the underbrush caught fire. Very quickly it became more than my younger brother and I could handle. The fire spread rapidly. I felt that I had to alert someone but I didn't know whom to tell. I was unaware that the airport had its own fire department so I jumped on my bicycle and pedaled as fast as I could. I had to find an adult. The first place I came to was a group of subsidized apartments that were also part of some former government project from the war years. They had probably been some kind of military housing for air cadets or civilian workers during WWII but now they were just somewhat rundown apartments. I saw a few children playing but no adults. Finally, I spotted an older black man although back then any decent African-American would have been insulted if he were called black. I was about three and a half years old the first time I saw a Negro. I thought it was the most amazing thing to see such a person. "Momma! Momma! Come see a man what is all black!" I cried out. We were living at a Veterans Hospital in Martinsburg, West Virginia, where dad worked right after the war. Momma came and received an ugly stare for her effort. Twenty years later when I attended the University of South Carolina I had a friend from Montana and she told me that she had never seen an

African-American in the flesh until she left Montana and did a tour with VISTA (Volunteers in Service to America).

At the time, I knew little of the long-standing race problems or prejudices that existed, and not just in the south, at that time. All the "colored" people that I knew were pretty decent folks, mostly professional or hard working people of good character. It's true that I did not have a lot of contact with other races with the exception of one Cherokee Indian family (only the husband was Cherokee, the wife was German). We always thought it was great to know a real Indian who was not at all like the bad Indians that we saw at the movies.

In 1961 when I was in basic training at Lackland Air Force Base in Texas, one of my buddies was a Native American. I do not remember his tribe or nation. He might have been Navajo but on that, I am not absolutely certain. The first time I was ever on a horse was when he invited me to go riding with him one weekend when we both had a pass. Today, sadly, even his name is forgotten but it may have been Montoya.

He was a small person, perhaps five feet three inches, if that, and did not talk much. Once when the entire squadron had to shower, I noticed he had quite a few major scars. I asked him about them later and he told me that he would tell me about them someday. The day we went horseback riding was the day he opened up about his personal life. "I never started a fight," Montoya told me, "but I finished a few." Montoya had scars of significant length that had come from knives and one somewhat round scar that he told me was from a bullet.

Montoya had had a date with an attractive Indian girl and had taken her to a movie. Three people, other Indians who were friends of the girl's boy friend, jumped him as he came out of the theater. They had knives and so did he. "What happened?" I asked him. "I won," was his answer in his characteristically modest way. "I did not even know that the girl was supposed to belong to someone," he told me. "I probably wouldn't have asked her out if I had known," he added, but he was smiling when he said it. He had told me that she was very pretty so I rather guessed that he probably would have asked her out anyway.

The bullet wound was a result of the same incident. It was not long after the knife attack that Montoya was out riding with his cousin who was also his best friend. They were quite some miles from anything that could be called civilization when shots rang out.

It has been over forty years now and I don't remember exactly where Montoya was shot but I think it was in the edge of his back. The bullet missed all vital organs. His cousin was not so fortunate. The impact of the bullet had thrown him off his horse and when Montoya reached him, he could see that his cousin was dead. The bullet from a carbine rifle had struck him in the back of the head. It was quite gruesome, not at all like the neat wounds that moviegoers saw in the 1950's and 1960's.

"I was in tremendous pain," Montoya told me, partly from his wound and partly from the realization that his best friend was dead. Montoya had to crawl back to his horse but once there he was able to get to his rifle. "My eyes were blinded from tears as much as from blood," he said. "I couldn't see to hit anything," he continued. When his attackers realized that he had a weapon and not grasping how badly off he was, they took off.

The murderers were caught. My shy friend had testified in court against them and before they were even transferred to prison, he decided to join the Air Force just to get away from it all.

I could hardly believe my ears! To hear this fantastic tale from such a quiet, reserved Native American, who may have been only five feet tall and not the five foot three I described, was quite incredible. He had all the scars to back up his story and I felt privileged to hear it. I did not tell him what I was thinking at the time but it was that if all Native Americans had been like Montoya we might not have had such a relatively easy time taking over this country.

Such thoughts were far from my mind that hot summer afternoon however. That day I only wanted to find an adult who would know what to do.

"The woods are on fire," I yelled to the black man who I supposed was a handyman of some sort. "Could you report it or call the fire department?" I cried out. The man looked at me as if I was crazy. I repeated myself and he continued to just look at me and not make a move in any direction. I couldn't believe it but I could see that he wasn't going to do a thing. I'm sure I must have been praying for help. Where else could I go? I was desperate. Even today, I am puzzled why it did not occur to me to ask any of the children to take me to their parents. Perhaps they were very young children. Instead, I jumped on my bicycle and pedaled as fast as I could. Down the road about the distance of two city blocks was a country store. There were no other buildings between the run down apartments and the store. As I approached the store with the gas pumps, I could see smoke in the distance about a third of a mile away. I was in tears.

"I need someone to report a fire," I said. Again, I got a peculiar look, this time of disbelief. "Look out back," I cried, "you can see it." Probably thinking that maybe there was a fire and that maybe it was right in back of his store the proprietor looked out the back door. The smoke was all too visible albeit in the distance. This person at least knew whom to call and he made the call. I was so relieved. "They already know about it," he told me.

I was physically worn out so I bicycled back at an average pace to the road where the fire had begun. By now, there were fire trucks and firemen, cars and pick-up trucks. The fire was almost under control and soon would be.

"I wonder how it started?" one of the firemen said to another but he seemed to be looking at me. I did not "fess up" as he may have hoped. "There are a lot of broken bottles around here," I said. "I've read that the sun can sometimes shine through a broken bottle like a magnifying glass and start a fire," I volunteered.A look of awe came over the fireman's face. "You know, I never thought of that," he replied out-loud to no one in particular. With the exception of broiling a few steaks with my cousin Darlene and my brother Mike in the 1960's over an open campfire on the beach near Southport, North Carolina, where the Cape Fear River reaches the Atlantic Ocean, it was nearly 40 years before I ever started a fire outdoors again.

The reason I knew about the possibility of the sun causing a fire through a broken bottle was that I read a lot. A love of reading was one of the greatest things that my mom ever taught me. Besides being quite literate, if I had to use one other word to describe the household I grew up in, that word would have to be theatrical.

Mom could have been an actress. At the age of 17, she was a veteran of school plays and even won first prize in an oratory contest sponsored by the Republican Party for the state of Rhode Island. Of course, she could hardly compete with adults who made their living by talking and the regional competition for all of New England was won by a lawyer who was a graduate of Harvard. Still, as a result of being state champion, mom was invited one weekend to be guests of the Vanderbilt family at their mansion in Newport. Their home is now a museum, open to the public for a fee, but mom was once their guest when they lived there.

Mom came from a family that was composed of mostly Democrats and she was doing her patriotic duty by helping out at the election headquarters of the local Democratic Party. How then did she win the contest for speaking for the Republicans? She overheard a local politician question another about her family and she also heard the answer. "Oh, don't worry about the Dunbar's; I have them in my back pocket." Mom could not believe her ears. That happened almost 70 years ago and that one incident made mom into a life-long Republican. People and nations need to be more careful what they say and what they do. Sometimes the consequences could not be imagined even if one tried.

Mom was an omnivorous reader and she once told me that before she was graduated from high school she had read all the books in the local library. Of course, she also told me that there were some she has never forgotten and that she wished she had not read. At 87, she still reads far more than most.

Mom has a love of words and their multiple meanings, which resulted in our hearing many literary jokes as we were growing up. She also evidenced a love and knowledge of Shakespeare. Hamlet, Macbeth, and others were frequently quoted to us. Mom would never just tell us to "Go tell your dad that supper's ready," but we would hear, "Stand not upon the order of your going but go at once" To be sure that we delivered a complicated message correctly (even if it wasn't complicated) we would frequently hear, "Speak the speech I pray you, as I pronounce it to you, trippingly and on the tongue, for if you mouth it as so many of our players do, I would as lief the town crier spoke my words." Now I cannot tell you what verse or even what play that is from but I heard those lines enough as a youngster that I can quote them from memory 50 years later.

After the excitement of the fire, life seemed very normal. I do not remember telling mom about it but I might have and of course, I would not dare have mentioned it to my dad as he had quite a temper although it has mellowed somewhat over the years. I think the reason that the fire spread so quickly was that we were in the midst of a drought and rainfall was scarce. Our vegetable garden was the talk of the neighborhood however. Although the weather was very dry, our vegetable garden was the greenest around. We had a bumper crop and more than one compliment was given to dad for his green thumb.

What no one knew (except us of course) was that dad had run a hose from our apartment across the yard and through a drainage pipe under the road and into the garden. The watermelons were big and the corn and squash were succulent because they were well watered. The Opportunity School had its own water supply and Dr. Wil Lou Grey never knew that that water supply helped feed the Pawley family. I was quite amazed when I visited the Opportunity School early in 2005 to discover that not one single building that I had remembered so well still existed. All had been replaced with newer modern buildings. Only the tree that dad had utilized to make us a good rope swing complete with a wooden seat was still there (the swing wasn't there, just the tree). It fact, with the exception of the road around the school itself, it was the only thing that was still the same. Even the vast fields that had been a farm to the east and north and that stretched all the way over to Platt Springs Road had turned into forest. The area that had once been our garden now had pine trees that were easily 40 or 45 years old and of considerable width.One could hardly imagine what the area looked like half a century ago.

4. The Rescue and the $5 Reward

Sometimes to save money, the fifteen cents that it cost to ride the bus, I would walk from St. Peter's Elementary School in downtown Columbia to the Opportunity School near the Columbia Airport, a distance of about six miles. Of course, I often tried the time honored method of sticking my thumb out and hitchhiking. Sometimes I only had to walk a mile or two. Occasionally I had to walk the entire distance. I tried varying the route from time to time and the most dangerous way I ever chose was to walk across the train trestle over the Congaree River just south of the City of Columbia. It would not have been a problem for me alone, after all I was 10 or 11, but my younger brother Bill was with me and he became frightened of the big spaces we had to step over in order to go from tie to tie. A fall was possible and it was the equivalent of several stories down to the rocks and water below us. Bill was only in the second grade and his stride was smaller than mine. He was about a hundred feet behind me and not even on the tracks when the first train thundered by me not six feet away from my crouched body. I had seen the train coming and climbed down on a side support beam. Bill finally joined me and we were about two thirds of the way across the river when Bill froze. Nothing I could do would get him to budge. I guess it was just the sudden realization of how far down the water was if he did fall. I wasn't big enough to carry him without risking both of us falling to our death. To make things even worse in the distance I could hear another train.

"Oh God!" I cried in earnest, "What am I going to do?" Although we had traversed two thirds of the way, the equivalent of more than a city block, Bill was afraid to move another foot. I noticed a couple of bigger boys, teenagers I guessed, fishing along the west side of the river. I called to them that I needed help. I explained to them in a shout that my brother was to scared to move and I could hear a train in the distance blowing its whistle. I was praying that they would come and help us and they did.

The oldest boy climbed up from the rivers edge to the tracks and then made his way across the third of the trestle that remained for us to cover. He picked Bill up on his shoulders and carried him the rest of the way across. We could see the slow moving train in the distance and had to move quickly. We had just gotten across the tracks and onto solid ground when the train, apparently oblivious to our presence, clamored on by. It had been a close call. When we told our parents what had happened they contacted the newspaper because they wanted to offer the boy who undoubtedly saved my brother's life a reward. The hero was located and received a check for $5 which had the purchasing power of more than $50 in today's money. My mother forbade me to ever go on the train trestle again but it was unnecessary to do so. I had no intention of ever trying to cross it again. I may have been inexperienced but I was not stupid.

I had almost forgotten this incident until 1986 when the movie "STAND BY ME" was released starring Wil Wheaton. In that movie another youngster barely makes it off the trestle before a train comes flying by. After seeing the movie I realized that probably quite a few young boys had crossed train trestles across the whole of America. Until "STAND BY ME" made me think about it realistically I had imagined that Bill and I were probably the only two to ever be in such a dangerous situation.

5. The Frog in the Classroom

St. Peter's Elementary School and the adjoining Ursline High School were taught by Ursline nuns. At the time the order dressed in black and white habits, clothes that were typical perhaps 450 years ago. No one could mistake them for anything but Catholic nuns. They were for the most part good teachers whose Christian mission in life was prayer and teaching. For this they received the necessities of life and little else. They did not receive a salary just a small stipend. Even if they were given something like a car, a hi-fi stereo record player, or money, they couldn't keep it. It would all go into a general fund to be shared by everyone much as the first Christians did almost twenty centuries ago. All my teachers through the ninth grade were nuns and an occasional priest. Some I liked and some I did not.

Even before I had begun to attend the first grade my mom had taught me to read and write and do simple arithmetic. Consequently the typical school work in a regular classroom was such a breeze that I was frequently bored (no such thing as an accelerated class as yet existed). I am sure I was a problem, only a minor problem, but still a problem for most of my teachers. One thing mom had never taught me to do was to sing and that is because she cannot carry a tune. She is, to put it bluntly, tone deaf. I don't know if such a thing is inherited or learned. I can whistle pretty good but even my wife has begged me more than once not to sing.

Once when I was in the fourth grade at St. Peter's the entire class was practicing the words to a new song and my teacher (a nun who shall remain nameless) said out-loud, "There's a frog in this classroom." She then proceeded to go around the room and listen to each student singing. When she reached me she listened for a few seconds and then she said, "Just pretend to sing. Move your lips but don't say anything out loud," and for the rest of my grade school, high school, and college years, that is exactly what I did. The teacher meant well, I'm sure, but I guess she knew even at that young age that I was a hopeless case when it came to singing. I seem

47

to remember that she spoke to each child so that none would be singled out but I was none the less humiliated and mortified beyond description.

It was around this time that a visiting Catholic priest gave a talk to the elementary students on faith in God. He had been captured by the North Korean Communists and tortured because he was a "foreign devil" bringing the "Imperialist doctrines" of the United States to the poor and downtrodden people in Korea. Why the North Koreans did not kill him I do not know. Perhaps even they were awed by his courage. I do not remember all they did to him in the name of "world socialism" but what I remember the most was how impressed I was when he told us how they had taken wooded splinters and soaked them in kerosene overnight. The following morning they drove the splinters up underneath his fingernails and set them on fire.

The priest spoke clearly to us and did not express any undue emotion about his captors and I was surprised at how he emphasized, like Jesus did, that we must pray for our enemies. The priest did not seem to harbor a grudge, much less any hatred towards these "communists". Although he looked physically normal in the typical black outfit that priests wore back then his fingers were distorted into claw-like appendages, something that I could not have even imagined at the time. His back was also a mass of scars from some kind of whipping. The fact that he undoubtedly had other scars of the kind that no one could see did not occur to me as I was too young to understand psychic scars.

I thought the communists must be the most monstrous barbarians who ever lived. At the time I knew nothing of the Spanish Inquisition or the Muslim hate for Christians and Jews, or of the history of so-called civilization and man's inhumanity to man over the centuries and in so many different places. Even in the 21st Century there are reports of children being used as slaves on 11 out of 12 cocoa bean plantations in Africa and the record of child sex slaves around the world is truly scandalous.

The following year I had a second humiliation that even my mom doesn't remember (again, maybe I never told her) but we used to get our lunches free because we could just barely pay the tuition to attend the school. I had saved my small allowance for a couple of weeks and purchased an instant pudding and pie mix for 15 cents. One day at home I baked a pie crust and brought it to school. I convinced one of my friends to give me his milk and together with mine I mixed up the pie mix in a bowl and poured it into the pie crust I had made earlier. My actions must have caused quite a commotion because as I was preparing to slice up the pie and share it with my friends, the priest who was second in command came over and asked what I was doing. When I explained he asked where I had gotten the money to buy the pie mix from and I told him that I had saved it out my allowance which was still 10 cents per week. "It only cost 15 cents," I told him. "Well, for someone who is getting his lunches for free it seems to me that if you had 15 cents to spend you should have given it to the lunch program," he replied. I was acutely embarrassed to have my friends discover that I was so poor I was getting "free lunches" and I have never forgotten the incident. I think I vowed that my kids would never have to go through that kind of financial embarrassment but I never had any. I wonder today if that might have been a factor in my lack of off-spring. I have never felt financially able enough to have children and consequently I have missed out on all the joys of parenthood, and the heartaches too, I suppose.

On a lighter note it was while I was in the fifth grade at St. Peter's that I had a crush on the prettiest girl in school. Her name was Adele and her family was descended from Middle East immigrants, Armenian or Lebanese. Adele had dark eyes and black hair. I did not know what the word exotic meant but if I did I probably would have used it to describe her. I never dated her (we were only in the fifth grade) but I did attend a birthday party at her house and she was the first young woman to whom I ever gave a corsage.

Behind St. Peter's Church was a historic old graveyard dating back into the 1800's. A walkway went from the side of the church to the back of the school and I used this as did many others to get from our classroom to the playground. Once I did some exploring in the graveyard. I was not in a mood to do any playing because the previous day one really big kid had knocked me down and just sat on me and since he was a big as an adult there was absolutely nothing I could do until he saw a nun coming and decided "to play" elsewhere.

I seem to remember once listening in on a debate on whether God has a sense of humor and I have become convinced that He does indeed. Look at some of the people He has created! One of these was Father Murphy. Father Murphy was actually Monsignor Murphy at St. Peter's School and Church and he served there for many years. He was always an older person to me which meant that he was older than my parents, more likely the age of my grandparents. He was also from the old school. He was a disciplinarian but whether he was actually from the old country I do not remember. He may have moved to the United States as a child but his English was flawless and he had no trace of an accent that I remember. He had served at St. Peters so long that he fully intended to die there. He even had his tombstone, purchased and paid for, and engraved with all the vital statistics except for the date of his death. As a ten or twelve year old I found that fascinating, a living person with a gravestone already set up in the cemetery that I walked through daily. It was when I was doing the exploring that I came across it. Well, part of Father Murphy's reward from God was a life so long that the church eventually retired him and he went to live his final days (and years) in his beloved Ireland before he went to his final reward. It has been many decades since I have seen that gravestone. Whether it is still there or in the interest of space has been removed I do not know. That God has a sense of humor I have absolutely no doubt and Father Murphy discovered that long before I did.

6. Numismatics and Judge Seabrook

Whaley's Beach House

It was in the early 1950's when I found a coin in change that I had never seen before. It was a Liberty Head nickel, a coin that was minted from 1883 until 1912, although five were secretly minted for a rich collector in 1913, the year my father was born. From 1962 until 2003 one of the five was missing, believed lost after its owner, North Carolina coin dealer George Walton, was killed in an auto accident. That missing 1913 Liberty nickel had entered folklore and much has been written about what might have happened to it. However, in the summer of 2003 it was once again "discovered" and not far from home. It seems that George Walton's sister recovered the nickel and other coins from the car wreck but someone told her later that the coin was not genuine. Believing what she had been told she marked that on the envelope containing the coin and it was still with her belongings when she died 30 years later. The nickel passed on to others who still had it eleven years later when Paul Montgomery of Bowers and Merena Coin Galleries decided to offer a million dollars for the coin if it could be found. He also offered $10,000 just to see it and that was sufficient to persuade its present owners to take a chance that just maybe the coin they had was real. The experts were able to compare the coin with the other four specimens where they had been gathered together in Baltimore in the summer of 2003. The long lost coin had been found. Examination proved that it had been struck from the same die as the other coins and that it was indeed genuine. One of the other coins sold for $3,000,000 that year and it is possible that the Walton specimen, missing for over 40 years could bring even more now that it has been located and the mystery solved. I guess the lesson here is to always get a second opinion.

I do not remember the date of the Liberty nickel that I found and it was probably only worth six or seven cents but it was a treasure to me. I had never seen one before and it made me wonder what other kinds of strange coins we might have once used for change. The existence of two cent and three cent pieces and even twenty cent pieces were completely alien to me at the time. The nickel I found was frequently called a "V" nickel by many because of the large Roman "V" for "5" on the reverse of the coin, followed, of course, by the word "cents".When I was growing up in South Carolina I occasionally heard the expression, "Oh, I was just joshing you!" The person saying this meant that they were just pulling your leg or playing a joke on you. I have not heard this expression in many years but it originated well over a century ago.

In 1883 when these nickels were first distributed they did not have the word "cents" under the large "V". A deaf-mute by the name of Josh Tatum was hauled into court for passing gold plated versions of the nickel. Gold coins in circulation usually just said "5 D." of "10 D." and older ones did not even have a denomination on them. Bar patrons thought the new coin was a five dollar gold piece and they gave Josh Tatum $4.95 change when he purchased a five cent beer. None of these people could testify under oath that Tatum had "said" they were gold pieces because Josh Tatum couldn't say anything at all. Very quickly, even for the mint, the word "Cents" was added to the new coin. That, I was told, was where the expression "I was just joshing you" came from and although it seems to have disappeared from the vernacular I wouldn't be at all surprised, if in the tiny communities, off the beaten track, far from any Interstate Highway, in the mountains of Appalachia, to hear that this expression was still, occasionally, in use.

Even in the 1950's finding a "V" nickel in change was an infrequent occurrence although the coin itself was not rare. The very common Buffalo or Indian Head nickel was what I often found although the Jefferson nickel had been minted by the millions for fifteen years. Today the Indian Head nickel and even that of the Liberty Head, or "V" nickel can be purchased in any coin shop for around $2 but are so rare in circulation that a clerk at a fast-food hamburger chain refused a worn "Buffalo nickel" a few years ago because she thought it was a foreign coin. I had some fun recently at a well known donut shop. When I went to pay for my purchase I used two paper dollars and then I reached in my pocket to get the remaining change. In my hand was a silver dollar, now worth about $10. "Wow!" said the clerk, a girl less than twenty. "What kind of giant coin is that?"

Well, silver dollars are readily available in almost any coin shop and the nickel from 1883 without the word "Cents" on it is also readily available for less than ten dollars. The government still makes mistakes at the mint and some modern ones are quite valuable. In 2001 someone at a Texas auction paid nearly $20,000 for a Franklin Half Dollar that was minted in 1961. This coin was stuck on a specially prepared silver planchet that was highly polished before striking in order to make a proof, a coin intended just for collectors who wanted the very best. Although there were over 3 million sets of 1961 coins minted in proof condition (a set consisted of a cent, nickel, dime, quarter and half dollar and specially packaged and sealed in cellophane) no one at the mint noticed that a number of the half dollars had the words "Half Dollar" and "E Pluribus Unum" clearly doubled. The original owner of the proof set with the very valuable doubled die Franklin half dollar in it had paid the mint $2.10 for it in 1961.

The "V" nickel that I found was the beginning of a lifelong interest in numismatics (the science and study of coins) although for years it was a sporadic relationship. I found a few Indian cents in circulation but as these coins were last minted in 1909 they were mostly worn or pitted. I came across a pawn shop between Main Street and Assembly Street that had a sign in the window that said simply "Coins". I discovered that this pawn shop had nice Indian cents in Fine condition that had no pits, had all the words of LIBERTY on the headband clearly discernible, and were available for a quarter. I was able to purchase a few different dates. Then one day I noticed in the back of one of my comic books an advertisement for a whole roll of 50 of these interesting cents that were first minted years before the last fight between the U.S. Calvary and the Indians had taken place. Since the roll cost $2 I saved my allowance for a number of weeks and purchased a roll of these interesting copper cents. I kept a couple of the best ones and sold the others to the kids at school, most of whom had more money than I did, for a dime each. That gave me more than enough money to buy a second roll but these were much harder to sell since I had pretty much saturated the market. After months of effort I finally had accumulated the princely sum of ten dollars which I made the big mistake of taking with me to summer camp. There I learned a hard lesson that spoiled the collecting of coins for me for almost a decade. The other youngsters at the camp were all Catholics who went to Catholic schools even. I thought of them much as my Baptist friends thought of themselves, or even as the Ancient Israelites thought of themselves (special, chosen).

It would be many years before I would discover that in God's eyes we are all special, but it was a rude awakening to discover that not all who were supposed to be honest, above reproach, and law abiding, actually were so. It was a hard lesson to have the money I had worked so hard and so long to accumulate, stolen.

That undoubtedly affected me in many ways but the only one I know for sure is that I lost all interest in coins until years later when I was in the United States Air Force. I don't think my faith in God was affected by the robbery but until the day years later in Texas when I found a dime in change that was worth three weeks salary my interest in coins was nil. I can't even say that my faith in people was affected by the robbery but it seems to me today, looking back as an adult, it must have been.

The robbery is the strongest memory I have of my last summer at summer camp but I also remember having to clean out a huge cast iron kettle in which I had boiled some crabs. Not being from the low country I didn't have a clue which parts were edible and which weren't and none of the other kids I asked seemed to know either so I simply walked away and left them. Within a day or two the stench was unbelievable. Since I had made the mess I was required to clean it up.

I have one pleasant memory from those final two weeks at Camp St. Mary's. During the time I was there I met a fellow camper. Her name was Dorothy VandeGrift and I developed quite a crush on her. When I returned home I carved her name high in a tree at the Opportunity School. It was the only time I ever did that. I was ten at the time and Dorothy was an "older woman" of eleven or twelve. Sadly, even that tree is long gone.

Summer camp was a solo affair for me but the entire family went on vacation a few times. We never went outside South Carolina though. In fact the only place we went was occasional trips to the coast. The ones I enjoyed the most were to a beach house owned by Judge Seabrook Whaley on Edisto Island. Judge Whaley was a retired law professor as well as a judge and as I understand it he established the first practice law courts in the nation at the University of South Carolina Law School. Actually he was quite famous in South Carolina and I remember visiting at his home in Columbia but I don't remember how we came to know the Whaley's.

Edisto Island was a small family oriented vacation island. There was only one general store when I was there in the 1950's and it was "Whaley's". I always assumed that it was run by one of Judge Whaley's relatives. I loved the quiet summer sunshine where the only sound was the breaking surf. None of the synthetic entertainment seemingly so necessary today existed at that time on the island. Fishing, crabbing, swimming and sunbathing was the extent of the activities. I thought it was an ideal place then and I still do.

Early in 2004 I had the opportunity to visit the island for the first time in half a century. Where once there had been only two roads there were now a dozen or more streets. Where there had only been a few dozen summer cabins raised on something like telephone poles to protect the buildings (somewhat anyway) from the high tides of hurricanes, now there were hundreds and hundreds of homes, some of brick, and some year round. There was even a tiny gated community at the far end of the island and what looked like a condo or apartment complex. Whaley's General Store had been replaced (or so I was told) by another store and that had eventually been torn down and replaced by a Piggly-Wiggly grocery store. There was even a liquor store and a restaurant. What surprised me the most besides the town hall was the fact that they even had a water tower. The old, slightly above sea-level bridge, was long gone although a small section of it was still visible from the island side. Now a tall span of a bridge, tall enough for the biggest sailboat to sail under, was there for all the islanders and visitors to use. Much had changed in the 50 years since I was last there but much had remained the same. The available entertainment, with the exception of television, and color TV at that, was as it had been when I was a youngster. It was still a family oriented vacation spot.

7. Carolina Clay, Suicide, and Land at $5 an Acre?

One day dad went to work a few minutes earlier than usual in order to get things set up for the class that was coming. He was surprised to discover that the door to the building was unlocked (it was one of the few separate buildings not connected to all the others at the Opportunity School). This had never happened before and dad knew that he had not left it unlocked. Although dad had seen plenty of death on the battlefield he was not quite prepared to find a fellow teacher hanging by a rope from one of the rafters. Dad had a hard time grasping that the teacher could be having such a terrible internal struggle that he would take his own life. Dad himself was having a difficult time with some of the administrators but the idea of someone he knew committing suicide was quite a shock to him. I had a friend over a decade later who did not want to go to Vietnam and kill anyone and his struggle over how to avoid having to kill ended when he took his own life instead. Tony was a fine person and quite sensitive but I had no idea how fearful he was of being drafted into the army and forced to kill.

Dad was searching for better opportunities than the Opportunity School could afford him and his growing family so after nearly three years he worked out some sort of verbal agreement with a landowner and developer on the other side of Columbia to build a house for us to live in and to start an art school in the attached studio which he also built. With the help of a few friends the four bedroom concrete block house at 4423 Bethel Church Road went up quickly. We left West Columbia in 1954 and relocated several miles east of downtown Columbia. The move meant a new school, a new church, and new friends. It was a big change for me and for my family.

Many of the people taking art classes with my dad were rich and some of them were very decent people. Others were outright snobs. I had to endure comments about our "brood" (my three brothers and two sisters at the time) from some of these people. Such comments undoubtedly had a sub-conscious effect on me (I know they had a conscious one because such talk always embarrassed me which is what I suppose such talk was meant to do).These newly rich seldom had more than two children, if that. "Tut! Tut! Must keep the money in the family you know" I could imagine some of them saying. In any event I've always liked children although I have none of my own.

There was a time years before this when I was about four or five years old and I happened to be playing with a doll (not a GI Joe action figure but an honest to goodness doll). One of the helpful neighbors on Greenbriar Avenue in Hampton, Virginia, saw me and said, "You shouldn't play with a doll. You're a boy. Boys don't play with dolls." My mom overhead this and before she could say anything she heard me answer with a wisdom that must have been divinely inspired. "Well, I'm gonna be a daddy someday and I have to get some practice sometime, don't I?" I don't remember the incident at all, only what my mom has related to me, but she told me that the neighbor was speechless.

Sometimes children can tell that I like them. I was sitting in a restaurant once when I noticed a young soldier eating at a table some two or three tables removed from mine. He was the only person in the place in uniform and I was on my lunch break from my job at IBM in East Fishkill, N.Y. Sitting with the soldier was a woman and a cute little girl in a high chair who was not quite two years old. I surmised that they were a family and I said a pray for all of them and I asked God to especially bless the little one. I had learned this practice from one of Dr. Norman Vincent Peale's bestsellers on positive thinking.I have frequently had children and even adults turn in my direction and sometimes smile when I have said a silent pray for them. It was as if they had suddenly felt some invisible ray of hope or light or love hit them from my direction.I was, however, unprepared for what happened next in that little restaurant.

Within seconds of my asking God to bless this little child she insisted that her mother take her down from the high chair in which she was sitting.The mother was clearly reluctant to do so but the little tyke was insistent.Finally her mother lifted her out of the high chair and placed her on the floor, whereupon she turned around and as quickly as her little legs could carry her practically ran past the intervening table's right up to the table at which I was sitting alone and eating my lunch. Then she put her arms around my leg, the only part of me that she could reach and gave me a big hug. Her mother, not knowing my part in this little drama, came over and said, "She must have mistaken you for someone else."I accompanied the two of them back to their table and talked for a few minutes with the little girl's dad who was stationed at West Point for six months. The family was from Ohio and I never saw them again after they left the restaurant but I went back to work feeling very special that day.

Life on Bethel Church Road was different from life at the Opportunity School. The house we lived in was adequate but not up to the standards of contemporary construction. Considering that dad spent most of his adult life teaching creative art and not creative construction it was a pretty decent house. How many men today, even with the help of a few friends, could build a house adequate for their families to live in for four years? It was a considerable accomplishment for someone who had never done that sort of thing before.

The house was poorly insulated which is to say that it was not insulated at all. The heat came from two sources, one large oil stove and one very large fireplace. The oil stove was adequate to keep the chill off but we really needed the fireplace to keep warm. I was not crazy about having to chop firewood after school every other day or so but the job I hated the most was gathering twigs and small branches into bushel baskets. We needed the kindling to start each day's fire. In the winter this was seldom necessary because we usually did not let the fire go out but it used to irritate me when dad would use twice as much wood as I felt necessary to start the fire with in order that we would have something to do on the following day. Even to this day I have a disdain for busy work, or pretend work, that which accomplishes nothing and which isn't really necessary.

The land immediately surrounding the house was quite poor and sandy but that didn't keep dad from putting in a garden, much smaller, of course, than the previous one at the Opportunity School. We had beans and strawberries and for the first time asparagus but the corn grew poorly and took up to much room. Overall the results were meager. I did not enjoy weeding this garden any more than I did the half acre garden in West Columbia.

The land on which the house stood and indeed what seemed like hundreds of acres around it belonged to Ray Stork who also owned a small brickyard just to the north of the house. More than once I watched bricks of good South Carolina clay being loaded into the furnace by Jesse or Julius, the two main workers. They may have been the only workers as it was a small brickyard. The bricks were then fired, baked to the hardness that we associate with firebrick. South Carolina has rich clay deposits and some of the clays were shipped to England when the Carolinas were still colonies of the British Empire. There they ended up in fine English china. I believe that at one time even the famous Wedgwood Company obtained some of their clays from South Carolina.

Only a very small trickle of a creek on a little strip of land with trees on it separated the brickyard to the north from our house to the south. In front of our house, across the street to the east, and up the hill was an older wooden house just visible from our house. Beyond that was a second house that faced a dead end street whose name I do not remember. The street didn't go anywhere and it ended a short distance past the single house that was on it and which housed one of the workers from the brickyard and his family. A nice family by the name of Neely lived in the house closest to us.

Mr. Neely had two teenage sons who were older than I was and he had a job involving the mechanical side of keeping the local school buses running. I recall that he was the only person I knew who changed the oil in his automobile every 1,500 miles when 5,000 was the most common change interval recommended and some cars had manuals recommending oil changes at 7,500 miles. His cars also lasted incredibly longer than most. Decades later I purchased the cheapest GM automobile made in the USA at the time and figuring that oil had improved over the years I changed the oil the first time at 1,000 miles and then faithfully every 3,000 miles after that. At around 100,000 miles I started to use an oil additive called Dura-Lube and once a year I used a quart of it in lieu of a quart of oil. At 193,000 miles I gave the car away because it was in need of a lot of little things to pass inspection and I did not want to bother with it. A year later I saw that car, recognizing the dings and dents and even some of the rust. The car now belonged to a college student at Marist College and had over 200,000 miles on it so I guess that changing the oil frequently really does help make the engine last longer.

Once Mr. Neely entered a raffle and won it. His prize was a tiny German car with the same name as the famous WWII German fighter aircraft, the Messerschmitt. The vehicle fascinated me because it was so small and looked so different from any other car I had ever seen. In fact, calling it a car was stretching it a bit. The vehicle had two seats, one for the driver and one for a passenger who sat immediately behind the driver. Today a Messerschmitt in good condition is worth ten times its 1955 or 1956 price of $750 as a collector's item. Then it was a novelty that interested few but I was one of them.

Behind the Neely's house was the house of one of the workers from the brickyard but I do not remember which one it was. I do remember that they had two children, one a girl who was about three years older than I was chronologically, but who was light years ahead of me in experience. Her dream was to go north to New York City and she simply could not believe it when my mom told her that in Harlem (at that time) that she might not even see a white person for weeks at a time. The girl eventually moved to Harlem and once she returned for a visit. Mom commented to her that her mother had said that she (the girl) had found a nice Christian woman to live with and my former teenage neighbor replied, "Yes, that's what I told her." We didn't know exactly what she meant by that but we knew that she meant something else.

Behind our green brick house (concrete block really but we always called it the "green brick house" because it was painted green) and to the west was a gently sloping incline of about 200 feet that ended in a slightly larger, but still small creek. This one however was big enough to house frogs and minnows and crayfish that were like thumb-sized fresh water lobsters. From there the lay of the land was upward with rolling tree covered forest and picturesque meadows where wild grapes and persimmons grew. I picked both on my exploratory walks. Once I saw a blue racer, a snake that could move incredibly fast. The glimpse I had of it was only long enough to observe that it was blue in color and then it was gone like a penny skyrocket, still legal in South Carolina, although now they come in clusters in more expensive packages for about a dollar.

The hills are still there but the lush almost forgotten wilderness is no more. Paved roads cover or at least crisscross where fields and meadows and long ago forests once flourished. Now dozens of upper-middle class homes align the streets that traverse the area. Our green brick house and the brick yard itself are gone, replaced with the Brickyard Condominiums. The Little People's Day Care is on part of the land that once housed the Neely Family and the government barracks up the road that housed the convicts in the chain gang when we lived there in the mid-1950's has been replaced with the Ravenwood Apartment Homes. So many changes the area is difficult to imagine as it once was.I can remember ads in the Farmers

Market Bulletin, a small weekly paper, in which farmers advertised what they had to sell. There was always an ad that said, "We will buy land anywhere in South Carolina for $5 per acre." That always intrigued me because even I knew that that was very cheap. Of course the phenomenon of growth is not a uniquely South Carolinian problem. It's happening all over the country.

"The people keep increasing but the land don't," an-almost millionaire with less than a grade school education told me once in Darlington County. I was hitchhiking and this person gave me a lift. He had a very nice car, a Lincoln Continental I think, and it was evident that he had had very little formal education. Because my family did not even own a car I tended to associate a fine automobile with education, money and prestige. The person who gave me the ride was a living breathing Jeb Klampert (the TV personality played by Buddy Ebsen in the series, The Beverly Hillbillies) although his fortune was not made in oil but in real estate. He was on his way to look at some property that he had purchased, a large farm with a farm house on it.He had already sold half the farm for what he had paid for all of it and he had kept the half that had the house on it. Now he was going to look it over again to see what ideas he might get as to how he could get the best return on the rest of his property. Again I was fascinated because here I was trying to get a college education so I could make my mark in the world or at least find fame and fortune (and I never really cared much about fame. "You can't eat it!" someone told me once). Here was someone who would never be famous except as a good example of what can be done with the barest of education, and with just a third grade education he was well onto making his fortune. Of course he had picked a very good thing to invest in. Since I graduated from high school in Florence, S.C. almost 120,000,000 new Americans have joined the swelling ranks of our population. Many were born here but almost as many have come from every country in the world to seek the American dream. More than eleven million have simply sneaked across the border, some dying in the attempt to get here. Sadly there are those who hate the idea of freedom and democracy and believe that only a world dictatorship can solve the problems of the world which are going to be far more serious in the years ahead. Some environmentalists have even said how wonderful it would be if mankind could just be eliminated but I wonder who it would be wonderful for if humans went the way of most other intelligent beings in the galaxy. Our government continues to pretend that there is something we can do to solve the Palestinian/Israeli conflict when both sides over there know that nothing Israeli can ever do (except go out of existence) will ever satisfy the Palestinians. But if we are willing to pretend then so are they. Since the Palestinians are having far more children than the Israelis their population will be larger within a decade or so. Of course I am more familiar with the population increase in the United States but what is happening over there will soon affect the whole world. Some would say that it already has. Of course this is hardly news to students of the Bible as all these things were foretold long ago. Information that someone hid in the Bible 3,200 years ago (THE BIBLE CODE) indicates the escalation of this conflict may even begin within the next twelve months, with an attack on or in Jerusalem.

Yes, it is truly incredible to see how much this country is growing. It's happening almost everywhere. A meadow that I drove past daily on my way to work nine years ago and upon which I observed both wild turkeys and deer (from time to time) is now filled with houses in the $275,000 range when I started writing this book but they are now $400,000 plus. Open space is disappearing in South Carolina as well as here in New York. Since the attack on the World Trade Center New York State has lost over a million acres of farmland. I understand now what I did not some 20 years ago when I was complaining to a dear friend from France about a good but expensive French wine. The demand was greater than the supply and the price just kept going up and up. The owner of the winery had said that he could sell thousands of more bottles if he could produce it. "Why doesn't he plant more grapes?" I asked my friend. "There's no more land," Sabine told me. "It would be necessary to tear down some buildings in order to plant more vineyards," she continued. At the time I was amazed just as I was upon learning that in the grass strip between what we call Interstate highways are planted crops in some of their European equivalents where land is scarce. I see it starting to begin here. Of course we still have a long way to go to match the population density of Europe but by that time only the rich will be able to own land, the way it has always been.

8. Not Quite Rock and Roll

The school I attended from 1954 to 1956 was Saint Joseph's, just two blocks from Dreher High School, which at that time was the high school that most of the rich kids attended. Saint Joseph's had grades one through six and my brothers Bill and Mike attended there as well. I was in the sixth grade which was as high as they went but the following year they added the seventh so I was able to attend two years before switching back to St. Peter's for the eight grade.

Besides history and geography and math and English there were school dances and birthday parties and occasionally games like spin-the-bottle to see which girl the guys would get to kiss. I liked the slow dancing because I could do it but I didn't have much of a sense of rhythm and so I usually skipped the "shag" or any other fast dances. Besides, even if I could have thrown the girl I was dancing with over my back I preferred to hold her close and nobody held anybody close in the fast dances.

I was drawn more to easy listening music like Nat "King" Cole (singer Natalie Cole's father), Theresa Brewer, Tony Bennett, Frank Sinatra, even Perry Como and the Platters. Oh, I liked some of the popular songs that Chuck Berry, Little Richard, and Marty Robbins sang but I could hardly be called a big fan of Rock and Roll. "Tennessee" Ernie Ford, Johnny Cash, The Everly Brothers, Buddy Holly, The Kingston Trio, I listened to them all. I even liked much of the "older" music from the 1940's. The only radio stations that I was aware of were AM stations and a few were more popular than others. These took requests for popular songs. Almost every night my classmates and I would phone the radio station with requests and then listen for the song to be played along with the dedication. Occasionally the radio stations we listened to would offer a free ticket to some popular movie to the first person who called the station after the advertisement stopped. I couldn't drive yet nor could most of my classmates. At that time in South Carolina a person had to be 14 to be licensed to drive alone on a public highway. Of course if you lived on a farm you could drive a tractor or a truck on the farm and across public roads to the other side if the farm work required it and you could do so at an even earlier age although not having lived on a farm I don't remember the actual age.

When I was in the eighth grade I had one older friend who was in high school. Ralph Stuart Singleton was his name and his goal was to go to Hollywood and become a producer. He had a great sense of humor and my mom enjoyed that even more than I did. More important than his sense of humor was the fact that he had his own car.I don't remember how we met. Perhaps he was one of my dad's art students or maybe his parents were. Once I remember driving around in Ralph's four year old Cadillac looking for Coke bottles to cash in for extra gas money. South Carolina didn't have a bottle refund law (I don't think they do yet) but the Coca-Cola Company and perhaps Royal Crown and Pepsi charged a two cent deposit on their bottles. I liked Coca-Cola and their bottles because most cities had their own bottling plant as many do today but back then each city had its name on the bottom of the bottle. It was fun to purchase a six-pack of cokes and see where the bottles came from originally. The farthest away I ever found one from in Columbia was from Albuquerque, N.M., where my sister Anne lived for many years. After all these decades the Coca-Cola Company has recently started making replicas of these bottles again.

My friend Ralph claimed to be descended from the Stuart line of kings in England and he may have been for all I know. His family owned a microwave oven (which was first invented in 1947) but which was still very, very expensive. I sold microwave ovens in 1974 for $795 but in 1957 a good microwave oven or an inexpensive new car cost about the same. Ralph himself owned a hand-sized transistor radio with five or six transistors. His radio was smaller than the battery that I had in my portable radio that had the old fashioned glass vacuum tubes. I seem to recall that his little radio cost about $80 which was almost two weeks wages at a regular job. Within a few years IBM was putting 100 transistors in something called "solid logic technology" and today silicon micro-chips no bigger than one of the transistors in my friend's radio may contain as many as 5,000 transistors. Other "chips" no bigger than half a dollar but squared in shape may contain more than half a million transistors. IBM scientists have discovered the limit of smallness in semi-conductor technology (I'm sure they have a better scientific name for it). The minimum thickness (or would that be thinness?) that a silicon micro-chip can have and still function is five atoms. Four atoms are too small and won't work but five atoms will. In any event, that is a very small transistor indeed. I worked at a company that has already produced these virtually invisible transistors.

One day I heard a commercial on the radio for a new Pat Boone movie. It was called "April Love" and the title song became a big hit. The radio announcer talked about the music and how great the movie was and then said that the first person who called a phone number that belonged to the radio station would get a free ticket to the movie. I wrote the number down and quickly called but the line was busy with many others doing the same thing. The next day I was listening to the same radio program and the same commercial came on. It occurred to me that they might offer another free ticket so I took the phone number out of my pocket or wallet and when the announcer said, "Tell you what, we're going to give away a free ticket to the next person..." I had already begun dialing before the number was given. The phone rang in the radio station as the commercial ended and I was the lucky winner. They asked my name and what school I went to and told me where I could pick up my free ticket. "This is easy," I thought, so I called Ralph to see if he would be interested in going to see the movie with me if I could win another ticket. He said, "Sure" so the next day I was at the phone with the radio nearby. I did not even wait for the free ticket part but began to slowly dial the five digits of the telephone number. Sure enough I hadn't dialed too early but had timed it just right. This time when asked my name I gave them the name Ralph Stuart Singleton and when they asked for the name of the school I attended I answered by giving them the name of the school that Ralph attended, Dreher High School. I was acting on his behalf, sort of like an agent, so I theorized that I wasn't exactly lying. I thought about continuing the next day to win still another ticket but decided that that would be greedy as I didn't really have a need for anymore tickets.

I provided the tickets and Ralph provided the transportation. I don't remember Ralph's opinion of the movie but I enjoyed it. I saw it once 40 years later and although it was OK it was not the same movie I had enjoyed as a young teenager. Of course, the movie was exactly the same; it was I who was different.

Ralph and I used to go to drive-in theaters which were very popular. We saw all the latest monster flicks and science fiction "B" movies. Some of them were truly awful by today's standards, but in 1956 a classic arrived which can still be seen today. It was FORBIDDEN PLANET and it inspired a generation of science fiction fans much as Buck Rogers had a generation earlier and STAR WARS would do a generation later. The only other movie I remember from the drive-ins we frequented was a romantic love story about a G.I. who falls in love with a Pacific Island princess. It was during WWII and all the soldiers or seamen had told their girls that they would return after the war and marry them. None did. (I had an older friend who was stationed in the South Pacific during WWII and I remember Jim telling me that from a distance the girls were beautiful but up close you could see that they had dirty fingernails and often needed a good bath).Anyway this island princess was still hopeful even though her friends made fun of her for still believing, after all the war was long over and where was he? Finally, in the final scenes of PLEASURE ISLAND, the guy returns with some plausible excuse on why he couldn't get back sooner. Everyone except the beautiful young girl is amazed that he really did return. PLEASURE ISLAND was probably one of the lesser known "B" movies that were one half of the very popular double features that were quite common at the drive-ins in the 1950's. Over the years I've watched for it on late night TV but I never saw it again. Funny how some movies and books and people will touch you in a way you could not have anticipated. Fortunately many of the old movies are being restored but some are lost forever. I don't even know if I would enjoy the movie today as much as I did back then but I have wondered if PLEASURE ISLAND still exists hidden away in a dusty attic or stored with who knows what on some actor's estate.

9. Another Rescue and Another Death

It was around 1955 or 1956 that someone gave dad his first automobile. It was a huge 1942 Chrysler limousine, one of the few cars manufactured in the beginning of that war year before all the factories and plants started making tanks and military aircraft. The vehicle was in relatively good condition and was certainly big enough for our family but neither of my parents had driver's licenses although my dad had driven jeeps during the war. He once drove the car about a mile to pick me up at a lake where I was fishing. I remember how surprised I was to see him driving that big old Chrysler. It was the first time I had ever seen him drive. When we moved from Columbia to Florence dad gave the car to one of the men who worked at the brickyard. Today that car would be worth $18,000 or more.

One of my mother's friends, Christine Whitlock, who lived about a mile from us, would often provide our transportation. Mrs. Whitlock was the only person I knew personally who had a family larger than ours. Eventually I had seven younger brothers and sisters but Mrs. Whitlock had three sets of twins in addition to her other six children. This was in the days before miracle fertility drugs and was a result of the fact that twins ran in both sides of the family. Mr. Whitlock was in the tobacco industry and among his talents was the fact that he could instantly give the answer to any number up to 5,000 multiplied by any other number up to 5,000. Until the electronic calculator was invented, his ability was an extremely important asset on his job.

Sometimes Mrs. Whitlock would take us to school and sometimes to school dances. She was a generous woman and a good mother and we were all shocked to discover that her oldest son Gordon died while in high school from something that they called double pneumonia. He had been a classmate and friend of my brother Bill. Young Gordon had been sick a day or two, enough to keep him home from school, but it was not until the once-a-week maid came to work, saw him, and told his mother, "Lordy, I sees the smell of death on him," that it was suddenly decided that he should be taken to a doctor. From the doctors office he was rushed to the hospital but it was too late. No one else had seen anything unusual or smelled anything and I used to wonder how the house cleaner had known that young Gordon was so close to death.

When I was in the seventh grade, I had crush on a pretty girl named Clare Burke. Her father was an officer at Fort Jackson and I wrote her little poems. I danced with her a few times but we never dated. In order to earn spending money I accepted an offer from an engineering student at the University of South Carolina. Bill Thomas was married and I think had one child at the time. He went on to become an executive of some sort at Union Carbide. Bill had a large paper route and I assisted him in rolling and throwing papers from his car over part of the route. One of the customers on the route was the Stevenson Family. Their daughter Miriam told Bill that she did not have a single date for six months after she was elected Miss Universe (or it might have been after she was elected Miss USA in 1954, she was both that year). Apparently, all the guys who had dated her previously were intimidated by her new titles. I remember Bill said, "I wished I'd known that back then." Back then, meaning in 1954, he had been single.

I saved my money and when Clare was thirteen, I gave her a $46 gold wristwatch. It took all the money I had saved for the better part of two years. Mom tried to convince me that the gift was too much, too big of a gift for a girl of thirteen, but I was, as they used to say once, smitten! Mom even called Clare's mother thinking that she would make her daughter refuse such an expensive gift, but her mother's reply was only, "Oh, no! I hope he doesn't get it for her because that's what we were going to give her." Even this knowledge was not enough to dissuade me. As far as I know, Clare received two gold watches on her birthday that year.

It is usually around the age of twelve or thirteen when baptized members of the Catholic Church make a personal commitment to Jesus Christ. We call it confirmation. We acknowledge that we are sinners and desire to deny evil in our lives (or to renounce Satan as we say it) and we ask Jesus to come into our lives, forgive our sins, and fill us with His Holy Spirit. Sometimes, if we have been properly or perhaps fully taught on what it is we are doing and what to expect, the result can be dramatic, a true spiritual awakening. More often than not, it is just one more step on the path to adulthood with the emphasis more on tradition than on expectation or change. I looked forward to this sacrament, which is only received once in a lifetime, as much as a young Jewish boy might look forward to his Bar Mitzvah. In addition to the public ceremony, which is performed by a bishop, we usually select the name of some heroic Christian of the past who led an exemplary life, someone worthy of being imitated. We read about the life of the saint whose name we had chosen and in my seventh grade class, we were required to write a paper on that saint. We were also required to read this paper to the class. When it was my turn to read the paper I had written about the saint whose name I had chosen I could hear gasps from some of my classmates when I announced, not that I was taking the name of Francis for St. Francis of Assisi, but that of his good friend Clare, who was also considered a saint and the founder of the order of nuns that was eventually named after her. Everyone, including Sister Phillip, knew that I was more interested in Clare my classmate than in the Clare who worked for the poor and was the Mother Teresa of her day.

My classmate Clare's father was soon transferred to Germany and she, her mom, and her younger brother Jerry all went with him. I never saw or heard from them again.

One of my classmates came from a medium sized Italian family and we were good friends. He was a tall outgoing person with a good sense of humor. During our Easter vacation, we decided to go fishing in the Congaree River, which divides Columbia and West Columbia. We packed some sandwiches and sodas for lunch and then we got some bait and fishing poles and walked the considerable distance of several miles to the river. There on the West Columbia side we climbed down the steep bank and made our way on some just slightly submerged rocks to a rock cluster about the size of a typical kitchen floor. Trying to be funny I told Robert that we had to leave by 2 o'clock because that was when they let the water out of the dam at Lake Murray (the world's largest earthen dam when it was built in 1930). I don't remember if I had a watch but I'm guessing that Robert did because of what I said. I was just making that up, sort of as a joke.

Lake Murray is a significant source of hydroelectric power in central South Carolina and the water behind the dam is the source of the energy for the huge generators. As I recall the water is several hundred feet deep at the center of the dam.

Time passed quickly as it usually does when you are having fun. Soon I noticed that I could not see the rocks that we had walked out on and even the clusters of rocks, the little island that we were on, had shrunk in size as the water rose. Rather rapidly, the water continued to rise.Soon our little island was no bigger than a door and then no bigger than two kitchen stools. We each clung to the rock we were on about ten feet apart from each other. I do not remember what Robert was doing. I believe he was praying. I know I was, especially since I couldn't swim and even an excellent swimmer would have had a difficult if not impossible time in these rocky waters. Years later when I was a student at the University and lived in a dorm on the "horseshoe" the oldest part of the University I had a roommate named "Buddy" Gray. One day "Buddy" decided to "run the rapids" in a large inner tube. "Bud" entered the river not far from where the zoo now is and although he is a good swimmer and had a good quality inner tube, he was two miles downstream before he could reach either side of the river and he survived his ordeal in bruised and bloody condition. The river is something one must never take for granted.

That day in Columbia, the rocks upon which Robert and I were clinging to were almost under the bridge. Only if a person were walking across the bridge (and not many people did) and that person decided to stop and look down, could a person above us on the bridge even see us. I don't know what is along the river's banks today but then there was no place, where an ordinary person on the shore could see us either. We needed help and I was praying as earnestly as I knew how. After some length of time, I looked up and was surprised to see someone looking down at the churning whitewater and us. Desperately we waved and tried with our arms to indicate that we were stranded and needed help. For a while, this person just looked at us and finally he waved back. If he yelled anything down to us as I thought he might have, we could not have heard it over the roar of the water. A few minutes later, he left and I prayed that he would tell someone about the two kids stranded in the river and not ignore us as the handy man had ignored me a few years earlier when I told him about the fire.

About half an hour later, when we were really beginning to wonder if anyone would come and rescue us, we noticed some commotion down steam. A group of people had gathered on the western bank of the river not far from where we ourselves had entered the water. There seemed to be about two dozen adults including the news reporters. Then I noticed that they were putting a good-sized aluminum boat into the water. It was about the distance of a small city block from where we were to where the boat was being launched by the firefighters from the local fire department.

It took a good ten minutes or more for the powerboat to navigate around and through the many submerged rocks. They really had quite a time of it. Finally, to my great relief they reached us. We were cold and wet and although I was grateful to be rescued, I felt very foolish at having allowed myself to get into such a situation. Consequently, when the photographers from The Columbia Record and The State newspapers took pictures of the two boys saved from the clutches of the raging river, I hid my face. Robert on the other hand, thought the publicity was great and with a big grin on his face, he stretched out his arms like Jesus reaching out to the multitudes. Not one picture was suitable to go with the story that appeared in the following day's paper. I was surprised to hear one of the firemen tell a reporter that the spot they had rescued us from was very dangerous and that several people had drowned there over the years. I was shocked, however, to hear that they really did let water out of the dam at 2 o'clock. I thought I had just made that up.

The news story appeared in the next edition of the papers and it seemed like everyone who knew us read it. Robert Amodio and I were both in the procession at St. Joseph's on Easter Sunday, and more than one hand from the overflowing crowd pointed us out as the boys who had been rescued from the river. I don't know why this embarrassed me but it did.

One day at recess in the seventh grade, I found a balloon. A classmate who was always cutting up and getting into trouble saw it and he thought it was hilarious. He kept saying, "Take it to Sister Phillip! It's not a balloon! Take it to Sister Phillip!" I had observed him enough to know that he was not to be trusted (years later I heard that he went to prison) so I suppose I should have just thrown it in the trash but I was curious why he made such a big deal out of it. Besides, if it wasn't a balloon I thought our teacher might tell me what it was. "Where did you get that?" Sister Phillip asked. I told her that I had found it on the playground and that so-and-so had said to bring it to her. She told me to throw it into the trash, which I did, but she never did tell me that it was a condom.

St. Joseph's did not add an eighth grade in the fall of 1956 so it was necessary for me to switch back to St. Peters if I was going to continue my education at a Catholic school. Once again, my teacher was also the principal. Sister Victor was a decent teacher. I remember her as being somewhat stern as compared to Sister Phillips but not a bad teacher. The work was not challenging and I was bored as I had been for so many years. One of the no-nonsense rules was that we were not allowed to chew gum or eat anything in the class-room. One day I made a big production out of chewing and Sister Victor said, "Richard, what are you eating?" I reached into my im-ported can of Japanese goodies and pulled something out by one of its legs. As I displayed it charred salty body for all the girls to see, I answered nonchalantly, "fried grasshoppers," and promptly chomped the grasshoppers head off. Several girls nearby shrieked, and Sister Victor was not amused. For the next five days, I had to stay after school for half an hour as punishment. My only thoughts on the matter were that it was worth it.

People used to tell me that I was so smart but I never felt smart. It never occurred to me that being second in the class was an ac-complishment of sorts. As I mentioned earlier Jean Hoeffer (Toal) South Carolina's Chief Justice of the State Supreme Court was my classmate and she was always the one with the highest grades in the class. Of course, she studied! Once when I was in the 8th grade, I hitchhiked to school in order to save the bus-fare. I was having quite a conversation with the driver until he asked me if I went to the University. I felt so self-conscious that I was only in elementary school that I said I was a student at Ursline High School right next door. Well, I would be in a few months.

I was graduated from the 8th grade at St. Peters in the late spring of 1957 and won a full tuition scholarship for the first year of high school at Ursline. The school, now long gone, was less than a 100 feet from St. Peters.The award was for $60 and today I would imag-ine that might cover a week's tuition (maybe), most certainly not a month, but in 1957-58, it paid my tuition for the entire year. The purchasing power of a dollar was considerably more before the Vietnam War and the War on Poverty and all the other government handouts since then. Not many years after that Congress passed legislation to take the funds in the Social Security Trust Fund and put them into the General Fund so that the money could be spent on the war in Vietnam and other things. That was the beginning of the problems with Social Security. So much for the "Trust" in Trust Funds. One day I am convinced we will look back at 2006 and re-member how cheap everything was before the War in Iraq. We are borrowing something like $2 billion and 400 million dollars per day to run the government and no one will ever be able to pay it all back. I do not even know if we will be able to inflate our way out of this debt, so tremendous has it become. However, before Congress went on a spending spree with our Social Security funds, $60 was enough to pay for a year's tuition at one of the only three Catholic high schools in the entire state.

The summer after I left St. Peters I decided to take a high school course in the public summer school. I do not even remember what the course was but it was taught at the local junior high school about half a mile north of St. Peters. I passed the course and obtained my first high school credit. The way things worked out, taking that course at age 14 and the subsequent one the following year may have started a chain of events that kept be ahead of the Vietnam Conflict. I was in the military and back out again before things really blew up over there. Taking those two courses might well have saved my life.

In addition to taking that summer school course I also had a part-time occasional job south of Columbia at a ranch owned by Burwell Manning. Mr. Manning was a real character. His father had once been governor of South Carolina. Mr. Manning told us that after WWI, he calculated the direction in which Columbia would grow in thirty years and he began purchasing land, gradually, in that area. To keep others away he allowed some less-than-desirable tenants to live rent-free in an old barely usable house. The term used in the South for such people who are frequently in trouble with the law (and who seldom have any visible means of support) is "poor white trash." No one wanted to live near people like that, and in time Mr. Manning was able to purchase quite a lot of land. When the time came, years later, to do something with the land the tenants were told that they would have to move. Weeks went by and the people living in the house were still there. They had not attempted whatsoever to move. Finally, they were told that they had 30 days in which to move and that the old house was going to be torn down. Still the people did not budge. On the last night before they were supposed to have moved about a dozen men showed up in several pick-up trucks around mid-night and while making a fair amount of noise went methodically around the house digging holes and laying wires. When asked what they were doing the men simply replied that they had orders to blow-up the old house with dynamite at dawn. The undesirable tenants who had for years never paid any rent quickly packed and got out before dawn. The explosion must have been a big one.

It may have been Mr. Manning who told me that there have been more millionaires made in this country through real estate than thorough any other medium. I don't remember all the stories he told us but I was fascinated by his dealings with the government. Mr. Manning dammed up a good-sized creek that ran through his property and named the lake after his wife, Katherine. I do not remember if there had been a small natural lake there or if the Army Corp of Engineers had anything to do with it but during WWII, the U.S. Army wanted to condemn the property so they could take it over and have plenty of water for Fort Jackson. Mr. Manning and his lawyers worked out a compromise solution where he continued to own most of the lake front property and the government got all the water they wanted for a dollar per year. The calculations that Mr. Manning had made as to where Columbia would grow proved correct and by the 1950's the land had become quite valuable. Of course, he owned other lands including the ranch where he raised polo ponies. There was a tiny one-room cabin on the ranch and Mr. Manning always left a single light bulb on in the cabin. "I have to pay C.P. & L. (Carolina Power and Light) so much money each month whether I use it or not," he told me once, "so I leave it burning to get my money's worth." The idea of conserving energy had not occurred to anyone yet!

I remember more than once eating my sandwich and soft drink lunch sitting on the limb of a huge tree that stretched out over the bank of the Congaree River, which was less rocky and more placid by the time it reached the ranch. It was a beautiful and peaceful setting and I could understand why Mr. Manning liked the area so much.

My dad only made one water fountain in his life and it was for Mr. Manning's front yard. It was a life-sized statue of a semi-nude maiden holding a water jar and the water ascended out of the top of the jar or jug into the air and then flowed into the surrounding pool. It was beautiful and in my opinion as nice as or better than some of the marvelous outdoor sculptures at South Carolina's famous Brookgreen Gardens near Pawley's Island.

We almost lost my sister Anne to an alligator at Brookgreen Gardens once. The "gators" are long gone unless some environmentalist has decided to "restore" them as they have the wolves in some of our western and mid-western states but in the mid-fifties the "gators" could still be seen, and large ones at that, at the waters edge and in the creeks and swampy areas surrounding the beautiful public gardens. Back then there was not even an admission charge to the gardens with their sculptures, some bigger than an elephant and some as small as a hawk. Many famous sculptors have works of art at this former 4,000-acre plantation including Augustus Saint-Gaudens who was a friend of President Theodore Roosevelt.Saint-Gaudens beautiful design for Lady Liberty was used on a $20 gold coin from 1907 until gold coins were outlawed in 1933. A single "legal" 1933 $20 gold piece sold in 2002 for over $7 million dollars. The Mint did not officially release any in 1933 but the story I heard as a kid was that a number of people who worked at the mint were allowed to substitute one of their $20 gold coins for the brand new ones and as many as a dozen may have ended up in collector's hands. When the government found out that a collector had paid a years salary to purchase one a decade later they suddenly declared them illegal and began seizing them at will including the one that the collector had paid so dearly for. An elderly collector told me once that one person threw his specimen into the Atlantic Ocean rather than let the government take it to destroy it. Gold was illegal to own in this country at the time (unless you were a collector) and King Farouk of Egypt managed to purchase one of the 1933 $20 gold pieces. American citizens, even collectors, could not own a 1933 $20 gold piece but a foreign king could and the government issued King Farouk an export license. This coin was the specimen that was recently sold for the most money ever paid for a single coin. Of course, the British and American sellers of the coin had to agree to give the U.S. Government half of all the money they got at the sale.

When gold coins were once again legalized in 1974-75 and the tremendous importation of foreign gold coins that followed proved that some Americans liked some form of money that could not be printed with paper and ink it was decided that the United States should have its own legal tender gold coins. Rather than use the designs of a contemporary artist Saint-Gaudens design was resurrected and modified. Lady Liberty lost 20 pounds (it seems that earlier 20th Century Americans liked their women with a little something on their bones, not the starving war-refugee look of some of today's models). Millions of U.S. Gold Eagles as they are called have been minted since 1986 in sizes ranging from a full ounce down to a tenth of an ounce, although the smaller ones are used more for jewelry than for a store of value.

Anyway, my family was visiting Brookgreen Gardens on a warm summer day in the mid-1950s. We had walked along the flower gardens and looked at the many sculptures and were standing behind a flimsy wire fence looking at the alligators. The largest was about 10 or 12 feet long. It came to the water's edge and then ever so slowly came out of the water and was about 15 feet from us when someone yelled at mom, "Hey, lady, you better get that kid out of there. That alligator thinks she's his lunch." Mom was a little startled. The alligators she knew from Roger William's Park in Providence, Rhode Island, were so lethargic in the cold New England water that you could almost walk across their backs with little fear. Still, there was a note of genuine concern in the man's voice. The creature had moved forward another foot or so and was now completely out of the water. Suddenly the fear that maybe these alligators were different from the ones she knew as a teenager in Providence gripped my mom. With a mother's instinct, she quickly reached down and picked my baby sister Anne up off the ground. As soon as she did, the alligator stopped coming forward and in fact retreated incredibly fast, back into the water. I was impressed with how fast the animal was moving away from us and it occurred to me that if it could move that fast away from us it could have moved that fast towards us if it had chosen to do so. We all realized that it had been a close call because the flimsy wire fence would not have stopped a beast the size of the one we had just seen.

I have visited Brookgreen Gardens a number of times since then and it is little changed. The biggest change, in addition to some newer works of art, is that there were no alligators of any size there the last few times I visited, and the department that runs the place had heard the phrase, "It's amazing that you don't charge anything to visit this place," from so many northern tourists that many years ago an entrance fee was initiated to help pay for maintaining the gardens. For those who appreciate the outdoors and the beauty of nature, and good art, the fee is well worth it. I've even taken friends from Europe there.

10. High School

In the eighth grade I only went out on a date once. Of course there were dances and parties but dating without the use or a car was not the easiest thing in the world and since neither of my parents had a drivers license I had to do the best I could without a car. Clare had moved to Germany and I developed a crush on a beautiful natural blond by the name of Patricia Hamburger. I had met her and danced with her once when I was in the seventh grade and she was in the eighth. Now she was in high school and I was elated when she accepted my invitation to see the new John Wayne and Natalie Wood movie, THE SEARCHERS. On occasion I would ride my bicycle four or five miles over to Pat's neighborhood in the hopes that I would see her but it did not occur to me to say that I was in the area and drop by for a visit. No one would have ever accused me of being shy but I guess I must have been where the opposite sex was concerned.

Pat came from a large family too, but at the time it consisted of just girls. We had made arrangements to meet at a particular place and time and I enjoyed taking her to the movie but I didn't know her well enough to kiss her. She was a really nice person and I distinctly remember shaking her hand as she got on the bus to return home. When I finally got to high school, Pat was, as I recall, going steady, and I still didn't have access to a car, so that as they say, was that.

I lived well over four miles from school and rather than spend the money I was given for bus fare I sometimes chose to walk home from St. Peters to Bethel Church Road. Sometimes I hitchhiked part of the way but because of the lay of the land it would take me three different rides to get all the way home. The city police frowned on hitchhiking in the city so a walk of at least a mile out past Providence Hospital was usually a necessity. There as the city thinned out and the suburbs began I would throw out the old thumb and take my chances. Although I was older and more able to walk the distance than I had been when I lived all the way out at the Columbia Airport or rather the Opportunity School I did not hitchhike as often.

Sometimes the time was more important than the money and I had an occasional baby-sitting job. I remember one Jewish couple who paid me $1.25 for 5 hours of watching their kids while they went somewhere. That seemed fair to me. It was what I agreed upon but both my parents and my mom's friend Christine thought it was cheap. "They should have at least given you a tip," someone said, but I had agreed to work for "what was fair" and had not set a price as I recall. I didn't feel cheated but thought that perhaps I had been when the adults made such a fuss about it. They never asked me to baby-sit for them again so I didn't know what to think.

The only problem I ever had while hitchhiking was with one driver who picked me up by the Covenant Road Elementary School. We had gone less than a quarter of a mile and being as gregarious as always I was rapidly into a myriad of topics when the driver, a decently dressed guy about my dad's age (mid-40's) asked me rather bluntly if I had ever had sex. I was taken aback! I may have been 13 or 14 at the oldest but I looked 10 years old. Of course at the time I didn't realize that I looked ten. "No, I don't even have a girlfriend," I answered. "No, I meant did you ever go out with the guys and have sex?" I can't imagine what my facial expression must have been but I noticed that we were going no more than 35 mph and I remember thinking that if I jumped from the car at that speed I might be killed. I had heard of homosexuals, men who had strange sexual longings for other men rather than for women, the way nature or God intended. This guy was soft spoken, did not look different from hundreds of others that I had met but he was different. He made no aggressive moves towards me and with every second I was getting closer to home. "Well, you can't fault me for asking, can you?" After a silence that seemed deafening and a time that seemed like hours but was no more than a minute or two I heard myself answer, "No, I guess not." I did not know what else to say. We had driven about a mile and the intersection appeared just as it should have. "I turn right here," he said. "Ok, thanks, I live right over there," I pointed to the left and I had the door open before the car had even come to a complete stop at the then deserted intersection. I wasn't in a state of shock but I'll bet I was very close. It was quite a while before I ventured to hitchhike again.

My freshmen year at Ursline High School was not the best year in my life. In fact it may well have been the worst year of my life. I've been robbed at gun point and rendered unconscious from an auto accident on three occasions and lost an entire years salary in a bad investment but I still say the 9th grade was the worst year of my life. Because I felt I did not measure up I tried to project the opposite. I felt inferior (although I didn't know this at the time) but what I projected or at least what was perceived was a superior attitude. I was desperately trying to compensate for what was missing in my life but I did not know what that was and I would have laughed if anyone had said something like that to me. I was always trying to fit in but never quite making it. My childhood tendency of coming on to strong as compensation for not feeling up-to-par did not diminish one iota until I had a wondrous spiritual experience the year that President Nixon resigned. My ego was such that even my friends wouldn't tell me how overbearing I was or if they did I simply did not "hear" them. My social ineptitude was evident even in the ninth grade.

It must have been some of my overbearing attitude that irritated some of the upperclassmen. Several of the sophomores grabbed me in the hallway when no nuns were present and dragged me into the men's room. The ring leader was a very intelligent but overweight kid name Judson. Someone told me years later that he was now a federal judge and I suspect that any criminals who come under his jurisdiction will think that they have met the re-incarnation of Judge Roy Bean, the hanging judge of Texas. Back then, however, I was just an incoming freshman and I was about to be initiated. I struggled to get away but there were too many of them and there was nothing that I could do to escape.

In seconds I was off the floor and upside down in the air. I could see what was about to happen and I struggled with all my might to free one arm which I succeeded in doing. Before I was plunged into the toilet, head first, I managed to pull the chain and flush the thing. That experience alone was quite humiliating but the worse part of all, the most embarrassing part of the whole episode was when I was drying myself off with paper towels in the hallway, Judson and the others were bragging to the girls present and passing by what they had just done to me. Some of the girls said "Yuck" and all of them moved quickly away from me. I have wondered if something like this might have happened to those two students at Columbine High School in Colorado.Timothy McVeigh, who killed almost 170 people when he blew up the Murrah Building in Oklahoma City in 1995, had the exact same thing happen to him and at another Catholic school. I remember how surprised I was when I read that he too had endured what I had endured. Could that great humiliation have been a factor in his demise into terrorism? I do not know. The actions of individuals and groups and even nations, often have consequences that were not considered or even imagined. The only consequence of what happened to me (that I am aware of) is that I made it a point to keep far away from the upperclassmen.

One of my classmates in the ninth grade was a nice young man named Bill. His father was the commanding general at Fort Jackson. Elvis Presley was all the rage at the time but I could take him or leave him. I enjoyed some of his songs but I thought that he was a bit outrageous.There was talk of Elvis being inducted into the army and Bill told me that his father (evidently not a fan) had said that he hoped Elvis got sent to Fort Jackson. Much to Elvis credit he did his stint in the army without complaint and he did an above average job but fortunately for him not at Fort Jackson but in Germany. Of course General Woodard might have been kidding.

I found a job as an usher on the weekends in one of the theaters on Main Street but I should have spent my time studying. I wasn't doing well in school. I especially hated Latin as I could not see what practical application it had. Algebra, too, was not a favorite and I missed too many classes for it to make much sense. I kept thinking that if I could just get away from everything, the classes, the harassment, everything, things would have to get better. Finally I decided to do just that. I do not remember why I decided that the Hawaiian Islands were the place for me. They were not yet a state but they belonged to the United States and they were as far away as I could imagine.

My most precious possession at the time was my collection of 45 rpm records (which I still have) and I dutifully packaged them and sent them ahead to a girl named Loretta who lived in East Point, just south of Atlanta. Her dad was an airline pilot and I had corresponded with her for some time after meeting her in church one Sunday when she was visiting relatives in Columbia. I packed my clothes and what money I had saved. The cheapest way to travel was by bus and one night after I got off work from my job at the theater I purchased a ticket and boarded a bus headed for Atlanta.

I had written mom a "goodbye" letter which I mailed before I got on the bus. She kept that letter for more than 20 years and then returned it to me. "Remember this?" she said playfully as she handed it to me. Of course I remembered it but I didn't remember how awful it was. I think I burned the pieces after I tore it up.

That night, however, was probably the worse night of my life. The bus I was on had not quite reached the Georgia border when it was stopped and searched by the police. My mom's intuition is better than most and when I did not return at the regular time she knew that something was wrong. When mom called the police they asked her what time I had left. She did not know logically or factually but she "knew" intuitively that it was around 9 p.m. The police told her that there was a train going north at that time and a bus headed to Atlanta.Mom knew I had relatives in the north because they were her relatives as well but she also "felt" that I would not be going there. Mom told the police that she was pretty sure that I was on the bus that was headed for Atlanta, which, of course, I was. It was near North Augusta, S.C. (which is just across the border from the Georgia state line) where the State Highway Patrol pulled the bus over. I heard them say as they boarded the bus that it was just a routine check for a run-away. When they came to me they asked for some ID but as I handed them my wallet I told them that I had left it at home, which was true. I had been smart enough to get rid of everything with my name on it but not smart enough to make fake ID's. Of course any kid today would know better from watching TV shows but my family did not yet own a TV although most of my friends had them. I fit the description of the kid they were looking for so they took me off the bus and carted me off to jail overnight. It was a very secure jail because three doors had to be unlocked to get to the cell in which they had placed me. I was very tired and fell asleep right away. A deputy awoke me around 5 a.m. and I found my mom and her friend Frances Turner (the German wife of the Cherokee Indian friend of the family that I mentioned earlier) outside the cell looking at me. Mom was in tears and Mrs. Turner said, "How could you do this to your mother?" I felt terrible for having made my mother cry. Suddenly all my problems didn't seem so important anymore. The police turned me over to the custody of my mother and Mrs. Turner drove us back to Columbia.

I knuckled down, hit the books, and crammed for my finals when the time came. I passed all my courses and decided to go to summer school once again. This time I took Sophomore English, a requirement towards a high school diploma. During the previous year dad had accepted a position as Art Director for the Darlington, S.C. school system. What this really meant was that he was the art teacher for all the city schools, black and white, elementary, junior high and high schools. For a year he commuted weekly from

Columbia to Darlington, a distance of about 80 miles. He'd leave on Sunday afternoon and come back on Friday night. Since he still had no drivers license most of the time he hitchhiked.

This weekend commute of 160 miles round-trip came to an end (at least for a dozen years) in 1958 when we all moved to a large house three doors north of what was then McClenaghan High School in Florence, S.C. We were now 75 miles east of Columbia but only 10 miles from Darlington. Dad was able to go to work each morning and return each night.

The house at 412 South Dargan Street was large enough for the eight of us (my two youngest sisters, Donna and Chrysa, had not yet been born). The houses were relatively close to each other with no more than a driveway separating them but we had a double sized back yard. It was "L" shaped and twice the size of most of the back yards. This meant that there was room enough for a small garden as well as a place to put up a badminton court. The rent was $50 a month in those days before the government started borrowing really big amounts and causing the inflation that has been so gradual but so steady, even more so since we relinquished the constitutional gold standard in the 1970s. The house was fairly substantial and in good condition and although it is now gone we lived there for two years.

Wanting to get the high school experience over as quickly as possible I told the administration that I was a year older than I actually was and that I had started school late and hoped to "catch up with my class".I hadn't really planned all this. It just sort of fell into place and since I had been smart enough to take Sophomore English in summer school the administration let me start my junior year in the fall of 1958. Consequently, I was never a sophomore at any high school (the summer course in 10th grade English had been taught at a junior high school). I always planned to someday correct the mistake that showed me being born the month after my parents got married but Mr. Lever, the principal, died and the school was replaced by a new modern Florence High School several miles to the west of McClenaghan and I never got around to actually doing it.

My junior year was relatively uneventful. I didn't have a car or a girlfriend. There were several girls I liked and they were all friends with each other. Some of them seemed to like me but I never had the nerve or the means to ask any of them out on a real date. All of their boy friends had cars of course and all I had was a bicycle. I did attend a few parties and got to dance a time or two with a couple of the girls I liked but the girl I liked the most was going steady with a college guy whom she later married. Last I heard her son was a teacher in South Africa but that was years ago.

It was only a three minute walk from my home to my homeroom but I frequently had to run to get there on time. Homeroom was a short session where attendance was taken and we were informed of any school activities or other events that would be of interest. Educational TV was fairly new in South Carolina and we had a TV in each homeroom. One of the programs I remember always being on, at least until the roll call, was a show called Captain Kangaroo. Bob Keeshan was the grandfatherly Captain with his bowl-cut hair and walrus moustache and he always reminded me of an 1890's fireman. I was surprised when he died in 2004 when I learned that he was only 76 years old. He seemed old to me even when I was in high school and I would have guessed that he had passed away long ago. I had no idea that the Captain Kangaroo show had begun the year my wife was born and that the program continued on the air until 1985, certainly one of the longest running shows in CBS history.

Fred Roger's of "Mr. Rogers' Neighborhood," died the year before Bob Keeshan. Both of these TV personalities lamented the increasing violence and declining quality of television aimed at children. This country has had some amazing people in it and two that I remember well were both teachers at McClenaghan High School.

Growing up I had many good teachers and two of them, Marie Gainey, who taught English, and Mary Manning Hanner, who taught history at McClenaghan, became friends. Over the years I would visit or at least phone and talk with them from time to time. Both lived well into their eighties.

Because of the prejudice against working women in the previous generation those who today might become doctors, lawyers, or even scientists, became instead teachers. As a result I was blessed to have a number of exceptional teachers. Miss Hanner's fiancé had been killed during WWII and she never married. I visited her at her home a number of times after I graduated from high school and moved from Florence and even South Carolina.

Marie Gainey had retired from teaching at a college level before becoming a high school teacher and in my senior year she signed my high school annual with a little quote that aptly described me at the time, "cheered up himself with bits of verse and sayings of philosophers," and then she drew a little double circle just the size of a single lifesaver candy. This meant that to her I was a lifesaver, someone who made her teaching worth- while. I was now a member of her "Lifesavers Club". I've always wondered how many of those she drew and how many of her other students were in the "club".

In 1974, when I had the same kind of spiritual experience that the 120 did in the upper room on Pentecost as told in the Book of Acts, just past the gospels in the Bible, I told Mrs. Gainey about it. From time to time we had discussed religion and the most profound statement she ever made to me, at least from a psychological point of view, was that, "whatever we gained by the Reformation was off-set by the loss of the confessional."

Mrs. Gainey, like the vast majority of South Carolinians, was a Protestant, and I thought that her observation displayed a great deal of thought and wisdom. When I told her about praying in new languages and miracles of healing she replied, "It sounds a lot like a church meeting I went to in 1911 or 1912." I was amazed at her recollection of the beginnings of the Pentecostal Movement in the United States and also of the fact that she was going to church be-fore either of my parents had been born. I was fortunate to have had her for a teacher.

It was in 1958 or early in 1959 when we purchased our first tele-vision, a used black and white model that cost about what we paid for a month's rent.My three favorite programs were GUNSMOKE with James Arness, WAGON TRAIN with young Clint Eastwood, and especially ADVENTURES IN PARADISE with Gardner McKay, a series about the captain/owner of a commercial sailboat, an old schooner, operating in the South Pacific. Each week the family gath-ered around to watch the ED SULLIVAN SHOW, a family favorite.

I had a bicycle and that enabled me to get a job delivering The Florence Morning News to the neighborhood to the south of where I lived. This gave me enough money for essentials and occasional movies but certainly not enough for a car. The first time I ever saw the moons of Jupiter was when I was collecting for the paper and one of my customers had a new telescope which he let me look through. I was able to see the four largest moons (I believe Jupiter has 17 or more). It was not quite dark but the moons were clearly visible. The most interesting thing I remember from my paper route was over-hearing a discussion one sunny day by one of my customers with a friend about a shipment of guns being sent to the freedom fighters in Cuba to help overthrow the dictator Batista. At the time I thought it sounded like a pretty good idea. Helping people find freedom from an oppressive dictator was a worthwhile thing to do wasn't it, much like getting rid of Saddam Hussein many years later. I did not know at the time that our government actually supported that dictator and had I known what kind of government would replace him I would not have been so approving.During my senior year I got a job on Saturday where I worked a ten hour day as a clerk in a dry cleaner for $5.Fifty cents an hour wasn't much but few part-time jobs for teenagers paid more.

Once during my senior year I rode my bicycle all the way to Columbia, about 75 miles to the west. Why, I do not remember. What I do remember was wondering if I would have the strength and stamina to ride all the way back to Florence. I'd have to be pedaling after dark and I didn't look forward to that. I had hitchhiked rides before, even at an airport on a small aircraft, but I had never tried hitchhiking with a bicycle. At the eastern edge of Columbia where the few stores ended and the countryside began I stuck out my thumb. There weren't many cars and some of them must have wondered about why I was hitchhiking with a bicycle under my arm. Of course, they didn't know how far I had to go. It couldn't have been more than ten minutes when I saw a car begin to pull out of the bowling alley in the distance, wait for traffic to pass and then turn in my direction. Out went my thumb and to my surprise the vehicle stopped. "Where are you headed?" the driver asked. "Florence," I quickly replied. "Well, I can take you as far as Sumter," the gentleman answered. Sumter was slightly over half way and that would have been a big help. We loaded the bicycle into the trunk as best we could.

His name was Jim Cook and he was an orthodontist in his mid-to-late thirties. We hit it off well and when I got on the subject of aviation I was surprised to discover that in addition to being a dentist Jim was also a pilot. I had thought that I would like to become a pilot someday and I had read a great deal on the subject. I also frequented airports more than most. Jim was surprised that someone only 16 knew so much about flying and aircraft and when we got to Sumter he told me that he would take me the rest of the way to Florence. The sun had set and I was grateful that I wouldn't have to pedal the last 30 miles or so to get home. It certainly would have been dangerous without a headlight and it would have taken me another three hours.

We continued to talk, mostly about aviation, and as we reached the outskirts of the City of Florence I was shocked to discover that Jim had not even been going to Sumter. It was his day off and he had played a few games at the bowling alley and was thinking about taking in a movie when he was puzzled to see this teenager trying to catch a ride with one hand while holding on to a bicycle with the other. I was so impressed that a total stranger would go 150 miles out of his way for someone he did not know that I determined not to lose track of him.

Years later, when I too was in my thirties, I saw a young woman in her twenties trying to catch a ride. I hate to see women hitchhiking. So many things can happen to them. I don't always pick them up but this time I did. She was a graduate student trying to get home to Connecticut for the weekend and I drove over a 100 miles out of my way for her so perhaps I'm not to different from Jim in this regard.

Before I left South Carolina to join the USAF Jim took me to a fine restaurant for dinner. Once we flew down to Hilton Head Island in his Navion aircraft. We ate at the Sea Pines Plantation and then flew back to Columbia. Eventually Jim owned his own aviation business as well as being a top notch orthodontist. My former classmate, Jean Hoeffer, had once been one of his patients many years ago.

I had known Jim for about two years, maybe more, when I happened to pick up a copy of American Legion Magazine. This particular issue had an incredible story of a young 24 year old WWII hero, a bomber pilot known as "The Lone Bomber of Rabaul." I could hardly believe what I was reading. There, in a story that might well have fit into Tom Brokaw's THE GREATEST GENERATION, was the saga of a B-25 pilot during WWII who had recently lost several buddies when just one aircraft was shot down. Pilot, co-pilot, engineer, radio operator, gunner, bombardier, all were lost. "Why did Washington insist on so many people on just one aircraft?" 2nd Lieutenant James E. Cook was thinking while waiting for his crew to show up. Actually he wasn't even supposed to be there, on that island, but he had flown a colonel who was going to give a lecture over to the island when he heard that there was going to be a mission.

Where was that crew? When Jim had heard that there was going to be a mission, what he was trained to do, he volunteered to help out. What he didn't know while he was waiting for his crew to show up was that the crew had been told that there weren't enough of them to fly. The other aircraft who were going on this particular mission had already taken off when a single Japanese Zero returning from somewhere and probably lost made a strafing run on the flight line. The engines of "Beautiful Girl" were running, the bombs had already been manually triggered, but no crew was in sight. What to do? A sudden inspiration, push forward on the throttle, get the craft off the ground and into the air. No need to get it shot to pieces just sitting there. The Zero was not piloted by a suicide pilot and Jim did not see it after he got his own craft into the air. The thought had already occurred to him that if he could complete this mission alone that would prove to the brass back in Washington that not as many men were needed on a B-25 as they claimed. If he didn't make it back, well, only one man would be lost, and he might get to inflict some real damage on those who were talking peace in Washington while they were bombing Pearl Harbor in Hawaii.

Radio silence was being maintained during the several hour flight to Rabaul, New Guinea. The reports they had received had indicated that there was some weather in front of them but what the squadron of the 13th Air Force met with was horrendous, so horrendous that they broke radio silence and scrubbed the mission. Apparently they had flown into the edge of a small hurricane although in the South Pacific they are called typhoons. Only Jim didn't know this as he had his radio turned so low he never heard the radio silence being broken and the mission being cancelled. Jim had not flown into the storm but had steered to the right of it and, as he continued on his way, he did not know that now he was really flying alone.

Soon he was approaching New Guinea. Coming in low from the sea in the early morning hours before the last vestiges of night had disappeared Jim could see that no damage had been done to this large encroachment of Japanese Military, 50,000 by some estimates. "What happened to all the other bombers?" Jim wonders. "Well, no point in returning to base with a full load," he thinks to himself as he makes his bombing run.

The Japanese can hardly believe that their massive base is being attacked by one lone American bomber. Little do they know that they are being attacked by one lone American. Suddenly all the lights in the world seem to be shining on "Beautiful Girl," as well as all the guns. From small arms to anti-aircraft everyone is trying to shoot down this one single B-25. Bombs rain down on the perpetrators of the sneak attack on Pearl Harbor. Dozens of direct hits are evident on Jim's aircraft as chaos reins on the airfields below. An artillery shell or anti-aircraft projectile careens entirely through the "Beautiful Girl" without exploding. It leaves a gaping hole five inches across where the co-pilot would have been sitting, if there had been a co-pilot.

Now devoid of its cargo but full of holes the craft struggles to gain altitude, first to make it over the mountainous terrain then to avoid the Zeros which had been ordered to shoot down this audacious American. Jim turns his aircraft back over the sea and heads for home. The clouds are thick and although the Zeros are swarming about like angry hornets they can't find him.

Hours pass. Jim hugs the sea flying in the calm place just dozens of feet above the water. Most of his instruments had been destroyed but he did have a hand held compass. With more than a few prayers Jim makes it back to the airfield on the island from which he started his journey. Barely flyable, the craft finally comes to a rest at the very end of the runway.

Jim has completed both his missions: bomb the enemy and prove that a full crew isn't necessary. He climbs down from his weary all night escapade. The flight surgeon comes running up and seeing the condition of the aircraft expects the worse. Seeing only Jim he asks, "How is the crew?" "There aren't any," Jim replies. Finding it hard to believe that everyone else in the B-25 has been killed he quickly boards the bomber and almost as quickly comes back out and looking somewhat dazed says, "There aren't any!"

"That's what I said," Jim tells him again. "I'm it!" The poor doctor looks like he's dealing with a mad man, but it's true. The "Beautiful Girl" isn't so beautiful anymore.

Hundreds of separate hits are counted on the wings, fuselage, and tail assembly of Jim's B-25.

"This is terrible," the general and commanding officer said in public. In private he shook Jim's hand and said, "If we had more people like you the war would be over a lot sooner." Within 30 days 2nd Lt. James E. Cook is 1st Lt. James E. Cook. The last time I heard, the "Beautiful Girl" was enshrined in San Antonio, Texas, as a memorial. There's a bronze plaque and some of the story I just told you.

I wish I'd read Tom Brokaw's first book before the second came out. I would have sent this story in to him. So many people did so much at that time in history to preserve freedom and a democratic way of life. Several thousand World War II veterans are dying every month because that was a long time ago and they are all elderly citizens now. Jim is younger than many of them but he hasn't piloted an aircraft or straightened a tooth in quite a while. I salute him and all like him to whom we owe so much.

11. Advanced Typing

The most valuable course that I ever took in high school was typing. The course itself had only been a one semester course called "Beginning Typing" or something like that. However I needed a full credit to meet the requirements for graduation and I was surprised to discover that there were only two half-credit courses in my final semester and I absolutely had to take one of them if I wanted to graduate. Those two courses were home economics and advanced typing.When I found that out it occurred to me that I had probably forgotten more about "home eck" than most of the girls even knew as I had assisted my mom in all phases of babys care and home care but when I discovered that I would be the only guy in the class I figured that not even an "A" grade would be worth the ribbing I'd get from the jocks on the football team and the basketball team, so I quickly elected to take the course in advanced typing. I was never very fast but the ability to type got me jobs in both military and civilian life.

I didn't go to the senior prom. I rationalized that I wasn't a good enough dancer and that the girls I might have asked most probably already had dates but the truth was I still did not have access to a car. I did not know another family besides mine that did not own an automobile. I'm sure there must have been some but I did not know them so it was just easier not to go.

I was grateful though, that I was, finally, finished with high school.

12. Myrtle Beach and Drug Smuggling

Florence is about an hour and a half by car from Myrtle Beach but the car that picked me up as I was hitchhiking to the beach could have made it in 45 minutes, if they made it at all. I had received my diploma from McClenaghan High School in 1960 and to celebrate I wanted to do "something." What I decided to do was to head for the beach.A lot more people do this today than ever before and Myrtle Beach has built up in so many ways as to be hardly recognizable compared to how it was in 1960, but the whole country has over 120,000,000 more people living in it today than it did when I was in high school. I do not know if that is counting the eleven million illegal aliens (some estimates are as high as 21,000,000) who are living among us. In 2005, I met a student, a young woman from Moscow who had a summer job in a restaurant in Myrtle Beach. "Such temporary jobs for students do not exist in Russia," she told me. I also met another young woman from the Ukraine, who had a summer job at a gift store (I was about to say gift shop but it was too big to be called a shop). Myrtle Beach has truly become international.

In 1960, Myrtle Beach had few visitors from any country except this one and a few from Canada and the summer jobs were completely filled by locals. The car that stopped to pick me up that day in June of 1960 looked ordinary, as did the two guys in the front seat. I did not notice the empty beer cans until I was in the back seat and we were going over 40 miles per hour. Before I could say anything, it was 60 mph. Soon it was 70 mph and 80 mph. I was beginning to become a little apprehensive. I glanced again at the speedometer and it registered 90 mph. I recalled a few years earlier when a student from Dreher High School in Columbia had been killed and decapitated when his 1957 Ford Convertible had crashed east of Columbia as he went through the swamp on U.S. 76. They did not know how fast he was going but the speedometer was smashed into the front of the car and the indicator registered 110 mph at the moment of impact. I looked again at the speedometer and we were going faster than that! There is an old saying (and this one is

probably true) that there are no atheists in foxholes. I'm guessing
that there are also probably none sitting in the back seats of automobiles traveling at these speeds by obviously drunk drivers either.
Somewhere in the Old English translation of the Bible it says, "The
fervent prayer of a righteous man availeth much." I'll leave it to
Providence to judge how righteous I am but I can assure you that my
prayers for survival that afternoon were very fervent. Finally, the
car slowed down and came to a stop. "Thish is where we turn off,"
said the driver. "Jus keep on thish road and you'll get to the beach."
I knew that but all I said was, "Thanks, thanks a lot!" I believe I may
have been looking up when I said it. Years later, I was watching
a Miss America pageant and when the name of a beautiful southern girl was announced as the new winner, the camera immediately
zoomed in on her. It was easy for me to read her lips. Looking up
she said, "Thank You!" and I knew that she was not talking to some
cameraman or lighting technician in the rafters.

I continued hitchhiking and with one or two more rides, I arrived at Myrtle Beach. I walked along the beach for a while then
went out on the pier to watch some people fishing. I believe it was
the same pier from which a couple of year's previously two high
school students had tried to attract a shark with a huge hook and
a three-pound chuck roast. They were successful. I read in the
Florence Morning News or The State how they dragged the creature into shallow water and then jumped in to pull it ashore. I distinctly remember that the shark weighed over 500 pounds and that
I couldn't decide if they were very brave or very dumb. The idea of
jumping into shallow water with a live 500-pound shark, even one
caught on a big hook, did not strike me as summer fun.I haven't
heard of sharks in the area since then but sharks seldom make the
news unless they bite someone.

The late afternoon and early evening found me hanging around
the Pavilion at what then was the center of town. I met a couple
of guys at one of the arcades and four or five of us went over to the
home of one of them to watch a game on TV.Who was playing what
I do not remember. As I recall they had beer and I had a cold soda,
as I had not yet learned to appreciate beer as a drink. I expressed
some dismay at having to hitchhike back to Florence in the dark
since it was already ten o'clock. "Crash here on the sofa and hitchhike back in the morning," said one of the guys. "Dad's away but
he wouldn't mind anyway," he continued. That's how I spent the
night in author Mickey Spillane's house in Myrtle Beach. The Mike

Hammer books and TV series are Mickey Spillane's creation and he is so popular a writer that once when he was just visiting friends at his former homestead just across the river in Newburgh, N.Y., I read about the visit in the Poughkeepsie Journal, New York States oldest newspaper. I never met the man personally but I did enjoy THE GIRL HUNTERS, the 1963 movie in which Mickey Spillane actually played Mike Hammer, and of course Stacy Keach's interpretation of Mike Hammer in the television series years later. Mickey Spillane left Myrtle Beach but eventually returned and settled in a small town south of there that is not far from Brookgreen Gardens. That town is, today, probably about the size that Myrtle Beach was back in the 1950's.

The next morning I left Mickey Spillane's house and hitchhiked back to Florence. I didn't really have any plans for the summer but since I had entertained the idea of becoming a pilot, it occurred to me that getting a few flying lessons under my belt would be a good idea. I did not have the money for lessons but I thought that I might be able to trade some of my labor for flight lessons.

The flying instructors at the Florence airport did not have any work that I could do in exchange for flying lessons but I did manage to catch a ride once to Columbia in a Piper Super-Cub. I don't remember how I got back to Florence, probably hitchhiked. All I remember was how great it was to be up in the air.

Later, after my family had moved from Florence to Darlington, I hitchhiked over to the airport in Dovesville, north of Darlington on Highway 52. There I told the flight instructor of my plight and he agreed to give me a lesson in exchange for some odd jobs around the flight line. I worked for two days and I remember pouring 50-pound sacks of agricultural chemicals into an Apache crop duster. The chemicals had a distinctive odor, not entirely unpleasant. It might have been DDT, now long banned.

Crop dusting was the main business at this isolated out-in-the-country airport. What effect breathing those distinctive crop dusting chemicals might have had on me had I continued to work at the airport I cannot say. In 1960, only a handful of scientists even suspected that exposure to certain chemicals could cause cancer.I had one flying lesson in a Piper Cub, the same type of aircraft that the missionaries had flown in Ecuador four years earlier. At least it was the type and color of aircraft that the 2006 movie END OF THE SPEAR showed them flying. Local Waorani natives killed all five of the missionaries and it made headlines in the South Carolina newspapers at the time. Their deaths moved me at the time because they all had families and I was surprised that such fierce tribes still existed in the Americas. The movie about the event, while quite entertaining and at the very end, even funny, was enough to bring tears to my eyes.

I got no more flight lessons that summer because dad wanted me at home helping him fix up the house he had purchased not far from the public square in Darlington.

It was some years after that that a large multi-engine aircraft, a former passenger airliner, apparently landed by mistake at the airport in Florence. The pilot acted suspiciously, keeping the craft at the far end of the field away from the hangers and the tower. The police were called and a huge shipment of marijuana was seized. Several years after that incident (and after I had moved to Poughkeepsie) I was down visiting my folks in Darlington and then left to drive back to New York. From Darlington, I drove due east and as I crossed the Great Pee Dee Swamp, a large multi-engine aircraft of a design I had never before seen flew over me at an altitude of only a few hundred feet. "What is that?" I said out loud to myself, so surprised was I at the sight of the strange and unfamiliar aircraft flying almost on top of me. The craft was as big as an airliner and it had four engines that drove propellers. It also had two auxiliary jet engines. I had never seen anything like it. It was flying very low for such a large aircraft and in a direction that would have indicated that it was flying towards the isolated Dovesville airport. At least that is what occurred to me a few years later when the operators of the Dovesville airport were arrested for smuggling drugs in from South America. I always suspected that the three events were related.

13. Darlington

Nineteen hundred and sixty was the year that dad purchased our first and only house. With the exception of the one he had built 6 years before we had always lived in rented houses. He had not planned to buy this house but Providence was with him when the opportunity presented itself. Some time after the previous owner had died the house was auctioned off to settle the estate. Sealed bids were solicited and dad put in his bid. He had never done anything like that before or since. The house was a short six minute walk to his classroom/art studio in St. John's High School. Most of my brothers and sisters graduated from this unusually named public high school. I always thought that one day the ACLU, the communist backed (at least in its founding days) American Civil Liberties Union, would bring a lawsuit against the city, county or state and force them to change the centuries old name but I guess it wouldn't get them enough publicity in South Carolina where the citizens are less likely to tolerate their shenanigans than in more liberal areas like southern California. A friend of mine who works for the court system in southern California sent me a paper on a recent situation that happened there. For probably the first time in history Jews, including Orthodox Jews (wearing their yarmulkes), showed up as part of 2,000 protesters in support of the Christian cross that was discovered by an ACLU lawyer with a magnifying glass to be a tiny part of the Los Angeles County Seal. The seal had been in use for half a century. It has six small sections surrounding Pomona, the Roman goddess of gardens and fruits. On the left of the seal starting at the bottom is a tuna representing the fishing industry, above it a Spanish galleon (Los Angeles was after all founded by Spanish Catholics who gave it the name City of Angels) and above that are some engineering instruments. On the right side of the Roman goddess is an oil derrick, below that the Hollywood Bowl along with two stars representing what Hollywood is famous for and a small cross, and below that is a cow. The cross symbolized the missions that were responsible for the taming of the California frontier. Well, history has been re-written once again in this country, the ACLU and three liberal supervisors have redesigned the 50 year Los Angeles County seal, the tiny cross has been removed and a building with no Christian symbol on it is taking its place. I was not surprised at this personally because I knew of a case years ago where the ACLU forced a city in the southwest to redesign their 300 year old coat of arms, older than our country itself, because in one corner of the coat-of-arms was a small cross. This was on city stationary and city police cars and might "confuse" people into thinking that these were "Christian police" or at least that is the argument I remember reading years ago. Growing up I was always fascinated that we as a country were so afraid of communism and yet there were those who supported the ACLU that was started and supported by followers of Soviet style "world socialism" as the best way to bring America to it knees and force it into a world socialist community. Because of the work of the ACLU some of our history has been re-written as much as any totalitarian regime has ever done and those who can success-fully re-write history can much more easily control the future or the masses. I have seen this on a scale that I never would have believed possible in this country since I finished high school. "People are funny," the comedian Art Linkletter used to say and nowhere is this truer than in politics.

Anyway dad submitted his bid on the house and promptly forgot it. An elderly woman had lived in the large old house for many years. She was very frugal and when she died something like $76,000 was found hidden in the house. This was a god-send to at least one of her relatives who was in ill health and was able to retire on their share of the money. Of course $76,000 over 46 years ago was worth about a half million of today's not backed by anything inflated dollars.

Dad had placed a bid at what he had thought was a really low amount, a figure well below what the house was worth. Apparently the other bidders really tried to steal the place and dad was the high bidder. He was more than a little surprised when the bank called and asked him how he planned to finance the house. Off course after the shock wore off he was quite pleased. As it turned out the monthly payments for the next 20 years were about what the taxes would normally be today.

So in 1960 the Pawley family moved from Florence to Darlington. Our new home on Orange Street wasn't really new. In fact, it wasn't even close to being new when the Wright Brothers flew their flimsy aircraft at Kitty Hawk, North Carolina, but it was new to us. It was a big gray wooden house with eleven foot ceilings and four bedrooms and three bathrooms and room enough for us all. The house needed some work as all old houses do but it was a good value for the money. I helped dad build a brick stairway to the front porch and then brick in the entire house all the way around the large foundation. This took considerable time and I was glad when the job was finally done. Summer was almost over and classes would soon begin at the University of South Carolina Extension which at that time was actually in the basement of the old Florence Library on South Irby Street. Of course I really had no idea what I wanted to study.

I've always admired and been somewhat amazed at those who knew exactly what they wanted to do or be when they were 5 or 10 or 15 years old. When Sarah Hughes won the gold medal in Olympic skating many people saw the video of cute little 5 year old Sarah taken years before saying that when she grew up she was going to win the gold medal in Olympic skating. It took years of practice and effort and everything coming together just right but she did it! Her younger sister Emily is also doing quite well as a figure skater.

Look at my junior high school buddy, Ralph Singleton. When he was 14 or 15 he told me and others that he was going to go to Hollywood and become a producer. Perhaps you have seen the movies CLEAR AND PRESENT DANGER with Harrison Ford, James Earl Jones, and Hope Lange, or ANOTHER 48 HOURS with Edie Murphy and Nick Nolte. Ralph co-produced them both. Reminiscent of the monster movies we used to see at the drive-in (but undoubtedly better) was Stephen King's GRAVEYARD SHIFT. Not only did Ralph co-produce that movie he also directed it. But as a youngster he already knew. As a college student I didn't have a clue.

I thought that I might like to become an airline pilot (one of my classmates from high school actually did become a pilot for a major airline until a triple by-pass heart surgery forced him to retire). The idea of becoming a city manager also appealed to me but it was the perceived prestige and the healthy income that interested me most of all. I've always been glad that I wasn't an only child or been born rich because most of those I've known who were either, had problems beyond what I would want to bear. Mark Twain (Samuel Clemens) said it best, words to the effect that if we all had to put our problems in a trans-parent knapsack and then place that knapsack for all to see on some back fence, and having seen them all we were then required to run and take one knapsack we would quickly run

and grab our own. I believe that what he said was true but I've still
envied those people whose life was not as haphazard as mine, who
knew what they wanted and who set about to achieve it. I have always felt such people were truly blessed. I still do.

Of course, there are many kinds of blessings in life and like most
human beings I don't always recognize mine. Certainly the ability
to go to college and the necessary funds to do so are a blessing. I
had both, at least for a semester.I also had a column in the Florence
Morning News. It was supposed to be about the happenings at the
newly formed University of South Carolina Extension in Florence.
There really wasn't that much going on at the tiny new school and
my ability to expand on the news, to dig deeper, was not exceptional.
Coupled with feelings of inferiority my columns tended to be long
on my experiences and short on content. Consequently, after a few
months the column was dropped. My grades were not exceptional
either, certainly not enough to warrant any kind of scholarship.

I did not have the money for a second semester so I decided that
I'd better get a job of some sort. The post office paid the most, $2
per hour, but the competition was severe. Even though I did well on
the exam my chances of actually getting a job at the post office were
nil. I had to find something so I looked into everything that looked
even remotely plausible. A good paying job was hard to find.

Finally I accepted an offer at American Bakeries in Florence.
Basically it was a bread factory. I caught hundreds of loves of bread
as they came out of a vast roller oven. The loaves were then placed
in a conveyer that carried them to a very precise slicing machine.

They continued on to another machine that wrapped each loaf
in a kind of waxed paper. The loaf then proceeded through a device
that heated both ends of the loaf and semi-sealed the waxed paper
by melting it together. It then quickly passed through a device that
applied a cold refrigerated metal plate about the size of a slice of
bread, or perhaps a little smaller, to both ends of the loaf thereby
sealing it.

One of my duties was to assure that everything worked the way
it was supposed to work. Occasionally a loaf wouldn't seal and the
quickest way to remedy that was to carry the wrapped but loose loaf
by hand and to run it through the sealing apparatus again. The extra
thickness of the second wrapper almost always solved the problem.
Only once did I have a loaf that required a third pass and a third
wrapper. As a joke I wrapped that loaf an additional nine times

and I had fun imagining the look on the face of the homemaker who eventually went to open that particular loaf of bread.

The bakery also made cinnamon rolls and all the new hires were told that we could eat as many as we wanted to eat. Within a week I couldn't stand the sight of them and five years passed before I ate another. Of course, I'm sure that the management knew that that was exactly what would happen and that is why they were so generous with their offer.

The main work, however, was the production of bread. My biggest problem, other than transportation (public transportation was virtually non-existent) was that we didn't have gloves but some sort of floppy mitt that had to be swung up into the palm of the hand to catch the metal bread pans as they rolled out of the oven in a never ending stream.

If it wasn't done just right you'd grab a hot pan with your bare hand. After three weeks of getting burned almost daily I'd had enough and quit. I could never figure out why they used these thick fancy pot holders and not real gloves. In order to keep my job I was willing to purchase gloves on my own but that was not permitted.

I began to entertain the idea of getting my duty to my country over with and perhaps, while doing that, I could get a handle on what I should be doing or working towards. Forget the Marines; I didn't even make any of the teams I had to try out for in high school sports. I wasn't quite a 135 pound weakling but that was my weight at the time and I had no interest at all in athletics. I didn't swim and that was a requirement in the Navy and I'd been around the Army enough to know that I didn't want to be a soldier. That left only one logical choice, the United States Air Force.

The local recruiter arranged the tests and I scored the highest possible score on general intelligence and administrative ability (or so they told me), not quite so high on math and a score equal to that on mechanical ability. I signed on the dotted line and in April of 1961 I said goodbye to my parents and caught the bus from Darlington to Columbia and Fort Jackson. It was my first step towards becoming an airman.

14. The USAF, the Destruction of LA, and the Fuel of the Future

Fort Jackson was not new to me as I had attended chapel there with friends. I had also visited friends whose parents were stationed there, but now I was being stationed there, at least for the first three days of my air force career. I don't recall all the preliminaries we went through but there were forms to fill out, medical evaluations to be taken, and even marching to do wherever we went. Soon I would be leaving South Carolina for the third time (the second time having been a five day trip I took with my dad and Ralph Singleton to New York City during the summer before my senior year in high school. The Big Apple was almost like a foreign country with its many different nationalities and peoples but I enjoyed visiting the various art galleries where dad tried to market some of his art work. Dad still didn't have his driver's license at the time and Ralph did all the driving).

While at Fort Jackson I made one friend that I still keep up with today. Mikael (not his real name) was of Swedish descent and his father was a Major General in the USAF. We went through the three day orientation together and when the time came the army took us to the Columbia airport and we boarded a flight bound for San Antonio, Texas, where Lackland Air Force Base handles basic training for all new recruits.

The flight to Texas was uneventful except for the fact that Mikael taught me to play chess on a small magnetic chess board. We changed planes once and it was about 5 p.m. when we finally arrived at Lackland AFB outside of San Antonio. The first thing that the USAF offered to do was feed us but I had eaten in the air and I was not hungry. Then began eight weeks of basic training similar to what most movie goers have seen in many films: marching, running, climbing, push-ups, the rifle range, studying the UCMJ (The Uniform Code of Military Justice) and even KP (kitchen police). The running was the most difficult part for me. We had to run around a review field ten times and by the sixth or seventh time I imagined myself running straight into the buildings surrounding the field and becoming unconscious. I never did but the thought that I could end it all at any time by doing so made the last few laps endurable.

Twenty years later when my younger brother Mike joined the Navy and went to Officer's Training School at Newport, Rhode Island, I counseled him to begin running at least three weeks before going for his training, running around the block at least once to begin with and then continuing to build up his stamina. Now a retired Commander in the Navy he believed me and started running that very day. Three weeks later Mike left South Carolina for the "South Carolina of the North" and his three months of accelerated officers training. At 34 he was the oldest man in training (the rest were 21 to 23 year olds). "Even with the three weeks practice," he told me once, "it was still the hardest part of the physical training. Without that extra preparation I would never have made it."

Mike was a college graduate at the time he joined the Navy and he was in training for three months to become an officer. I, of course, had only one semester of college when I enlisted and my basic only lasted eight weeks. Still the exercise was more than I'd ever done and the food was excellent. In eight weeks I acquired 20 pounds of muscle that I'd never had before.

I had been advised to never volunteer for anything while in basic training and I usually followed that advice. The one time I did volunteer was on May 5, 1961, and I am glad that I did. Partly it was to get out of KP (I had spent a 12 hour day washing huge pots and pans and sterilizing glasses in a large steamer at the base hospital just a few days earlier) and partly it was a sense of adventure. Given a choice of going to Brooks Air Force Base less than 20 miles away, for some experiments and tests, a number of us gladly volunteered. Brooks was where our new astronauts were receiving part of their space training and to be in any way connected with that was heavy stuff indeed. Since we had all volunteered we were given a quick guided tour of some of the latest astronaut training equipment and labs and we were duly impressed. At least I was.

I was selected for some sort of hearing experiment but my hearing has never been great. When I proved unsuitable for whatever they were trying to learn I was given the day off. I remember it all so well because it was the day that Scott Carpenter became America's first man in space. Actually they just shot him up 50 miles in a rocket and then he plummeted back to earth. Still it was very exciting, and I was able to hear some of it, as it was happening, on an intercom system broadcast to the various labs where he had trained. Our understanding of short-term space travel was so very primitive then but it was a beginning and when the movie, THE RIGHT STUFF, was released it brought back many memories of those times. Before the movie and the book from which the movie was made, General Chuck Yager, the first person to break the sound barrier was not well known by the general public, but he was a boyhood hero of mine along with General "Kit" Carson whose frontier home I once visited in Taos, New Mexico. Carson was sort of the Daniel Boone of the West and he spoke many native dialects. Of course this was before I learned how Col. Carson had forced the Navaho's to endure a 300 mile "Long Walk" on their way to four years of captivity in New Mexico. Many elderly, sick and pregnant Indians died on this forced march. I have wondered if his hardness towards the Native Americans had stemmed from the fact that his first wife, a Native American left him after several years because she said he was never home.

Camelot was in full swing. The term "Camelot," the legendry site of King Arthur's palace and court, was used to denote the supposedly idyllic thousand days of John F. Kennedy's presidency. The times were good. There were those who thought that Kennedy could never be elected president because he was a Catholic. I remember a Baptist preacher coming to McClenaghan High School and telling us why we should convince our parents not to vote for a Catholic, but nothing was said or done about it in 1960. I complained at the time to my mom that it didn't seem right to me for him to be saying what he said without a rebuttal. Three years later, of course, the Supreme Court went overboard and re-interpreted the Constitution so that not only behavior like this was illegal but that any mention of God, whatsoever, in public schools was also illegal. No Bible studies were allowed, no prayer, nothing. (We used to say The Lord's Prayer, the "Our Father," in homeroom each day before classes began. The Jewish students were exempt from saying it although it was the same "Father" to whom we prayed). According to the "new" interpretation, public schools were effectively to be a culture without religious morals. Since all morality derives from a belief in God the lack of any moral influence soon became apparent. Like some Pandora's Box being opened the very year that the Supreme Court kicked the Supreme Being out of the public school system a lot of "other" came in. What scientists call "statistically significant increases" came about in school crime, drug use, teenage pregnancy, murder, rape, robbery, and many other indices of a stable society began to give way in our public schools and they have been giving way ever since. Some say it is only a "coincidence" that these "problems" began to dramatically increase the same year that the liberal court kicked God out but I have seen the charts and graphs and numbers and they convinced me that something very big happened to American society that year. If it wasn't the Supreme Court decision then I don't know what else it could have been. It was almost as if an invisible force field or shield of protection had been removed from over the public schools of America.

Some scientists are of the opinion that life as we know it here on earth will not be able to continue beyond another 70 or 80 years, if that. The earth does seem to be going through some sort of major change. Global warming is a fact but how much of it is caused by the activities of man is not known. We do know that the last ice age came about very rapidly, in something like 20 years, and not the gradual cooling that we were taught about in school a few decades ago.

Although I haven't heard anything about them recently well over a decade ago a number of small volcanoes were discovered off the coast of California. I have a hunch that someday in the not to distant future the movement of the tectonic plates that cover the mantle of the earth may rapidly accelerate. A movement of around 30 feet in these plates deep in the ocean caused the tsunami at the end of 2004 that killed around 200,000 people in the area of the Indian Ocean. A really big shift (100 feet or more) could cause a wave that would kill millions all over the world. The mathematical code discovered in the Bible mentioned the 2004 disaster and correlated it with the child sex slavery that is so prevalent in that part of the world but, of course, modern man in all his wisdom doesn't believe in things like this. The Bible speaks of a "new heavens and a new earth," and the preachers always interpret that spiritually but if the Bible means what it says and the earth shifts again on its axis as it rotates around the sun then that ancient prophecy would surely be fulfilled. A survivor in Israel might look up and instead of seeing the North Star he might see the Southern Cross. There might be so few survivors that another Biblical prophecy might be fulfilled, a thousand years of peace.

If the earth did wobble on its axis such a change might cause one or more unbelievably large earthquakes and not surprisingly the Bible also says that one day there will be an earthquake bigger than there has ever been since men have been on earth. It does not say that there will be an earthquake bigger than any that has ever been, only that it will be bigger than any earthquake that has ever been SINCE MEN HAVE BEEN ON EARTH.

No human beings were yet on earth the last time the earth shifted its rotational direction.

In the 1970's a scientist told me that the equator once ran through the United States in very ancient times. If it happened before it could happen again. We know almost nothing about the causes of such phenomena. The latest discovery involving volcanoes is something called a super volcano. The last one erupted less than 74,500 years ago and apparently destroyed 90 percent of the primitive humans living on earth at that time. Thousands of times bigger than the St. Helen's eruption this super volcano covered the earth with 12 feet of ash as far as a thousand miles away. I don't lose any sleep over these things but I do find them fascinating.

In 1965, a minister in or near Los Angeles, California, had a vision of the destruction of the City of Angels. It must have been quite dramatic because when he shared the vision with his church and two others some 600 people quit their jobs, sold their homes, and moved to Tennessee. At least one national news weekly picked up the story of the his vision of volcanoes and earthquakes destroying Los Angeles because that is where I read about it in McKissic Library at the University of South Carolina where I was a student.

"If the vision was true," someone asked me once, "how come nothing has happened in all these years?" The only thing I could think of was that a whole generation of people has grown up knowing only the verdant hills of Tennessee as home. They have no emotional ties to the area, nor any friends or close relatives living in the area. A movie, VOLCANO, was made about the Los Angeles earthquake in 1997 but of course in the movie the hero saves the day and the city is saved. Unfortunately I do not believe that even Hollywood will survive the real quake. I'm sure movies will still be made, but from the place that will replace Hollywood, and that remains in the future.

Even the hidden computer code discovered in the Old Testament of the Bible predicts the coming Los Angeles earthquake just as it predicted the one in Kobe, Japan. The mathematical genius and famous scientist Sir Isaac Newton spent decades of his life trying to find the code that he believed was hidden in the Bible. He even learned Hebrew in order to find it. That was over 300 years ago but lacking a super-computer, he failed.

However, with the aid of a super-computer mathematician Eli Rips and Physicist Doran Witztum discovered a fantastic code hidden in the 3,200 year old manuscript that reveals much of the history of the world.

Admittedly, Michael Drosnin's amazing book, THE BIBLE CODE, does not say Los Angeles but the scholars did find LACALIF and GREAT EARTHQUAKE and the year 5770 in Hebrew which begins in September of 2010 on our modern calendar. They also found the Hebrew date 5754 all in close proximity to the other words and date. I knew an engineer, Bill Rapp, who lived just about a mile from the previously undiscovered fault that was the cause of the 5754 earthquake, 1994 on our calendar. I suspect that the CIA or perhaps NSA has done a lot more research on this subject than the general public knows but unfortunately I am not privy to that research.

In the early part of the last decade, before any of this was public, a science fiction movie was made in which a police officer was put into suspended animation and revived some 40 years later to solve a crime. The movie was DEMOLITION MAN starring Sylvester Stallone. In the film he asked what had become of his wife and he was told that she had died in the Los Angeles earthquake of 2010. That, of course, was fiction and the date picked by the screen writer just happened to be the same one that was found later by scientists using their computers and searching the Old Testament. When I saw that movie on late night TV I was reminded of how I had just "made up" that the water was being released at the Lake Murray dam at "2 p.m." shortly before I was stranded in the Congaree River decades earlier and was quite surprised to discover that the water had actually been released at that time. Apparently it is possible to know things without knowing that we know them.

Many scientists (but not enough in my opinion) have become increasingly concerned over the past 20 years of the probability of an NEO (Near Earth Object) hitting the earth.

A small one hit Russia in 1908 (actually it blew up before hitting but destroyed everything in an area about the size of the State of Rhode Island). Fortunately it was in a very remote part of the country. Another hit the Indian Ocean in 1991 during Desert Storm.

One military official said that if it had smashed into the desert at the typical 35,000 miles per hour the explosion would have been such that everyone would have thought that an atomic bomb had been detonated. A few years later in 1995 or 1996 another small one with the power of an atomic bomb crashed into the icy wastelands of Greenland. A large mountain sized "something" apparently hit the earth 65 million years ago near what is Yucatan, Mexico, and that seems to have caused the rapid demise of the dinosaurs. Mankind has no memory of such a huge loss of life on a planetary scale.

The newest part of the Bible, written just over nineteen hundred years ago, tells of a vision that Jesus' close friend John had on the Island of Patmos where he was exiled, the only one of the original 12 associates of Jesus to die a natural death. "I saw something like a burning mountain crash into the sea and it killed one third of all the creatures in the sea," John wrote. He did not mention how many millions of people were killed by the giant tidal wave that would be generated by this huge impact. In 1996 a comet passed overhead that was emitting X-Ray radiation. This had never been discovered before. If such a comet were to crash into the sea the radiation would add to the death that it would bring. The possibility of a "star-like object" threatening the earth has been discovered with several different dates in THE BIBLE CODE, the first being 2012. A friend of mine, Dieter, a German engineer who lives in Vermont, pointed out to me that the ancient Mayan Calendar also ends in the year 2012 as well.

Hollywood has tried to guess or imagine the effect that such a great impact would have upon our planet. Most of the movies have been pretty good but the most accurate one was called DEEP IMPACT. I saw this movie when it first came out in 1998 in the huge old Roosevelt Theater in Hyde Park, NY, before it was subdivided into several smaller theaters. Located across the street from the home of Franklin Delano Roosevelt, the 32nd president of the United States, this big theater had a depth to it that really added something to certain movies. I saw the first STAR WARS movie there in 1977 and it was there that I saw DEEP IMPACT. As I sat in the theater with my wife on my left side and my friend Russell on my right side I listened to the music that is often played before the coming attractions are advertised. In the otherwise dimly lit silence of this formerly huge theater I suddenly heard in the stillness of my spirit the following clearly distinct thought, "Someday, something similar to what you are about to see, will happen." You can be sure I paid very close attention to the movie after hearing that. Will this happen during my lifetime? Will this "something like a burning mountain" crash into the earth in the next 50 or 100 years? I have no idea. I am just glad that God is still in control and that He still speaks to people today if they have a heart to hear.

If a star-like object doesn't hit the earth in our lifetime we will all be faced with two other problems almost as serious. First, the world is running out of water. The old theory was that there were underground rivers and reservoirs and that rainfall replenished them but the evidence is that water, like oil, came with the planet that human civilization inherited. Half of all the people on earth get their water from ground water. In Kansas it is 90 percent and in Florida it is almost 100 percent. Unfortunately, all over the earth, water tables are dropping as it is necessary to go deeper and deeper to get water. In the capital of China the wells must be at least 3,000 feet to reach water. At such depths mankind will long have since disappeared before the water table is replenished by rainwater. Much of the groundwater is used for irrigation to produce food and thus allowing for the earth's population to increase dramatically increase. We have learned how to take ever increasing amounts of water out of the ground but have not even thought about what will happen when the wells run dry. When the ground water decreases so will the food supply as is already evident in Africa and even the Bible (the last book of Revelation) says a time will come when it will take a days wage to earn a days food.

The second problem the world is facing is that we are running out of carbon based fuel. Now there is plenty of coal and oil and gas in the ground but the demand, like the demand for water, is beginning to exceed the supply. What many Americans don't realize is that the production of oil peaked in this country in the 1970's and has been going downhill ever since. It also appears that Middle East oil has or will peak very soon regardless of optimistic government reports to the contrary. Some experts are saying that because of increasing demand and decreasing supply, oil prices could triple in five years. Being an optimist I only believe they will double, at least at first.

The only technology that exists that I know of that could replace carbon based fuel (and greatly reduce greenhouse gases at the same time) is called "Pebble Bed" Nuclear Energy. A "Pebble Bed" reactor was first proposed by Farrington Daniels, a team member of the Manhattan Project, the year I was born but was nixed by

Hyman Rickover in a race to beat the Soviet Union with a nuclear submarine. I remember the thrill I had as a child reading about the launch of the first nuclear powered submarine, named after Captain Nemo's submarine, the Nautilus. That sub was powered by what we call a conventional rod-fueled water-cooled reactor, the same as our electricity generating nuclear power plants. This older technology is now considered so potentially dangerous that none have been built in the United States in over a quarter of a century.

In recent years China has built over 100 new coal powered energy plants, which produce a great amount of pollution. China has built two conventional nuclear energy plants this past year and has plans for 50 more. Already over one third of all traffic on Chinese railroads consists of coal trains moving coal from the northern coal mines to the electric plants in the south. The Chinese have already constructed a small "Pebble Bed" reactor and have plans to build a large commercial size plant as well.It is, however, South African scientists who are really on the forefront of "Pebble Bed" Nuclear generating technology, having refined and redesigned the system to be 35 to 45 percent more efficient than conventional technology. What is the advantage of the "Pebble Bed" method and why is it so much better? Primarily, because it cannot melt-down, accidentally or intentionally. They also cause less pollution than any other known technology. They are cheaper to construct, needing none of the expensive shields and containment that used rods require. Even the tangerine size "pebbles" are easier to dispose of when "spent" and cannot be used to make nuclear weapons. This means that rogue nations can generate the electricity they need without being a threat to democracy loving nations, and as the price of gasoline doubles and triples in the years ahead only hydrogen seems to be capable of replacing gasoline. Oh, did I mention that hydrogen can be produced by these "Pebble Bed" reactors in sufficient quantity to power automobiles as they make the electricity we need in the future?

The only real danger to the full sized commercial "Pebble Bed" reactor which the South Africans expect to have up and running within 48 months is that politicians and companies that have their own agendas might try to slow down the development of this safe, virtually non-polluting energy source, much as someone completely stopped the development of the 1986 British experimental gasoline powered automobile that could carry four passengers at speeds in excess of 100 miles per hour and much more importantly, got in excess of 110 miles per gallon without fancy hybrid technology and

$2,000 car batteries. I have been told that such developments in automotive technology have been purchased for huge sums by those who stand to lose if such a product came on the market, and that part of the transaction is or was a non-disclosure agreement.

In April of 2005, Senator Pete Domenici, Chairman of the "Senate Energy and Natural Resources Committee" spoke of how the choices we make today will determine how successful we are as we move from a carbon based fuel to a hydrogen society. Senator Domenici has stated that he believes that only high temperature nuclear reactors offer the ideal source for the hydrogen we will need, in the amounts we will need, for automotive purposes. General Motors is spending hundreds of millions of dollars on hydrogen research for automobiles although our own Department of Energy seems to think it will be 20 years before we can produce safe high-temperature reactors that can easily produce the necessary hydrogen. Fortunately for the world South Africa will have the first such 160 megawatt pilot project Pebble Bed Modular Reactor up and running by 2010 if they are allowed to do so. China has plans to build 30 nuclear power plants in the near future and hopefully these will be the safer cheaper "pebble bed" type. In the past three years China has opened several dozen coal powered plants and even with all this additional power they still have brown-outs and even black outs as the demand exceeds supply. They need nuclear energy but they do not need the possibility of a Chernobyl and only a "pebble bed" reactor can truly eliminate the possibility of that. South Africa and China are in the forefront of the new refined and redesigned "pebble bed" nuclear technology and America needs to get back on the bandwagon regardless of what our big companies want.

Of course, I knew none of these things that day in 1961 at Brooks Aero-Medical Space Center. I was just glad to be there on that historic day when we launched our first man into space. It wasn't long after that, perhaps another week or two, when we got our first pass to leave Lackland AFB and I was equally glad to be able to tour the Alamo. The two things that stood out the most in my 18 year old mind on that visit was how small the Alamo really was - I had imagined it to be much bigger - and I was surprised at how many South Carolinians had died there.

I visited Brackenridge Park north of the Alamo where I rented a paddle boat and saw the biggest goldfish I had ever seen in my life, a Texas sized giant that would easily have been big enough for a meal for two or more people but I had never heard of anyone eating a goldfish before except as a stunt. Later that day I walked along the river or creek that eventually flows through downtown San Antonio. At lunch time I tried a local Mexican restaurant. It was the first time I had been in a restaurant that offered three levels of hot sauce. I do not remember what I ordered but with the option of mild, medium, or hot, I opted to try hot. It was a mistake. Figuring that it might really be hot I didn't try much but it made no difference. It was as if I had put red liquid fire into my mouth. Tears flowed involuntarily and I grabbed for my soft drink. I even remember that it was a 7-UP, something I don't often drink today. I tried to appease the inferno in my mouth but the cold liquid only made it worse. It was truly beyond description. I had not yet learned that a piece of bread would have done a much better job of absorbing the volcano that had been my mouth just a few moments before. I like somewhat hot sauce but this was ridiculous.

Some people like Mikael only went through six weeks of basic training at Lackland and then completed several more weeks of basic, part-time, at whatever base they were sent to for training in their appropriate career field. The lucky ones, though I did not think so at the time, were those of us who had to stay for the full eight weeks before being sent to their next assignment. Their basic training was completed and they were regular airmen at their next base. I was one of these. The extra time at Lackland allowed me the opportunity to go horseback riding with my Native American friend that I mentioned earlier. Of course, in 1961 we called them Indians, not Native Americans. Since that time there have been some amazing discoveries here in North America, some very old skeletons found in various parts of the country. These skeletons are in the neighborhood of 9,000 years old. Since all these ancient skeletons are Caucasians there is accumulating evidence that the White Man may well have been here before the Red Man. Consequently the story on who is the most native "Native American" has yet to be written.

I completed basic training in June and returned to South Carolina to visit my folks. Mom was having her last child, my youngest sister Chrysa, so I applied for an emergency leave (an extension) so I could help with my six younger brothers and sisters as I had always done before while mom was in the hospital. It was a nice visit and I enjoyed being back in South Carolina but the days passed swiftly and soon it was time to return to Texas where Chrysa and her six children live today.

Within two hours of catching a bus in Darlington I was back in Columbia where Bunny (Mrs. John Richard Craft) picked me up at the bus terminal. I had dinner with her and her husband at their home, a beautiful place on Kipling Drive hidden away on a semi-private pond, just off the main thoroughfare. I spent the night there and early the next day Bunny drove me to the train station where I caught the train to Memphis, Tennessee, on my way back to Texas. It was the fourth time that I had left South Carolina.

The trip to Memphis took a full day and night. The train traversed halfway across South Carolina, into North Carolina, then through the Appalachian Mountains and all the way across the state of Tennessee which is the equivalent of going through Georgia, Alabama, and Mississippi combined. I arrived in Memphis on the eastern side of the Mississippi River early the next morning. It was about 8 a.m. and the train I needed to catch didn't leave until 8 p.m. so I had a day to explore or do whatever I liked. I took a bus by Graceland just to be able to say that I had seen it but, of course, I didn't go in because Elvis Presley still lived there when he was in town. In the early afternoon I went to a movie that was in Cinerama, a then-new technology where three projectors were running at the same time, all synchronized and overlapping on the screen. The movie was shown on a very wide screen. At the time it was quite amazing but today any visitor to EPCOT at Disney World can see travelogue movies on screens completely surrounding the viewer.

Later in the afternoon I walked along the cobble or brick lined landing leading along the eastern bank of the Mississippi River until I stepped one step too far and my foot sunk into the mud. The landing had ended but I hadn't noticed. When I pulled by foot out the shoe remained and I had to pull the shoe out with both hands and then wash it off in the river. The shoe was still damp when I finally caught the train to Little Rock, Dallas, and eventually San Angelo, Texas.

I had been assigned to Goodfellow Air Force Base on the outskirts of San Angelo to attend an intelligence school. This was operated by the Air Force Security Service under the auspices of the then super secret National Security Agency. At least I think it was. It was difficult to be sure about any of the structure of the NSA (the initials in 1961 were supposed to stand for No Such Agency). This very important organization has greatly contributed to our security in this country and would be an even greater asset if their intelligence gathering were utilized more effectively by other departments of the government. The most amazing book that will ever be written on this ultra-secret agency is BODY OF SECRETS by James Bamford. Unless Congress overturns President's Bush's restrictions on the Freedom of Information Act by Executive Decision never again will Americans learn so much about their government and what is really going on? If we are to remain a free society we need to know what our government is doing in our name even in the age of "terrorism."

A lot of math was involved in what I was being taught and I found it increasingly difficult. I hadn't realized that I had joined the Air Force to go back to school again. I found solace in joining the Nexus Club, a young adults club at a church in San Angelo. A small group of us took a memorable trip to Sonora, Texas, one weekend to visit some caverns that had been opened to the public not to many years before. One remarkable formation looked as if a butterfly had landed on a stalagmite and been frozen in crystal. I have heard that over the years many new caves have been discovered within the Sonora Caverns and that the areas open to the public is much bigger today than it was in 1961.

Some of the airmen in my barracks were jealous of the fact that I had permission to go off base to attend the young adults club and one Sunday night when I returned to a darkened barracks I quietly crossed the long open room where all the beds were laid out in a row much like they had been when I was a child and my family and I were living for a couple of weeks in the Columbia Museum of Art. I took off my uniform, hung it up, and prepared to go to bed. Many of the other airmen were already asleep. As I put my weigh on the bed it suddenly collapsed with a thunderous boom that woke every one up who had been asleep. Some of my fellow airmen had disassembled the metal bed and rigged it to fall apart when I put my weigh on it. I couldn't see to fix the bed in the dark and voices all over the room were complaining about the noise as if I alone had been the cause of it. It was also awkward and uncomfortable to sleep on because they had reversed the spring and a bulge existed in the center of the bed where none should have been. It was not until morning that I was able to take the bed apart completely and then re-assemble it properly so that it would no longer be awkward to sleep on.

I wondered if this little prank had been arranged by the group who had invited me to accompany them to Cuidad Acuna just across the Rio Grande River in Mexico. Being interested in new places to see I had almost agreed. They had all but convinced me when one to them started bragging about how pretty, and how young, and how inexpensive the girls were there. I quickly realized what kind of "girls" they were talking about and what kind of trip this would be and I backed out. It was a 300 mile round-trip and they were trying to get a large enough group to drive expenses down to a few dollars. I recall that they were not too happy at my refusal. I decided it was better to just ignore what had happened and let matters drop and I did not mention it again.

Riding a bicycle had always been a recreation for me and while stationed in San Angelo I purchased a used professional Italian racing bicycle. It had ten gears and stainless steel toe guards on the pedals to keep from slipping off at high speeds. The bicycle also came with two stainless steel clips that went around the bottom of ones trousers to keep them from tearing or being caught in the gearing mechanism. Although I don't remember the name of the bike it was certainly the Ferrari of bicycles and I think that some of the airmen may even have been jealous of the fact that I had the bicycle although most aspired to have an automobile and one or two of them secretly did off base.

One day I was whizzing along somewhere in a neighborhood in San Angelo and I must have startled a patrolman much like the two 90 year olds startled the sleeping state trooper by flying their ancient aircraft under the bridge and setting off the auto alarm in the excellent movie SECONDHAND LIONS with Michael Caine and Robert Duvall. Anyway I was soon pulled over, not being able to out-pedal a police car, or even wanting to do so. "This is a 25 mile an hour zone." I was told. "You were going 35 mph. You could get killed just as easy on this thing...no easier" the officer mused. "Yes, Sir," I replied, not knowing what else to say. I had no idea how fast I was going as I didn't have a speedometer on the bike. I felt that they took to much energy to operate and my legs were the engine doing the operating. I may have said something else because the officer replied, "Well, slow down and take it easy."I was grateful not to get a ticket although I didn't know if they would really have given me one for such an offense. I wasn't even in 9th gear and I could never get the bicycle into 10th gear so I don't know how fast I could have pedaled if I really wanted to speed. The fastest I have ever heard of someone pedaling was about 120 miles per hour but he was doing it between two speeding trains which created somewhat of a vacuum in which he was able to pedal. I had no interest in setting records though; I used a bicycle merely as transportation.

Once, when I was really working, pushing hard and pedaling up a small hill and sweating in the process a dog came tearing out at me and I did not even see it until it was nearly on top of me and then it started barking at the top of its voice. I was so startled that I put on the hand brakes, jumped off the bicycle, and picked the bike up over my head and waving the bicycle in the air I growled at the dog as loudly as I could. It was medium sized dog, and could have delivered a good sized bite, but the poor creature had never gotten such a response and it turned and ran off yelping in the opposite direction apparently as fast as it had come. I never would have imagined my reaction but it was non-the-less effective and may have saved the dogs life if it cured him of chasing bicycles. Some people are really scared of dogs. When I was six years old I had a dog, who used to chase bicycles. One day she chased one and the fellow doing the pedaling swung at her with a pipe. The fellow did not miss and my dog died from the impact.

Another time I was pedaling out in the desert west of San Angelo and I saw a black something or other run across the road in front of me. It looked fuzzy and since I was curious what kind of creature it was I speeded up. There were no other vehicles on the road that hot summer day and I swung over to the left side to see just what it was that had almost reached the other side as I approached. It was as big as my hand with the fingers outstretched and turned out to be a Texas-sized spider, undoubtedly a Tarantula.

Goodfellow Air Force Base was a place where the song lyrics, "the stars at night, are big and bright, deep in the heart of Texas," were literally true. Of all the places I've been in this country I've never seen such a star-filled sky as I saw on base on a clear summer evening, no smog, no city lights, nor hills nearby to interfere with a sky that looked truly magnificent. The rising sun or moon was also greatly magnified by the clearness of the atmosphere and the flatness of the terrain. One night I looked up and saw the balloon-like Echo satellite pass across the sky and one morning an ancient C-46 flew in from the east with smoke streaming from on of its engines. The smoke was quite impressive and I really thought we were going to see a crash. We were all standing at attention on the flight line watching it as it headed our way. The sun had just cleared the horizon when the craft finally made it to the airfield. A sigh of relief came from me upon seeing that the aircraft had made it. I could imagine how thankful the pilot must have been as well. Goodfellow had some of the best mess halls in the USAF. More than once they had won the coveted Hennessey Trophy for the best food served on any air force base in the entire United States Air Force.

I made friends with a young girl on base. She was too young to date, only 14, but we got along well together and I corresponded with her for several years. Her father was stationed at Goodfellow and when he was transferred to Alaska his family went with him. They went to Elmendorf AFB outside of Anchorage and they lived off base. In 1964 a devastating earthquake, the most powerful to hit North America in modern times, hit the area doing a lot of damage. My young friend wrote me how glad she was to move onto the base because she was now one mile further away from the fault. I suspect that the earthquake that THE BIBLE CODE says will strike "LACALIF" between Sept. 2010 and August 2011 will be even more powerful than the 1964 Alaskan quake and could kill more than 38,000 but that is another story. Sadly I lost track of my friend over the years.

I don't think I was having to difficult a time adjusting to the military discipline although I did think there was an awful lot of pettiness and trivialities involved but I was having such a rough time in the school I was attending that I finally decided to opt out of it. I still had not developed good study habits and the material was complicated. I did what was necessary to get re-assigned and while waiting for that re-assignment I was required to do odd jobs like helping an officer and his family move their belongings from one house to another. I vaguely remember doing some painting and one night I was required to do CQ. This meant that I had to stay up all night in the squadron office, take phone calls if there were any, and most important of all, wake the sergeants who would wake the troops at 6 a.m. All went well until about 5 a.m. when I had been awake for 23 hours and I simply couldn't keep my eyes open any longer. I don't remember closing them but I was not awake on time to wake the troops and a couple of hundred airmen were late for breakfast and classes. It was the only time that I was assigned to that particular duty.

"Richard, Richard, what am I going to do with you?" the Base Commander asked me once. I said nothing. "Do you know what your problem is?" he continued. "No, Sir!" I answered. "Your problem is that you don't think your problems are problems," he replied. It sounded wise, even profound, but I did not have a clue as to what the Colonel was talking about. The last time I was called before him he had apparently already made up his mind about me but he was only doing his job. I must have truly exasperated him. He asked me, "Richard, do you know the best thing you could do for the United States Air Force?" When I answered, "No, Sir!" with some trepidation, the Colonel simply replied, "Join the Russian Air Force!"

I heard someone mention that the Colonel had a grudge against the base commander at Sheppard Air Force Base in Wichita Falls, Texas, and that is why I got transferred there but that was just a rumor and I have no facts with which to back it up.

Wichita Falls is a little over 200 miles north east of San Angelo and just a few miles south of the Red River which separates Texas from Oklahoma. Sheppard AFB was a much larger base than Goodfellow and with several functions other than training. It traces its origin back to the days of WWI when it was called Sheppard Field and novice pilots used to train in primitive Jenny's. Somewhere I still have some more than 85 year old photos from those interesting early days at Sheppard Field only 15 years of so after the Wright Brothers first flight.

I had been assigned to electrician school which did not exactly thrill me. I could see where it could be quite messy at times so within a few days after arriving at Sheppard I decided I had to get out of it and find a job I liked. My color vision has never given me a problem in real life but I have always had a problem with the color charts that are usually used to detect the problem. When I failed these tests at Lackland AFB during basic training I was sent to the School of Aviation Medicine where an entirely different kind of test was administered to me. In a completely darkened room, with time enough for my eyes to attempt to adjust to the dark; I was shown two pin points of light like two tiny stars on a very clear night. They were reference points and I was told that their color was white. This was helpful because I could just barely tell I was seeing them. I was then shown a third pinhole of light and told to identify what color it was using the supposedly white lights as reference. This was done several times and once the person giving me the test said, "Guess again," which I did, apparently getting it right the second time. In any event I passed and there was no problem with my color vision at Lackland AFB.

During my first few days as an apprentice electrician at Sheppard AFB I noticed quite a few different colors of wire. Some were easy to identify, some were a little more difficult. I theorized that the USAF would not want me to connect the wrong colored wire on a bomb, a jet, or even a house (I had no idea what kind of electrician I was being trained to be). I also guessed that the more sophisticated color test that I had passed with a little help at Lackland in San Antonio might not be available at Sheppard in Wichita Falls and they would have to use the old stand-by of "what numbers do you see." Since I have never been able to pass all of those successfully I figured that I had a good chance of getting out of 16 weeks of electrician school which was a lot like more basic training if I told them that I had problems with color. At first I don't think they believed me since my records indicated that my color vision was normal. I have never had a problem with traffic lights which are green and yellow and red but weak pastel shades such as those on my alkaline battery charger are a bit of a problem. Anyway I told them of the special color test I had been given and how I had passed it. This was enough to create some doubt and I was scheduled to take a color test within 48 hours. Sure enough, the doctor pulled out the same old color charts that I had been failing since I first took them in grammar school. I tried my best and passed some of them easily but there were some numbers I simply did not see and others that I saw differently than a person with normal color vision.

"Well, you definitely can't be an electrician," the doctor told me. "Oh!" was all I said in reply. In my mind I was jumping up and down. I had already decided what I wanted to become.

15. Information Specialist and West
Texas Politics

In the United States Air Force, the career field of "Information Specialist" covers a number of areas but for me it meant journalist. I applied for and received assignment as a staff writer on The Sheppard Senator, the base weekly newspaper. It was an on-the-job training assignment and one afternoon a week was devoted to the theory of journalism: Who, What, When, Where, Why and How.

Some may argue that this wasn't true journalism because feature stories were rare and we seldom dug up the news. We were told what to write and oftentimes we were given the facts with which to compose the story. The military version of a weekly newspaper is something like a trade journal but there were some opportunities for creativity. I only recall doing one feature story but there may have been more. My primary responsibility was one page. I wrote the stories, composed the headlines, and arranged the layout. The actual typesetting was done in an old fashioned print shop in Bowie, Texas, about 50 miles southeast of the base.

We rotated turns and once or twice a month I would join Sergeant Snyder and drive to Bowie, Texas, where the type was set and the paper was printed. A middle aged printer would set the words on something like an ancient typewriter and machinery that seemed as old as Texas itself would come to life, grinding and clanking and thumping as the words were cast in hot lead and appeared, line after line, as we had written them or rather as the typist had typed them.

The newly cast type would be assembled in a frame that represented one page. I would put together the headlines by hand from larger letters but I usually deferred to one of the older civilians who worked there as to the proper size to select. When one page was completed, a paint roller would be dipped in black ink and rolled over the newly formed type. Then a blank page of newspaper would be pressed upon the wet type with an ancient rolling device. That would produce one page, a proof that we would then read for spelling errors and continuity. The process was probably not too different from the one that Johannes Gutenberg had used five centuries before me. If a mistake was found, and it was occasionally, then that section would be removed from the frame and new type would be cast as the typist or printer re-typed it. When the paper was finally printed, the type went back into the melting pot. The lead was used over and over. The headlines, which were composed of individual steel letters, were saved and those letters were put back into their appropriate box sizes to be used again.

One mistake I did not catch nor did anyone else until the paper was printed and back at the base being distributed was in the final issue for that year. The headline read, "What Will 1962 Bring Us?" and it was a story or report by Gen. Thomas Moore, the base commander, telling of new plans, construction, and such like, that we could expect during the coming year. Unfortunately, this edition was printed at the end of December in 1962 and what 1962 would bring us, it had already brought us. What I had meant to quote the general as saying was, "What Will 1963 Bring Us?"

Sergeant Snyder and Sergeant Baumgartner both talked to me about that one and nothing like that ever slipped by me again.

One night as we returned from Bowie with the freshly bundled newspapers ready for the next days distribution we noticed a glow in the sky in the direction of Wichita Falls and Sheppard AFB. We were still about 20 miles away and as we drove closer, we could see flames in the distance. The fire was on the other side of Wichita Falls and fairly close to the base. It burned for two days. I do not remember how many gallons of oil burned, perhaps 200,000 gallons, but the tanks were huge. I was told that these large tanks had wooden tops that floated over the oil and they would rise and fall depending on how full the tank was at the time. This seemed primitive to me, and an open invitation to fire, but I was told that this was crude oil, less susceptible to flame than the refined product. For years, I believed that until I saw the fires that Saddam Hussein ordered his Iraqis troops to start in the Kuwaiti oil fields in 1991. Tens of millions of gallons of crude oil were burned up in retaliation for his not being allowed to keep Kuwait and the fires were so large and dense that they could easily be seen from space. If we had gone and arrested him, and charged him with a crime against the environment perhaps we would not be involved in what many hope will not be a multi-decade's long war. We can hardly afford any war right now and are borrowing over 2 BILLION dollars per day as I write these words. Since this is three quarters of the savings of everyone on earth, it is not likely that this rate of borrowing and debt can keep going for much longer. To bad, we don't follow the ways of the Bible, just cancel everyone's debt, and start over every 50 years. Some experts believe it will take at least 20 years to come out of the inflationary financial crisis that is approaching our doorstep. Time will tell and not even an executive order from any president can cover up the size of the problem. It is going to be awesome!

In Wichita Falls, there were two huge oil tanks not far from the main entrance to the base but the firefighters succeeded in keeping the fire from spreading to the second tank. I do not know how thick the metal was on the sides of these tanks but the heat was so tremendous that the top side of the tank downwind from the breeze actually melted and let burning oil pour out over the side of the tank. We could look out one of the windows from Base Headquarters and see the firefighters in the distance doing their best to contain the fire. It took them a couple of days to do so.

I was learning about the theory of writing and at the time, I lived in the last barracks on the corner of the base next to the base golf course. My roommate at the time was a nice kid my age from Amarillo, Texas. He had red hair and his name was Larry Minor. One Saturday he asked me if I would take over CQ for him and man the phone in case anyone called. We were all required to take turns doing this so messages could be relayed in case of emergencies of any kind. Larry offered me three dollars to do this for him and at first, I agreed. I got to thinking about it and I decided that although the offer was a fair one (three dollars in 1962 would purchase what $20 will buy today) I didn't want to hang around the barracks on my day off.

"Well, will you at least go the service club and bring me a snack?" Larry asked. Feeling a little guilty that I had changed my mind, I agreed and left shortly thereafter for the nearest service club, about a ten block walk round-trip. I made the purchase and in the change I received, I found a 1916 Winged Liberty Head dime in almost very fine condition. Back then, of course, the majority of people called them Mercury Dimes because the figure of Liberty looked a lot like the Roman god Mercury who served as messenger of the gods and was the god of commerce and thievery in ancient mythology. Only a few years later these coins were removed from circulation because

like the early Roosevelt dimes, they were made of silver and that
was replaced with copper-nickel dimes much as the Roman Empire
diluted their coinage as they approached the end of their greatness.
This particular design was used on all our dimes from 1916 until
1945. Such dimes can still be purchased in a coin shop for $2 and
sometimes less. In 1916, the "Mercury" dime was minted at three
mints, Philadelphia, Denver, and San Francisco. The dime from one
of those mints was quite valuable. I had had little involvement with
coins since I was robbed at summer camp when I was ten years old
and I could not remember if it was the Denver coin with a small "D"
mintmark or the San Francisco dime with an "S" mintmark that was
valuable. Larry, however, was an avid coin collector.

"Hey! Larry," I called out to him when I returned with his snack
items. "Look what I found at the service club," I said as I pitched the
coin through the air as if it was the fifty-cent coin I expected it to be.
Larry's eyes widened and the look on his face was such that I knew
I had found the key to the set, the rarest coin of the entire series. It
was worth about three week's salary back then. I wish I'd kept it. It
is worth over a month's salary today.

Once again, I became interested in coins. Soon I met others on
the base who collected coins. One was Mario who told me that five
years earlier he had served with the U.S. Embassy in Japan where he
made frequent trips all over the country. In every town and city, he
would stop in the curio shops and the junk shops and ask to see the
coins. He purchased only American, Canadian, and British coins.
He would purchase the silver coins and often he would be given the
copper ones. One freebie I distinctly remember was a brown uncirculated 1911-s Lincoln cent. Today that coin would easily be worth
a hundred dollars. Another silver quarter had cost him 37 cents. It
was an extremely fine or better pattern quarter or experimental design from the 19th Century. Today it would be worth a few thousand
dollars. Mario did not have a 1916 Denver minted "Mercury" dime.
He traded me a rare 1883 Hawaiian silver dollar in choice extremely
fine condition and a similarly graded 1926-S dime for it. Mario had
two trunks full of coins that I saw and I offered to catalog them for
him just for the privilege and pleasure of being able to see them.
Mario declined because he was planning to retire in a few years and
he wanted to do that for himself.

The following year, in 1963, when silver dollars could still be
obtained in a bank for a dollar, I found the key to the regular set of
Morgan Silver dollars in a bank in Darlington, S.C.All 1893 silver

dollars are valuable but the one minted in San Francisco is the rarest and it was worth a week's salary even in very good condition. Today, of course, it is worth at least a months salary. No, I wasn't smart enough to keep that one either.

I don't remember volunteering so my job must have required me to be a member of the auxiliary air police. This extra duty did not consist of much. It was really just a practice for a national emergency. One day, however, in the fall of 1962 we were all posted at real potential targets. We were given live ammunition and I and one other airman were given the job of guarding 7,000,000 gallons of jet fuel. The thought occurred to me that if an enemy truly wanted to destroy the jet fuel the air force probably wouldn't be able to find enough of me to bury but this time I kept my thoughts to myself.

We were told nothing about the nature of the emergency but we had heard rumors about Russia, Cuba, and Castro. I did not know for years how close we really came to a nuclear confrontation at that time. Only President Kennedy's calm resolve avoided nuclear war.

The day after I was issued live ammunition I telephoned my mom and suggested to her that she go out and purchase an extra two weeks groceries. "Something is going on," I told her. "I don't know what it is but it's big." Mom had been keeping up with the news and she seemed to know more about the problem with Cuba than I did. Whether it was public information at that time that one of our spy planes had been shot down over Cuba and its pilot killed, I do not remember. Years earlier during President Eisenhower's administration an American spy plane was shot down while spying over Russia and more than a dozen Americans were killed. The whole affair was so top secret that at the time that only the president and those directly involved knew anything about it and the president made those who knew swear on the Bible that he knew nothing of it.

In any event, mom purchased an extra large order of groceries in case something did get out of control. Of course, a few more bags of groceries would not have made much difference if nuclear war had broken out but fortunately for the world Russia, or rather the Soviet Union, took their missiles out of Cuba. We were told very little of this at the time, just that the crisis had been averted, everything was now OK, and we gave back the live ammo that had been issued to us. What no one in the free world knew at that time was that along with the missiles, 161 nuclear weapons had also been delivered to

Cuba, more than enough to annihilate the United States.They too were removed.

Life quickly returned to what passed as normal. Once I was in my quarters, the last barracks at the extreme corner of the base where the flight line ended and the golf green began, and someone yelled at me, "Have you ever seen a tornado?" The tone of voice of the person asking the question led me to believe that he was seeing one at that very moment. If that was so, shouldn't we seek shelter, I thought to myself, but I quickly yelled back that I had never seen one. "There's one out front and it's moving away from us," came the reply.I ran to the front door and I could see that it was so. On the other side of the flight line, perhaps a mile away, was a funnel shaped cloud running along the ground and moving away from us.

That same year I went home on leave to South Carolina for three weeks (at least I thought it was for three weeks). When I returned, my commanding officer asked me where I had been. "What do you mean, where have I been?" I asked him; after all, he had signed the papers authorizing my leave. "You were supposed to be back yesterday," he replied. "I don't think so," I answered as I pulled out my papers and re-read them carefully. He was correct and once again, I had made a mistake. Twenty days may be two thirds of a month and twenty days may be almost three weeks but twenty days is not twenty-one days and I had been AWOL (absent without leave) for a day without even knowing about it. Of course, I had to be punished because the military cannot have its members being AWOL intentionally or unintentionally. Rather than being made to do something constructive, for two weeks I had to scrub tiles in the latrine with a toothbrush. Of course, I was never AWOL again so I guess the punishment worked.

The biggest surprise I had, however, in leaving South Carolina yet again and returning to Texas was not in discovering that I was AWOL but in discovering that an empty barracks behind the one I had lived in, which had been a two story building when I left was now, three weeks later, a one story building.The building next to that one, fortunately also empty, was missing altogether. "We had a tornado," I was told.

One Saturday I took a day trip up to Lawton, Oklahoma, about 50 miles to the north. While there, I went up Mount Scott, the tallest mountain in the Wichita Mountains northwest of the city. I remember seeing a majestic eagle soaring below me and I was awed by the rugged wilderness of the area. I also visited a coin shop in

Lawton where I met a gold prospector from Alaska. I was impressed by his watch or rather the watchband. The prospector had made it himself and it consisted of a solid stainless steel band to which he had welded gold nuggets that he himself had found in Alaska. The clip was a five dollar gold coin of the type last minted in 1907. Alaska, then a state for three years, was the only place, the prospector told me, where you could make a purchase for a dollar, hand over a twenty-dollar bill and get 19 silver dollars in change. "They don't like paper money," he continued.

I have a hunch they might like the Sacagawea golden dollar even less. The coin has no silver in it, and it certainly has no gold in it, and any numismatist could tell the government that it will never replace the paper dollar until they stop making the paper dollar. We are the only major country in the world that has a paper bill for a value as low as a dollar. The reason I think is simple. First, as I have already said, we have a paper dollar and Americans will use that as long as it exists. It might be nostalgia or it might be that enough Americans have talked with the citizens of those countries who have more valuable coins than our seldom-used half dollars and for the most part, they do not like the bulkiness in their pockets. Still the real reason might be that the Phillip Crane Company of Massachusetts has been supplying paper to the U.S. Government for over 135 years. There is nothing wrong with that. I am sure it's a lucrative contract. Massachusetts also has powerful democratic congressmen who try to help their constituents whenever possible. Nothing wrong with that either. The solution it seems to me would be to guarantee that the BEP (Bureau of Engraving and Printing) continue to buy the same amount of paper as they do now but to use that paper to print $5 and $10 bills. A ten dollar bill today isn't worth as much as a one dollar bill was when the Phillip Crane Company began selling paper to the government and a $5 bill is worth less than a $1 bill was worth when I was in the service and before the Vietnam War and the War on Poverty and all the other inflationary spending that our government has done for us for the last 45 years. If we really want to compete in the 21st Century (primarily with Europe) we will need to print bigger denominations of bills like the old $500 and $1,000 bills that could still occasionally be acquired at some banks as recently as the 1990's when someone would bring one of these collectors items into the bank for smaller denominations. Although Europe already has a large $500 Euro note we are not likely, however, to print new $500 dollar bills any more than we are to start reprinting the $100,000 bill that was issued early in the 20th Century. The president on that bill was Woodrow Wilson. "Payable to the bearer on demand, one hundred thousand dollars in gold," that note had printed on it. Of course, if you get right down to it we shouldn't be using paper money at all. The constitution says that no state shall issue any money but gold or silver and it's true that no state does. Newer laws forbid any state from making its own money. Our paper money was once backed by gold and silver but that proved too much of a hindrance on government spending. They say there isn't enough gold in the whole world to back our mountains of paper money (and debt) but that isn't really true. It's just that gold would have to be $20,000 per ounce and I have read serious analysis of the possibility of gold someday being even higher than that. Today our money is just backed by faith and credit in the government and the Federal Reserve Banks of the world.

Amazingly, the cryptic last book of the Bible says a time will come when all buying and selling will be done through some sort of mark (or microcomputer) imbedded in one's right hand or forehead. This "implant" will apparently be required by law and the Bible says that even a king won't be able to buy or sell without it. How could John who wrote that last book of Revelation know one thousand and nine hundred years ago that a time would come when gold and silver would no longer be accepted as money?Undoubtedly, gold and silver coins will be outlawed when that happens just as gold coins were outlawed in the United States from 1933 until 1975. I hope that that will far in the future but I have already heard talk of such things. I believe they call it feasibility studies and the FDA has already approved the implantation of micro-chips into human beings in 2004 so it's just a matter to time.

The company I worked for until 2005 will probably build some of the microscopic computers that will go inside ones arm or fore-head. They have already built many of the chips that are used in the new "smart cards" that contain all ones financial records, and military personnel no longer have to carry a handful of records wherever they travel. Now a credit card sized piece of plastic containing microchips has all the data instead. When my friend Ralph bought that five or six transistor radio back in the 1950's a single transistor was about the size of medium size fingernail and about as thick as two nickels. Today single transistors are being made so small that they cannot be seen with the naked eye. You could have one in the palm of your hand and not be able to see it.

Even using silver for coins is considered "to expensive" nowadays for day to day transactions but that day in Oklahoma the coins in my pocket were all silver (except for the cents and the nickels) and some of my money was in silver certificates.Like the gold certificates of an earlier generation, some of these bills still exist but they are no longer redeemable for silver, only for more paper. Pre-1933 American gold coins were available and if I had enough money I could have purchased one of these collectors items. Even in the old Soviet Union and here as well, collectors were allowed to collect gold coins if they could afford it. Of course, I have read that the government didn't tell people that collectors could keep their gold coins until months after they were supposed to have turned them in. Some law-abiding citizens had their fine collections go into the melting pot while those millionaires less inclined to follow the whims of Congress and the President were rewarded with a 67 percent profit when the government revalued their gold. Gold had been $20 per ounce and the government revalued it at $35 per ounce. Today the price of gold floats and changes day to day (actually hour to hour) and it is considered just another commodity like soybeans or oil but it really is money, at least until the politicians decide to outlaw it again because of our astronomical and unpayable national debt.

I looked over the coins that were available in the shop on the Main Street of Lawton but the ones I wanted I couldn't afford and the ones I could afford I did not want. The coin dealer had a fish bowl filled with ancient coins, some from the Roman Empire. "Every coin at least one thousand years old - Your choice 50 cents!" the sign read.I thought recognized some emperors but I've never been overly impressed with any empire so I passed them up. Finally, I purchased an old sock with a handful of foreign coins in it for 50 cents. Later when I went to attribute them, I was able to find out where all of the coins came from with one exception. The one I was unsure of was a dime-sized silver coin dated 1917. It was a 10 Kopeks piece obviously from Russia but the catalogs showed that 1916 was the last date of issue. I thought that I might have discovered a truly rare coin but, alas, it was not to be. A year of writing to foreign dealers, experts, even museums, resulted in my finding out that the coin was not unique. Mr. Dupont of the Dupont Chemical Company was supposed to have had an uncirculated one in his collection that might have been worth $35. My coin was worth far less because it had a hole in it. The coin was rare but so was anyone who would want to buy it or trade me for it. Its actual value might have been $5 but

I had more fun giving it to a collector of Russian coins than I ever could have gotten selling it. Today the coin is listed in the catalogs and it still might be worth $5. A brand new or uncirculated one is now listed at $75.

After leaving the coin shop, I caught the Greyhound bus and headed back to Texas and Sheppard AFB. We had just crossed into Texas when the wind increased rapidly.It was only minutes to the main entrance of Sheppard but before the driver could get there, he had to pull off the road and stop. The wind was blowing so hard that he could not steer the bus. It was not a tornado but it was quite exciting nonetheless.

While I was stationed at Sheppard, a new hospital was being constructed to replace the old WWII Army Hospital that was still being used. The air force as a separate branch of the armed forces wasn't formed until 1947 so they simply inherited what the Army Air Corp had used. Although somewhat bigger than the Opportunity School, the hospital buildings were familiar to me because they were of the same design as the buildings I had lived in when I was eight to eleven years old. The year after I left Sheppard AFB the new hospital opened and patients and some equipment were moved out of the old one-story- several-square-block hospital. Plans for the old hospital were never realized because just a few months after the move a powerful tornado came through and completely destroyed the old hospital, one aircraft hanger and at least one KC-97 Strategic Air Command tanker. Seven people on base died. Some years later an even bigger and deadlier tornado hit the city of Wichita Falls and that storm was so severe and so damaging that film clips of it are sometimes shown on Educational Television when the subject is tornadoes.

Windstorms were not usually as damaging as tornadoes in northern Texas but sometimes they were spectacular. Once while walking across the base on a sunny afternoon I noticed that everyone else seemed to be walking rather quickly. A few were even running. I hadn't heard a siren or any kind of warning.Something was going on but I had no idea what. I yelled to someone who was running in the direction I was heading, "What's going on?" and he yelled back that I had better take cover because a storm was coming. The sky was clear. The sun was shining and the air was pleasantly warm. It was then that I noticed a thin reddish orange line in the distance about where the Red River and Oklahoma were situated. It was about the thickness of a pencil held horizontally at arms length. It would have taken me 20 minutes to get back to the barracks where I lived so that was out of the question. The nearest public place was a base service club, which sold sandwiches, hamburgers, coffee, soft drinks, newspapers and cigarettes and maybe beer. I had never been in this particular one. I headed in the direction of the "club" and then I noticed that the reddish orange horizon to the north was now the thickness of four pencils. I had never seen anything like it, but it did not dawn on me what I was seeing. I was running now like the few who were still outside on this bright sunny day. By now I could see that "it" was coming as fast as a freight train and I was about ten feet from the door when I found out what everyone else seemed to know. A burning sensation blasted my arms and face as I leaped for the door, which opened as if by magic. I turned around and it took all of my strength and that of two others to close the heavy glass door, which was framed in either steel or aluminum. The red sands of southern Oklahoma blasted that door at 60 mph for a few seconds and then were gone. Cold pelting rain immediately followed the sand and instantly turned the sunny day into a somber gray one. It didn't last long but the glass door was lightly etched as I would have been if I hadn't have run the last 50 yards. I shouldn't have been surprised as I once saw the temperature drop 19 degrees in seven minutes while I was stationed in Texas and that is what I call a real cold front! On another occasion to illustrate how hot it was one summer I accompanied a photographer for a photo of an egg frying on the wing of a jet aircraft sitting on the runway in the summer sun. I don't remember the temperature but as soon as we cracked the egg open and it touched the wing of the jet it began to sizzle and turn white. There are storms and tornadoes in South Carolina and in New York but I have never seen such varied weather as I did when I was stationed at Sheppard Air Force Base outside Wichita Falls, Texas.

My barracks was on the last street parallel to the flight line and on the same street as the barracks that housed the WAF (Women in the Air Force) squadron. Both barracks faced the flight line. It was at the WAF barracks that I put my name on a list of available baby sitters. Baby-sitting was one of the few things in which I had sufficient experience to enable me to earn some extra money. I had made a friend who lived in the barracks as well. She was a beautiful blond girl from the tiny town of Bethune in South Carolina. I seem to recall that Leah or Lela was an orphan raised by a local minister in Bethune and that she had a sister, but that was a long time ago.

I presume that she met someone and married because a year or so after I left Texas she stopped writing.

I think it was Leah who phoned one day and asked if I could handle two families, a double baby-sitting job, a total of six children under the age of seven. I obtained the details and figured that it wasn't anything I hadn't done before. In that I was more right than I knew! The two families lived off base in a town called Iowa Park about nine miles from Sheppard. One of the husbands picked me up at the base and drove me to one of the homes where all the children had been gathered together. After getting emergency phone numbers and instructions the two sergeants and their wives drove to a party in Oklahoma. After six hours or so they all returned. The children were well behaved and caused me no problems. Most of them slept the whole time. What caused me some concern was the parents. The wives seemed OK but they were staying home with the kids after having been out a good part of the night. Part of the deal was that I would be provided with transportation back to the base at the end of the evening and the sergeants prepared to drive me back. Unfortunately both had had too much to drink. There was no other way for me to get back and both of them decided to take me back to Sheppard. I didn't want to get into that car. Suddenly it was déjà vu all over again. I was in the back seat of the car praying that we would all arrive safely much as I had when I hitchhiked to Myrtle Beach two years before.

At one point just shortly after we left their home the driver went down a medium sized slope or hill. They were supposed to stop and turn right at the bottom of the slope onto the highway. It was impossible to see the traffic coming from either direction unless you did stop at the stop sign and look. We never even slowed down until we had run past the stop sign, sailed across both lanes of the highway and onto a then unpaved road on the other side of the highway. "Ought-oh!" the driver exclaimed as he came to a complete stop on the dirt road and then, without really looking, backed out onto the highway, and turned in the direction of the air base. Fortunately it was after two in the morning and there were no other cars on the road. If there had been it is unlikely that I would be writing these words. After running off the road a time or two more we made it to the base. The sergeants must have straightened up and looked serious because the guard at the gate did not stop them. Finally around 3 a.m. I got back to my barracks. I said a silent pray that the two of them would get back to their homes safely. Six orphans and two

widows were a possibility. I heard nothing and I didn't read anything about them in the newspapers so I presumed that they made it
back OK and I made a mental note not to baby sit for them again.

One of the big stories in the local Texas newspapers at the time
was supposedly a huge scandal involving Billie Sol Estes, an en-
trepreneur who was supposedly being paid by the government to
store fertilizer in huge tanks, which he owned. Apparently the fertilizer did not exist and the government was quite upset to discover
this. Stories like this can sometimes take on a life of their own and
this one was no exception. It was the major news event for weeks
(months?) on end. I was not even particularly interested but day
after day the headlines kept up the barrage.Somehow, from what
I read back then, it did not seem so terrible to me. The government paid farmers not to grow crops. If they paid Billie Sol Estes
to store fertilizer for those non-existent crops and the fertilizer too,
was non-existent...well, I guess I just didn't understand it all.

After I wrote the above paragraph I decided I'd better look on
the internet and try to verify some of the facts as I remembered
them. Wow! The internet was loaded with stories about this colorful character who was apparently loved and hated by many. I did
not know that the whole episode had become part of Texas folklore.
What I had remembered was some of what had been reported at the
time but not necessarily the truth.

I was surprised to discover a recent item on Billie Sol Estes
that had been printed in The Washington Post on April 2, 2002 on
page A14. It was a letter to the editor from Robert Lewis who was a
Deputy Administrator at the Department of Agriculture during the
Kennedy administration. In his letter Mr. Lewis said that Mr. Estes
never stole a cent from the government. Billie Sol Estes' grain storage tanks were approved by the government as storage facilities in
which farmers could store their grain as collateral for price support
loans. Estes rented them out to farmers who did not lose money
either.

As for the tanks that I had remembered as being non-existent:
they existed and so did some of the anhydrous ammonia. If anyone
was cheated on these transactions (and I'm not sure anyone was
cheated), it was not the government nor the farmers but possibly
the bankers who demanded to see the fertilizer that was collateral
for money loaned to Mr. Estes. Apparently, not as much fertilizer
existed as the banks were led to believe.

Other stories on the internet tell of some fantastic allegations that Billie Sol Estes made against the late President Johnson and of his association with then Senator Johnson. I do not know the truth about any of these allegations. However, President Johnson's scandalous cover-up of the killing of 34 Americans in an un-provoked attack by our allies, the Israeli's, on the USS LIBERTY, while Johnson was president would surely be enough to impeach any president. The evidence, though there are those who still refuse to believe it, shows that those few Israeli's who carried out the attack knew what they were doing in destroying our "spy" ship and were trying to cover up their own actions. I believe all nations have a right to protect themselves against invasion but that does not apply to friends and allies who are not in any way a threat.

In 1997 Admiral Thomas H. Moore, former Chief of Naval Operations, called the lack of a Congressional hearing on the USS LIBERTY affair "a national disgrace." Interestingly, the Bible says a time will come when all the nations of the world will unite against Israeli. Because of God's promises, I do not believe that Israel will ever be wiped off the face of the earth as it was over 2500 years ago, but until I learned about the destruction of the USS LIBERTY in never occurred to me that Israel could bring this opposition down upon herself. I have come to believe that "as you sow, so shall you reap," applies to nations as well as to individuals. That is why I am concerned that the United States of America be truly involved with "justice for all" and not just political expediency. I have also come to believe that only God knows the truth of all things, but He does know. Nothing done in secret escapes Him and while He is a God of healing, love and forgiveness, He is also a God of Justice.

I have also wondered if West Texas politics is as colorful today as it was over 40 years ago.

16. Jerry Van Dyke and the UN Representative

One morning when I was at my desk at base headquarters a celebrity came by and although it wasn't my job to interview him I did get to talk with him. He was in the Air Force Reserve and was doing his 6 months of active duty. Now there are a number of people from Hollywood that I would enjoy meeting and talking with today (Michele Greene and Jennifer Love Hewitt come to mind) but then I was just as fascinated by what Jerry Van Dyke had to say. He told us of his upcoming TV series and I remember asking him about some of the popular actresses of the day. He was a regular guy and if he had not been a movie/TV star he could have been anyone's next door neighbor. From time to time other celebrities and actors came by the base or were stationed there but Jerry Van Dyke was the only one I actually talked with and he is the only one I clearly remember.

If I had been a student of military history I could have surmised that something was going on in Vietnam. I remember they had to say the name twice before I could remember it. In the barracks directly behind mine lived student pilots from the South Vietnamese Air Force who were being trained to fly American helicopters. I didn't really have much personal contact with them but I was amazed that some of them were only 16 years old. I did pick up on the idea that if I went overseas that going to Saigon might be a pretty nice place to go. Since there were no base facilities at that time I thought that having the government pay me a per diem salary sounded great. I looked into it and I seem to remember that I would be getting in the neighborhood of $900 per month for room and board. I could get my own apartment and I knew I could save a substantial amount of that because I, too, had inherited or learned my grandfather's thrifty ways.

The idea of going to Japan also appealed to me. Ever since I'd seen the movie SAYONARA starring Marlon Brando I'd been fascinated with the Orient. I did make some friends with some Philippine officers who to me were just regular people. It did not occur to me at the time that they might just have desired some inter-active fellowship with Americans but since they were "people of color" that might have been hard to come by in Texas or even in the USAF in 1962. Of course, as an enlisted man I was not supposed to associate with officers but I figured that rule was for American officers.

As far as the U.S. military goes there exists a caste system separating enlisted men from officers that is in force as much as the caste system of India. I did not feel comfortable with this but I tried to follow the rules as best as I could.

The lieutenants and captains from the Philippine Air Force invited me to their officer's quarters for dinner and I enjoyed the authentic cuisine as well as the friendliness of the people. It was a small cultural exchange and I learned things that I never would have known otherwise as I have never been to the Philippines although one of my poems was published in a weekly magazine there, submitted by a pen pal, a Philippine nurse who worked for the magazine.

Associating with those Philippine Officers was the kind of thing that I was often doing without considering the military ramifications of my actions. Some people love the military life. We certainly need the five branches of service. In fact, the army, navy, air force, marines, and coast guard of the United States are undoubtedly the best in the world. Still, some people are just not the military "type" and I was one whose effort "to do my best" as we said in the scouts just didn't measure up to what the military life required. I was too independent in my basic core values. I certainly wasn't a trouble maker but I seemed to get into trouble more than most over things that I thought were ridiculous but which the military thought were very important.

Once when I was being reassigned from electrician school to the base newspaper I was put in a transient barracks where I had my own private bedroom which was normally reserved for non-commissioned officers. I was there for three weeks - I think the Air Force forgot me - until I overslept on a Saturday and missed a parade. I might still have been "left" there which was fine with me but another division assigned a sergeant to my room and he was quite upset to find someone of my rank in a private room. He could see by the look of the room that I had been there for some time: calendar and pictures on the wall, flowers in a vase on my desk. The sergeant raised such a stink that I was quickly reassigned to the corner barracks opposite the flight line and across from the golf green.

More than a few times I would skip the several block walk to the mess hall and eat instead at the golf club which had some reasonably priced favorites of mine. Of course I had to pay at the golf club but the food was good and the club was much closer than the mess hall. Of course I always wore civilian clothes at the club.

I didn't get an apartment in Saigon but I did get one in Wichita Falls. I didn't think to ask anyone's permission and I got in trouble for that. I saw an ad on the wall of the service club or maybe in the newspaper and the price seemed right to me. I figured that if my half of the room I had on base was spotless and inspection ready that all would go well. We were required to have a blanket stretched so tightly on our beds that a quarter would bounce on the bed when one was flipped onto it. My bed was perfectly made and it was always inspection ready because I didn't sleep in it. This arrangement only lasted about two months because the other airman was under investigation by the Office of Special Investigation. They wouldn't tell me but I figured out that they suspected that the other guy was a homosexual. Consequently, I too, was questioned by a couple of investigators, one of whom had definite bad vibes about him. He was clearly different and only one other time in my life have I ever met someone so clearly alien to all I knew or had ever experienced. If someone had told me that he was a professional assassin I would not have been surprised. The other person was someone I seem to remember was a government agent from a country that I will not mention in Africa. The incident happened a few years after I left the air force. I had ridden a Greyhound bus from New York to Washington, D.C. on my way back to South Carolina. It was in the mid-1960s and I sat next to and talked with a United Nations Representative from that country for a couple of hours. The fellow was the first true African that I had ever met and he was quite friendly. We talked about many subjects until I finally had to ask him why he was riding a bus to Washington. I had imagined that all UN diplomats or attaches would have limousines and chauffeurs. "I like riding in buses," was his answer and I believed it was the truth. He enjoyed seeing the countryside such as it was and he certainly seemed to enjoy talking with me as I did with him. When we reached Washington, I had to change buses so we got off together and he introduced me to someone from his country who had been sent to meet him at the bus terminal. At the time I thought that the person he had introduced me to might have been a communist but I said nothing. This strikes me as a little odd today but I guess "a communist" was the greatest evil I could think of at the time. Whatever he was I feel that looking back from my perspective and understanding today that he was indeed evil and might have been something far worse.

However, that day in Texas, I answered numerous questions to the best of my ability and I was eventually told that I couldn't live off base because of my rank and I had to move back to the barracks. I never found out what happened to the other airman.

The funniest thing I ever saw while living in the last barracks on the corner of the base next to the golf course was the crash landing of a small private aircraft. The accident wasn't funny, the craft had a good bit of damage to it but fortunately no one was seriously hurt. What struck me as funny was that the craft had crashed onto the greens surrounding one of the holes on the golf course. The fire trucks and rescue vehicles raced out to the crash but stopped just short of driving onto the perfect manicured grass. No fire was coming from the small aircraft (the USAF hates it when you say "plane") but I was puzzled as to why they had all stopped just short of their goal. When I asked, someone told me that the drivers were afraid to drive on the grass because the golf course was the general's pride and joy. Of course, I'm sure that if the craft were burning and lives were at stake the fire-fighters and ambulance driver would have gone where necessary.

I don't remember why but at one point I felt I had better write my congressman and my letter to Senator Strom Thurmond succeeded in getting a red "P.I." written on my military records. I didn't know if this was good or bad even when I discovered that "P.I." meant "Political Influence". I missed out on the opportunity to go overseas but since Saigon was the place I was most likely to have gone (because I would have requested it) this was undoubtedly a blessing in disguise. Within two years thousands of American servicemen and women began going there and other places all over Vietnam, many never to return.

When I left Texas and the USAF it was with mixed feelings. I had envisioned making a career out of the service but that was before I had actually experienced what military life was like. I never wanted to be a fighter pilot but I had thought that I would like to become a pilot of some kind. Someone was watching out for me even here because if I had become a pilot of any kind I would undoubtedly have had to serve in Vietnam and a lot of good pilots died over there without ever knowing that it was never actually America's goal to "win" that war. Of course some who fought there were frustrated to the extreme when they realized this, even if only subconsciously, and the use of drugs among our troops increased in proportion to that frustration. One thing I am absolutely sure of and that is if it is not one's intention to win a war then fighting such a war can never result in success. It is a waste of time and talent, resources and lives. As the computer in the movie WAR GAMES said about the game Tick-Tack-Toe and implied about the war game Thermonuclear War, "What a strange game, the only way to win is not to play." We won WWII because that was our goal and no sacrifice was too great.

One of my wife's co-workers at IBM, who was also a part-time college professor, once told her that although she and her family had to hide out in a cave after one of the nuclear attacks on Japan in 1945 she believed that the use of those bombs actually saved lives. The Japanese of that time were such fanatics, she told Sharon, that they would have fought to the death and taken millions with them, something that the fanatic Moslem fundamentalists would like to do in their quest to destroy the world or at least all non- fundamentalist Muslims in it.

17. Home Again

South Carolina was like a breath of fresh air. I was home again, but still without a clue as to what I really wanted to do or what career path I should pursue. One of the wonders of this great country of ours is that with determination and perseverance a person can become anything he or she chooses, but of course you have to know where you are going before you can get there.

Being a teacher my father was convinced that education was the key to all success. That is true, up to a point. I met a bus driver once who had a doctorate in English but he preferred to make his living driving a bus, even though he taught a class or two at Columbia University. I knew a factory worker who has multiple college degrees including a doctorate in Nuclear Theory and I have argued with him that he could be doing so much more but he is content with his job working alongside those who have only a high school education or a few years of college.

In the fall of my first year back as a civilian I again enrolled at the University of South Carolina Extension, now no longer in the basement of the Florence Library, but in a new building on a 100 acre estate about seven miles east of Florence. I lived at home with my parents and my seven younger brothers and sisters.

It was a seventeen mile drive to the university from Darlington and I still did not have a car or even a driver's license. I made arrangements with Sam, a fellow student, and we drove to classes in his car. Sam was an impeccable dresser, always with a white shirt and tie. He eventually became a minister. One morning I opened my eyes for a few seconds and saw Sam standing next to a highway patrolman (in New York they are called State Troopers). Sam's white shirt looked just awful. "I've never seen him looking like that," I thought and then fell back into unconsciousness for another day and a half. The dirt or whatever I thought I saw on Sam's shirt was actually his blood but I was too dazed to realize it at the time. In fact I did not realize that we had been in an accident until I regained consciousness in McLeod Infirmary the next day and someone told me. Twenty years later I was in a similar accident on Route 9 south of Poughkeepsie, N.Y. that made the front page of New York's oldest newspaper, The Poughkeepsie Journal, and it was three weeks before I regained any memory of that accident but I never regained any memory at all of the accident on the way to what eventually became Francis Marion University. Sam, however, was able to fill me in on what had happened. He had been driving down a long stretch of road going the speed limit when a car passed us then pulled back in front of us rather quickly. Suddenly the driver of the other vehicle realized that his turn off was just ahead and he braked hard so as not to miss it. Sam braked even harder on the two lane highway to avoid crashing into the car in front of us. Sam's car careened off the road and hit an embankment which caused the vehicle to spin around with us in it. Fortunately the car did not turn over. Cars were not routinely equipped with sea belts although the Tucker Automobile had had them as early as 1948. The other driver was decent enough to stop and I seem to remember hearing that he offered Sam money. Sam had a good sized gash in his forehead and I was unconscious. I also had a blood-clot on my right ear drum. One of the physically most painful experiences in my life was the dislodging of that blood-clot by a high pressure air hose. Usually the doctor says something like "this won't hurt much" and then it hurts like the dickens but this time the doctor told me that it was going to hurt and to grab onto the steel table with both hands and to hold on tightly. The pain was something that I hope no one reading this ever has to experience. It was indescribable but it was over quickly. The second "treatment" the following week was far worse because I knew what was coming and for 15 minutes I stood outside the doctor's office in a cold sweat as a spirit of fear enveloped me. I did not yet know that such a spirit is easily controlled by an informed Christian and is different from a natural fear (such as a fear of falling). Of course, an irrational fear of falling could be a spirit as well but since I knew nothing of this at the time I had to endure a feeling almost of terror and something that was equally as painful as the physical pain of the air pressure on my ear drum.

I do not remember how I overcame that fear and mustered the courage to go back into the doctor's office for the second attempt to completely dislodge the blood-clot. As a youngster I had had tremendous earaches up until the age of five but when my tonsils were removed the earaches stopped. My hearing after this accident was only slightly impaired and not noticeable on a day to day basis.

Other than the pain and fear of the second treatment the only thing I remember from this accident was the pressure that the insurance company put on me to sign off. They even offered me a week's salary as a bonus to expedite the matter.

I had purchased an old 1949 Buick Convertible from a former high school classmate for $75. It ran and it would have been a wonderful car to restore but I did not have the money to do that. Eventually, after about a year, I sold the car at a loss. The main reason? I still didn't have a driver's license. Finally I decided that I had to have a drivers license and the only way I could do that was to take professional driving lessons.

Dan Schipman had been a driving instructor at McClenaghan High School and he also had a business of driver training. Since I didn't even have access to a car in which to practice I came to the conclusion that this was the most reasonable way to go. Mr. Schipman had two beautiful daughters, Peggy who was a little older that I was and Faye who was my junior. Back in 1960 South Carolina had one of its once-in-a-decade big snow storms and five inches of snow fell on Florence. With the help of my younger brothers and a little help from Faye we built an eight foot snowman. The citizens of Florence had never seen anything like it and for days people came by to take pictures of their children next to the giant snowman. A nice photo of me, my brother Bill and Faye along with the snowman made the front page of The Florence Morning News. Had I been smart enough to send the undeveloped roll of film I took of the snowman directly to Life Magazine rather than having it developed first, pictures of that snowman would have been seen all over the nation or so they told me at Life Magazine. Now I was taking some driving lessons from Faye's dad, the first time I had actually driven more than a city block since I was thirteen years old.

My dad, who by this time had finally gotten his drivers license, questioned why I was getting mine. I remember he said, "The next thing you'll probably want is a car." I said nothing because arguing with my father was useless, but he was absolutely right.The truth was that I did not know a single person outside my family who did not own and operate a car and all of my friends had had automobiles for years.

One of my former classmates from St. Joseph's in Columbia was written up in the newspapers once when she was stopped by a police officer. The story was not about her not having a license because she had one, it was just that the police officer could not believe that her license was real. "Cookie" hadn't been driving long and she made some minor mistake as new drivers often do. The officer asked to see her driver's license as officers always do. This officer must have been a fan of the popular TV show CANDID CAMERA where jokes were played on unsuspecting people. The license in his hand looked real but the name was Rockefeller and since he couldn't conceive of anyone else having that famous name, he was convinced that someone was playing a joke on him. I once found myself in a large crowd at the University of South Carolina standing next to and making small talk with "Happy" Rockefeller, and she was a member of that famous family and the wife of the governor of New York State, but that's another story.

After a couple of lessons I passed the driving part of the test as well as the written test which I had passed eight years before. I have since driven close to a million miles in about twenty different vehicles.

18. Back to Columbia

The University of South Carolina Extension at Florence eventually became Francis Marion University (named after the legendary patriot of the Revolutionary War, the "swamp fox" who was the inspiration for the "ghost" in Mel Gibson's good but overly violent movie, THE PATRIOT). The athletic teams at Francis Marion today are even called "The Patriots" but then it was just a USC extension and I did not stay there long.

Moving back to Columbia to attend the main campus of the University seemed the right thing to do. At the same time about 80 miles to the north of Columbia a cute little girl was enrolling in the first grade in Gaffney, S.C. She, too, would grow up and leave South Carolina but she would go on to fame and fortune as an internationally acclaimed actress. Her name: Andie McDowell.

I did purchase a car, a five year old German Ford station wagon for $200 and it lasted for 19,000 miles and for the first time in my life I got my own apartment on Maple Street for $45 per month. Of course I shared the apartment with my younger brother Bill so I guess it wasn't really "my own apartment" but I thought of it as mine. It was an upstairs apartment in an older private home. It had a small kitchen with a gas stove, a small living room that besides a sofa and an easy chair had a small dining table and two or three chairs. The bedroom was fairly large and it had a single bed and a large double bed that the owner told me once belonged to General Wade Hampton.

Gen. Wade Hampton had been born in Charleston, S.C., descended from Revolutionary War patriots. His grandfather, Major Gen. Wade Hampton, fought in the War of 1812 and was said to be the richest planter in America (in his day). His grandson not only led Gen. Robert E. Lee's Calvary Corp after the death of Gen. "J.E.B." Stuart but in the Centennial Year of 1876 won election for governor of South Carolina and returned home rule to the State of South Carolina. Federal Troops and carpetbaggers left South Carolina the following year. Re-elected governor and then senator, Gen. Wade

Hampton lived to see the automobile but died the year before the first flight at Kitty Hawk. I believe that Hampton, Virginia, where I lived as a child before moving to Columbia the first time, was named after one of the generals relatives. I never did think to ask which General Hampton the majestic bed belonged to but I slept well in it and never once dreamt of battle.

The owners of the house on Maple Street in which I rented the upstairs apartment were a retired couple and they were up in years. Mr. Scott had retired from the Highway Patrol a number of years before and he was a bit of a character. Once I noticed him shooting at squirrels in a large tree right next to his house. I was surprised to see him shoot the 22 rifle in the city and I pointed out to him that when he missed the bullet would come down somewhere in the city and the possibility existed that someone could get hurt. He told me that it had never occurred to him. What surprised me even more was the rifle he was using. It had a silencer on it and it made less noise that I did when I sneezed or clapped. I thought such things were illegal but all I asked him was where he got it. "Took it away from a criminal back in the thirties," was his reply.

This reminded me of one of my classmates from high school, Melvin Purvis, Jr. His dad owned WOLS radio, a popular Florence radio station and he was famous for his work as an FBI agent. Agent Melvin Purvis, Sr. was present in the Ohio cornfield when gangster "Pretty Boy" Floyd was shot and killed. He is also usually given credit for killing the infamous outlaw, John Dillinger.Actually, according to this southern gentleman, he and the other agents involved felt that there was no great honor in killing a man, even if the man was America's Public Enemy No. 1. Purvis, a Florence, S.C. native (he was actually born in nearby Timmonsville just on the outskirts of Florence) was head of the Chicago office of the FBI at the time, another person who had left South Carolina for a while. Melvin Purvis and the other agents present agreed not to reveal who fired the fatal shot that killed Dillinger and as far as I know none of them ever did. Still it was Melvin Purvis who became a national hero as a result. During WWII Purvis served as a Colonel in the Judge Advocate Department and worked on war crimes cases in Wiesbaden, Germany. He died while hunting when I was a student at McClenaghan High School in Florence. The rumor was that he had terminal cancer and that the accident was not an accident. I did not know the family personally as the younger Purvis was ahead of me in school but cancer was still a mysterious scourge in the late

1950's worse than AIDS was in the 1980's. The treatments were primitive and some cancers are excruciatingly painful.

An extremely painful cancer caused one of my favorite actors, Richard Farnsworth, to end his life with a gun. Farnsworth was not nearly as well known as my favorite actress, Audrey Hepburn, but he was very good in the roles he played. Richard Farnsworth did not even become an actor until he was 57 and at 79 he was the oldest leading man ever to be nominated for an Oscar when he portrayed Alvin Straight in THE STRAIGHT STORY. Drastic and violent as such actions are we cannot really judge them unless we have been in the same situation. I only wish that those patients with really painful terminal cancers were allowed to have access to marijuana when other painkillers have proven ineffective. Terminal cancer patients in England, hospitalized for pain, have even been known to be able to leave the hospital and go home where they lead relatively normal and useful lives up until the last week of their lives when they had access to medicinal marijuana. I believe it is kept from American cancer patients because there is no profit in it to the big corporations who profit from the conventional and sometimes useless painkilling drugs.

I once spent two years studying everything I could find on the avoidable causes of cancer. I wrote to scientists and doctors and spent a great deal of time in the library reading all I could on the subject. I even wrote 120 pages of a book that I was writing on the subject until I lost interest. I came to the conclusion that inadequate and unbalanced nutrition, smoking, and over-exposure to sunlight and some chemicals were responsible for over 85% of all cancers. I was fascinated that the oldest recorded case of cancer was in hieroglyphics, an account of breast cancer in one of the Pharaohs of ancient Egypt while the oldest known case of cancer happened over 65 million years ago and was discovered in the bones of a dinosaur. I was amazed at how much was known about cancer but it was not common knowledge and one had to dig for it. I guess until I did the study I had some fear of the disease. I can remember the days in the 1950's and 1960's when physicians scoffed at the notion that not eating whole unprocessed foods could have anything to do with cancer. Today, fortunately, most of them know better, but I'm told that medical schools still do not teach more than one course in nutrition, if they teach that.

The apartment on Maple Street was about a 30 minute walk east of the campus. One night when my brother Bill was walking back

LEAVING SOUTH CAROLINA

from the campus he was mugged by some low-life's who jumped out of a car to attack him. (One of my classmates at the University was born and raised in NYC and in 18 years had never even been threatened while in New York but during his first semester at USC he was mugged while cutting across the State House grounds from Main Street on his way back to the campus two blocks away. Of course it was 2 a.m. but both he and my brother were fortunate in that both survived).

As Bill was being assaulted by several criminals another car turned onto the street where the crime was taking place. Apparently the approach of the car scared off the muggers as they jumped into their car and sped away but not before the Good Samaritan copied down their license plate number.

Bill was drifting in and out of consciousness but was able to tell the gentleman who rescued him where he lived. The man helped Bill into his automobile and drove him to our apartment in the nine hundred block of Maple Street. Together with Mr. Scott the police were called, the incident reported, and the license plate number given to the desk sergeant or whoever answered the police telephone. Then, having done more than some would do, the rescuer left. Soon the police arrived to file a report. Apparently they or their supervisors assumed that the witness who helped my brother would be waiting for them. The good Samaritan had done all that he thought necessary but he had not left his name and phone number or even a copy of the license plate of the criminal's automobile which was unfortunate because the police had no record of it at the station, so the punks were free to maim again. We always wondered if the car actually belonged to some State Senators son or the son of some important businessman but of course we never found out. Hopefully by today all such phone conversations are recorded and no assumptions are made on such matters.

The police officers who came to the house did take my brother, who was still not fully coherent from the attack, to the University Infirmary where he was treated for concussion.

I narrowly avoided "something" one night myself a few years later as I was walking towards an apartment I had in the big colonial house at 1804 Green Street just a few blocks east of the campus. I noticed the car with several occupants slow down to observe me crossing the street, slow enough where someone could surely have jumped out if they chose to do so and if I continued in the direction I was headed. They seemed to be waiting for me to walk up to the corner where our paths would have intersected. Their car had come to a complete stop at the corner but they were not moving on as would have been the normal thing to do. I sensed something was wrong so I turned onto a short walkway of perhaps ten feet and walked up onto a porch of one of the houses between myself and the corner. As I reached the front door of the house I opened the screen door and then reached into my pocket as if I were going for keys and out of the corner of my eye I noticed the car finally start to move again and then turn the corner and drive out of sight. Since it was unlikely that they would back up on the street I only waited a few seconds before getting back out on the sidewalk and carefully continuing to the corner. I didn't see the car on the street so I quickly crossed over to the other side and immediately cut across to the campus where there were no streets and only walkways. I think it had been a close call.

The building with the tall white columns is still at 1804 Green Street and the house on Maple Street is still there too. I liked the apartment on Maple with its huge magnolia tree which was almost as big as the house itself. I was fortunate to get a part-time job right around the corner on Millwood Avenue where the South Carolina Educational Television Network was located at the time.

My first job at SCETV was adding to the picture "morgue" which was a kind of library of drawings and photographs and pictures. As I recall this photo "morgue" had been started by Ron Chapiesky and Leigh Lehocky to enable the art staff to have access to thousands of pictures and photos on virtually every subject they might ever need for inspiration and reference for the various programs produced by SCETV. Leigh Lehocky was a year ahead of me in school but his younger brother Alan and I had been classmates in grade school and I knew them both well enough to have visited them at their home. Leigh graduated from college and went on to become a Catholic priest and was Monsignor Lehocky at St. Peters Church on Assembly Street a few years ago.

While working at SCETV I did a few minor interviews and I even wrote one TV script which was produced as a pilot but never as a series. It wasn't completely original because I was told what was wanted but I did the best I could and I enjoyed watching the video with words I had written being produced. The story involved a talking tree, an owl that lived in the tree, a professor and his talking dog. The idea was to teach children about science through a series of debates on various subjects. The first and only one produced by SCETV went like this: one day the tree off-handedly says to the owl that he went swimming once in part of the ocean, whereupon the owl goes into a fit saying that what the tree said was impossible because he (the owl) had seen the ocean once at Myrtle Beach and it was 150 miles away and the tree had roots and couldn't go anywhere. The dog comes along and the owl tells the dog about the ridiculous assertion of the tree. "What do you think?" I had the owl ask the dog. "Well, I don't know all the facts," I had the dog reply, "so let's wait until the professor comes and we'll ask him." "It's utterly ridiculous" or words to that effect the owl mutters to no one in particular. Finally the professor arrives. He walks over and sits on a bench beneath the tree and becomes involved in the discussion. The owl makes his complaint. The professor wants to get all the facts before he gives his opinion. When the owl gets the tree to repeat to the professor what he said about going swimming in part of the ocean the professor picks up on the words "in part of" and thus begins an explanation of the rain cycle and how rain falling on the tree could be interpreted as swimming in water that had once been part of the ocean.

Actually I thought that the finished product was pretty good but the series never materialized. It was my first and only attempt at script-writing. Years later I heard that one of the people who were working at SCETV at the time was from Canada and that within a year of this pilot project the person quit his job and returned to Canada where he had worked for Canadian TV previously. Coincidentally (so I was told) the Canadian Educational TV people soon thereafter produced a series with a professor and a talking dog. I had no way of independently verifying this but I have always wondered if the story I was told about what eventually happened to "my story" was true.

My boss at SCETV at the time was one tough lady. I was impressed by the fact that not only was she a judo expert but she always carried a .38 caliber pistol with her. Unfortunately our personalities clashed so much that we both wanted me transferred so the rest of the year and a half that I worked there was as a photographer under John Lilly. Sometimes I took photos of visiting VIP's but more often than not I worked in the photo lab developing and printing the photographs. I had developed my first photos as a hobby at Sheppard AFB and now I was doing the same thing to help support my way through college.

I still had no idea what I should be studying or what I should be aiming at as far as a degree and a career were concerned. Liberal

Arts seemed to cover it all and I eventually finished the core requirements. If someone had absolutely forced me to come up with an answer I could only have told them that I wanted to make a lot of money, get married, and have a family, though not as large a family as my parents had had. I realize now that back then and for many years afterward I was terrified of making the wrong choice, of marrying the wrong person. This fear undoubtedly affected my relationships with the opposite sex. Fear is always an enemy, never a friend. Didn't General Patton once say that he never took counsel of his fears?

I was raised in the Catholic tradition of Christianity and one of the basic rules of Catholicism that was somehow imbued into my spirit was that God hates divorce. Of course so does any caring psychologist or sociologist. To see the havoc in the lives of victims of divorce, especially young children who often feel that they are the cause of their parents separation, is a sad thing indeed. I noted with interest that the 9th grader, who shot all those students in Santee, California, in March of 2001, was a product of divorce. He and his father lived in California while his mother lived in South Carolina.

All Christians believe that God hates divorce because it says so in the Bible but that doesn't mean that he forbids it in every situation. In some denominations the worse thing a person can do (in the popular perception) is to drink. I grew up around many who believed that cheating is wrong and sexual infidelity is worse but drinking was the sin that they and their denomination considered the worse possible evil and that is the one I heard about the most from my friends as I grew up even though I didn't drink and neither did my parents. Well, the popular perception in the Catholic Church when I was growing up was that divorce and later remarriage (to someone else) was the worse possible thing. Such people were reduced to a sort of second class status in the Catholic Church, unable to receive the blessings (the sacraments like communion, the breaking of bread) intended for regular members. Jesus did say that those who divorced their wives to marry another were committing adultery but I recall that he also criticized the religious leaders of his day for adding to men's burdens rather than trying to alleviate them. And what if a person sought a divorce because their partner refused to accept help because they were alcoholic or addicted to internet pornography or beat their wives? Such people were not divorcing to marry another. If sometime later they met a mature and responsible person and fell in love and married it would seem to me that the words of Jesus would not be applicable because they weren't divorcing to marry another.Jesus also said, "What God has joined together man must not divide" and I have often thought that God had very little to do with some marriages.

Because I had more than a casual interest in spiritual things my Catholic friends often asked me if I had an interest in the priest-hood. Perhaps if the Roman Rite of the Catholic Church had not come up with another man made rule (that priests can't marry and have families) I might have been interested. It is my understanding that in Eastern Rite of the Catholic Church priests have always been allowed to have families if they chose. Even in the Roman Rite there are exceptions for ministers of other denominations who convert to Catholicism. They can keep their families if they have them and become priests as well. Of course if they don't have them at the time of conversion then the same restrictions binding those born Catholic apply. When I first found out about that exception I re-member thinking that being a convert to Catholicism was certainly preferably to being born into the Church as I had been.

Years ago a priest told me that the church expects a priest to give up any interest he might have in pursuing a sexual relationship but that they don't tell him how to do that. Of course all organizations have rules. Some rules are changeable and some are not. Some rule changes would change the organization so much that it would no longer exist. If the Boy Scouts of America allowed girls to join they would no longer be the Boy Scouts. All churches and religions have man-made rules. The Catholic Church is no exception.

The oldest church in the world promoting the teachings of Jesus is the Catholic Church. Since they are the oldest they are burdened with the accumulation of nearly two thousand years of customs, tra-ditions, disciplines and laws upon laws (rules and regulations). This is understandable but they, like many of the newer Christian church-es, need to get back to basics. The purpose of the Christian church is to reveal God to the world, through word and deed. Christians are supposed to be shining lights for the depressed and downtrodden. They are supposed to reveal God's love and truth and mercy to the world. There is no other reason for the existence of the church, any church.

Two generations ago Jesus told a woman in England, "All of my followers know, love and live by the simple rules I taught when I lived on earth as a man. Many of them would have no response to all the rules of your churches. Seek simplicity in all things" (paraphrased from the classic paperback GOD CALLING, edited by A.J. Russell). The Bible says that "Judgment begins in the House of God." The last time that corruption was rampart in even part of the Catholic Church the result was the Protestant Reformation when masses of people rebelled against the injustices that they perceived in the Church. Some of these were real, others imagined or invented. It will be interesting to see what the long term result will be of the rampant liberalism in some segments of the North American Catholic Church that has spawned the acceptance of non-celibate homosexual priests. Fortunately only a small percentage of these are pedophiles and some of them are going to jail. Some of their sentences seem light to me, three months for one, three years for another. Some are doing "hard time" though and that is as it should be.

"Justice delayed is not justice," the late great FBI agent Melvin Purvis Sr. used to say. He was only partly right. Justice delayed is better than no justice at all. The Bible says that God is slow to anger but He is also infinitely just. The Law of Sowing and Reaping is no less universal than the Law of Gravity. It does not seem to require belief. It is a principle of the Universe. It may, however, take some time to see it all play out. Besides the millions of everyday Catholics who suffered through the recent sex scandals, some of the upright and righteous priests who are in the majority were too embarrassed to even wear their collars in public. Some are afraid to show the fatherly affection that they used to demonstrate for fear of it being misinterpreted. If demons can dance in hell they are surely doing so over what transpired in the Catholic Church in the United States and Canada at the beginning of the 21st Century.

Not long after I got out of the air force I mentioned to a priest who did not seem to happy to me to be a priest, that I thought that the church and the military had a lot in common. He quickly retorted that their purpose was different. What I had meant was that the structure, the chain of command, the promotions, the transfers, even the uniforms, if you will, had similarities with the military. If Christians are supposed to be the army of God fighting evil in the world (and in themselves) then the similarities may not be accidental at all. I've known some really wonderful priests and I've known some who would have been better in another profession or at least I'd hoped that they would have done better at something else. It was small comfort to me that even here, not everyone knew what they really wanted or how they wished to spend the rest of their lives.

19. Leaving South Carolina

In 1964 I joined a young adults club at St. Peters and it was there that I met one of my life-long friends, Judy Clair. Like me she came from a large family and had been born north of the Mason-Dixon Line, in her case, Chicago. Judy grew up in Sumter, S.C. and was in her final year of nursing school when we were introduced. At that time in South Carolina it was not necessary to have a college degree to be a nurse. Separate schools of nursing existed, affiliated not with a college or university but with a hospital. When Judy graduated, to celebrate, we took a day trip to the mountains northwest of Greenville. We did not date in the conventional sense but attended a number of group functions, picnics, and that sort of thing, often with the young adults club. Neither of us had a "significant other" but we were friends, and so we remain to this day.

A few years later I was listening to a radio program on opportunities in nursing in the U.S. Army and I thought to myself, "Judy should hear this. I'll bet it would be of interest to her." Imagine my surprise when she told me later that she had been in the audience where the radio program originated. Judy liked what she heard, joined the army, left South Carolina, and served two years in Germany. She spent some time in California but the lure of South Carolina and friends and family brought her back.

More than once I told her that I thought that a college degree would help her career and Judy eventually enrolled in the School of Nursing at the University of South Carolina and earned two degrees in nursing. I probably wasn't the first to suggest to Judy that she purchase her own house but I thought the rent she was paying at the time was outrageous. It was undoubtedly a fair price for a luxury apartment and was probably less that what a room would rent for today. It wasn't to long after that when Judy purchased her first house. I've often wished I'd taken my own advice because 40 years of rent receipts won't buy a cup of coffee but I was always blessed at being able to find a place to rent at rates I seldom talked about for fear the word would get back to the owners at how reasonable they were.

I made friends with several of the Chinese students at the University, Wan Lee, Peter Cheu, Yvette Zee, and a few others. Their culture fascinated me and they were all superior students. One of them, Joan, a refugee from Shanghai, had a famous grandfather who, in the old empire, was the governor of two provinces in China. This was a rare occurrence and in the last thousand years had only happened two or three times. Once Joan asked me who I thought was the better student, Peter or Wan Lee. I had no idea really but I picked one of them. "You only go by appearances," Joan answered me. She told me that the one I picked only studied to get "A" grades while the other studied to learn all he could. Of course, all three of them were "A" students, something I did not even aspire to be.

Some weekends Peter would come with me to visit my parents in Darlington. My mom enjoyed his humor almost as much as she did Ralph Singleton's in the previous decade. One weekend I couldn't make it home but Peter was going to visit my folks. It was like a home away from home for him. I remember giving him a message to give my mom. Peter came with me and Judy on occasion to some of the events sponsored by the young adults club at St. Peter's and one of my favorite photos of my youngest sister, Chrysa, then 4 years old, is of her sitting on Peters lap at Sugar Loaf Mountain, the only hill in the state park north of McBee, S.C. Peter left South Carolina and moved to New Jersey in the late 1960's and is a professor to-day. One of his stepsons, Henry, became a doctor and served with my sister Chrysa's husband, Keith, in the same Air Force hospital in Texas. It's a small world.

I did not really know Henry although I had met him when he was a youngster. I was, however, shocked to learn that the aircraft he was piloting crashed and burned, killing him and his five year old daughter. I do not know if Henry was instrument rated but he had at least as much experience as John Kennedy, Jr. Neither of them were beginners and whereas Kennedy was already flying his second aircraft, Henry was on his way to look at a second aircraft that he planned to purchase when his aircraft crashed in a storm. I did not know John Kennedy, Jr. either but I was more moved by his death than I was by the death of his father. I can only suppose that it was partly because a little bit of me died with him. His death, the TV coverage, the search for the aircraft, even the irony of his pilots license washing up onto land that he himself owned, all brought home to me in some vivid way how tenuous all our lives are on this small speck of dust we call earth.

There is a mystery to much of life. We can uncover enough of it, if we work at it, to make it through this earth school of ours, but some of it will remain a mystery until we cross over to the other side. There I suspect that some of what is a mystery to us here will be so evident that we may well be amused that we did not see it sooner. A wise person who just happened to be a priest once said that life is not a puzzle to be solved but a mystery to be lived. Of course that is easy to say and harder to do.

Not long after John Kennedy Jr. died on the way to his cousin's Rory wedding, or what was to have been her wedding (it was postponed a month as a result of the crash and all the publicity that ensued) I found myself talking with an Irish nun, an artist by the name of Sister Mary Ann Cullen. We talked about a number of things and eventually got to discussing all the tragedies that had befallen the Kennedy Family. Sr. Cullen told me that she had written a letter to Ethel Kennedy right after Robert Kennedy was assassinated and suggested that if the baby she was carrying was a girl that Mrs. Kennedy might consider naming her in honor of her husband using the ancient Celtic or Gaelic name for Robert which is Rory. She already had a son named Robert. I had always wondered how the family happened to pick that particular name and now I knew.

In September of 1965 I met a young graduate student from France at the Thomas Moore Student Center on Green Street.She was working on her Master's degree and was teaching French at the University. Her name was Sabine and we quickly became friends. Although she married and moved to Africa for seven years, Sabine and her husband Edouard returned to the United States in 1973 when their second daughter was born and we are good friends to this day.

It always fascinated me that Sabine did not attend school until she was twelve years old but had instead a private tutor. I do not know how it is in France today but somewhere in the neighborhood of one and a half million American children including several of my nieces and nephews are being tutored at home. This way they are not being exposed to the constant amoral or morality-free education that has come to permeate the public schools of America. I find it interesting that over 70 percent of the public school teachers in one of our major cities, a city with a population almost as large as that of the state of South Carolina, send their own children to

non-public schools! For some reason the educators in this country
have become convinced over the last 35 years that they can teach
students to become good citizens without teaching them anything
about morality, a far cry from Daniel Webster, the founder of the
public school system in America, who said that, "Education without
the Bible is useless."

Of course, with the discovery that there is incontrovertible mathematical proof that the ancient Hebrew Bible contains a computer
program (perhaps is a computer program) that contains much of
human history, that a 3200 year old scroll tells of much that did not
happen until the 20th Century and much that will happen in the 21st
Century, perhaps this ancient revealed Word of God will once again
have the importance to mankind that it once had. Of course those
who have always opposed God and the Bible are also opposing The
Bible Code too. Well, this coming decade alone will reveal the truth.
Will it be the mathematicians and the believers or the doubters and
the atheists who have a greater grasp of reality? Will Jerusalem experience a vicious unnatural man-made attack and LACALIF a violent natural one as discovered in The Bible Code? Time will tell.

Later that year I left South Carolina once again. My girl friend
had ended our relationship because I had skipped one to many
classes to be with her, or at least that is what she told me. Gina (not
her real name) and I had only been going together for a couple of
months but I had really fallen for her. I met her for what I thought
was the first time at the University in Columbia where we were both
students but we had actually attended the same high school together
in Florence a few years earlier. After high school Gina had had an
emotional breakdown and ended up in the state mental hospital as
her family was poor and could not afford private therapy. She was
convinced that I would drop her like the proverbial "hot potato" if I
found out that she had been "mental" as she put it. Even stronger
than her fear of that was her desire to be honest with me. I distinctly
remember the night we were sitting in my little German Ford station wagon and she told me that there was something that she had
to tell me. Gina was in tears as she spoke, so fearful that I would
reject her once I knew, but so brave in wanting me to know the truth
about her. I listened intently to the story of her suffering. "Shall I
leave now?" she asked me with one hand on the door handle of the
car as she finished her story. "No, of course not!" I answered and I
took Gina in my arms and told her that I loved her. Now I was the
one being dumped.

She told me that she was looking for someone more mature. The last I heard, Gina, still looking for stability, for someone or something to believe in, had married a military psychologist. I did everything I could at the time to win her back but it was not to be. I recognize now that we were both a help to each other at that particular time in our lives and it would be difficult for me to ascertain which one of us was most in need of healing. Wherever she is today I hope she is well.

Of course, in 1965 I could never have said that I needed healing, but I did. I have come to believe that such "inner healing" is to some extent a life-long process. All I knew was that my life was not what I wanted it to be and I didn't really know what I wanted it to be. I decided that I needed to leave, to get out, and to go someplace different. The problem was that I was taking myself with me.

I didn't want to go someplace where I knew absolutely no one and I wasn't aware enough to know to pray for guidance and direction in any but a general way. The only place where I knew anyone who wasn't in South Carolina or a relative was in upstate New York. That was where my old air force friend Mikael (not his real name) was living.

Mikael had turned down a job offer from IBM when he got out of the air force because he wanted to go to college but after a short stint at Georgia Tech where he made straight "A's" he decided that the college life was not for him. He really hated it. I, on the other hand, had just barely passed some courses and making an "A" was a rare occasion for me, but I loved college life. It was my own personal life with which I was not at all happy.

When I left South Carolina again it was with mixed feelings. I drove all day and much of the night until I found myself at 2 a.m. somewhere in Manhattan. I remember seeing a really huge cat and then being shocked to discover as I drove closer that it was actually what I would call a giant rat. I'm told they are called wharf rats but the only kitty cat that could tackle one of these would have to be a mountain lion. I was truly lost in Manhattan and where I was there were very few people. In fact I did not see a single white person. Finally I pulled over to one person who was almost as black as the night and asked in what direction I should go to get to...and then I realized I didn't know how to pronounce the name of the town which was about the size of Florence in South Carolina. Poughkeepsie! Well, "dough" is pronounced "doe" so I guessed "Pough" was pronounced "Poe". "Do you know where Poe-keepsie is?" I asked with some trepidation. I don't know if he saw the South Carolina license plates. "I think you is in the wrong place" was the reply I heard. "I sure am!" I truthfully answered but asked again what direction I should be heading to get there. He pointed north and I thanked him and continued to drive for about another two hours and finally reached Wappingers Falls. I pulled over unable to keep my eyes open any more and slept in the car in the parking lot of a long gone Grand Union supermarket. Later that day I learned how to properly pronounce Poughkeepsie.

IBM was in its big-growth days and had been persistent with Mikael and written to him again a few months after he had been at college. By this time he was ready to accept a job. He worked at the main IBM plant on South Road, Poughkeepsie, and I got a job at a company that today might be called a computer graphics company. They promptly sub- contracted me to the same IBM plant. In fact we worked in the same building and had the same hours which made transportation a lot easier.

I worked under the auspices of the Systems Development Laboratories but not actually in the labs but in the manufacturing area. I was little more than a clerk but it was exciting to work on the biggest computer that had ever been built up until that time, the Model 95 of the System 360. Several were being constructed simultaneously. As I recall one was for the Pentagon, two were classified (probably for the National Security Agency), and one was for France, then more in tune with America than they have been of late. With all the components bunched together the Model 95 was about the size of a small bus. I do not remember the computing power of these multi-million dollar machines but it was probably on a par with a $1,000 home computer today. Back then these expensive giants were huge and the men who put them together were the best and the brightest that IBM had gathered from all over the planet.

One night, when I had little to do, one of the engineers asked me to assist him in setting pulses. This was described to me as something like shooting electronic bullets through a small opening in a speeding train. Another time I sat and listened in during a coffee break while these top scientists and engineers discussed the cryptic "mark of the beast" which the Bible says every man and woman on earth will someday have in their wrist or in their forehead and without which they will not be able to buy or sell anything, even food. Of course we know that it will be more than just a mark because the Bible says that it will be "in" their body, not on it as a mark would be. The Bible also says that whoever accepts this "mark" will not be allowed into heaven. Apparently by the time this comes about the world's financial system will be in such chaos that this system will seem to be the answer and the people of this world will welcome it with open arms much as they did Hitler when Germany was in such financial chaos in the 1920's and 30's. Never mind that the acceptance of this "mark" or microcomputer will also mean that you accept the world leader as the living God. Thank God we have no "world leader" yet!

That day, 40 years ago at IBM, the scientists were pretty much of a consensus that this "mark" had to be some sort of futuristic computer about which they could only guess. Today, a generation later, this technology not only exists but is being used. For a decade now thousands of dog and cats have been returned to their owners because the animals had been scanned and had a micro-chip under their skin that told not only the their name and their owners name, but the address where they normally lived, the animals license number and even the shots the animal had received.

In May of 2002 the Jacobs Family of Boca Raton, Florida, became the first "chipped" family in America. Of course, their imbedded micro-chips were for medical reasons and were entirely voluntary. In Mexico a couple of hundred of the top security personnel have micro-chips imbedded in their arms and a wave of their arm over the electronic scanner allows the doors to top secret or at least secure areas to open as if by magic. What we well have in another generation I can only imagine but I am expecting some sort of severe inflationary crisis with over 400 percent inflation long before that. How long will it take for the world's financial situation to go to pieces I do not know? The tremendous amounts of money owed by those who must have the latest of everything, our huge state deficits, our colossal Federal deficit, even our unbelievable trade deficit is such that I am constantly amazed that we get along as well as we do. The presses keep printing hundreds and fifties and twenties and tens, 24 hours a day, seven days a week. Financial managers who know what they are talking about have had a hard time convincing their clients that the old Wall Street adage of "put ten percent of your assets in gold and hope that nothing happens" is not out of date. They are wrong because even ten percent won't be enough when our house of paper assets comes tumbling down around us. In November of 2004 a meeting was held by the chief economist of one of the top financial investment firms in the country, a name that would be instantly recognizable. The meeting was for mutual fund managers and was not open to the press or the public but of course notes were taken.The old adage, "two people can keep a secret if one of them is dead," seems to have applied. The fund managers were shocked to hear that in the opinion of the speaker "we have only a ten percent chance in this country of avoiding a financial Armageddon...and maybe a sixty percent chance of stalling it for a couple of years."I do not believe we have any chance of avoiding it. We are so in love with paper investments in this country that we have even found ways to buy paper gold and paper silver. We want to see the percentages of annual return on our paper investments and we don't want to hear some financial Noah tell us that it's going to rain and ruin our plans. After all there is no danger of living downstream if the dam doesn't break. We don't want it to break so if we keep pretending and believing that the stock market is the way to go and that inflation is a thing of the past, all the while the waters of our financial debt keep rising. Our entire system of finance is designed to be one of gradual inflation. It is only considered dangerous when that "gradual inflation" gets out of hand.

Looking back over the last 40 or 45 years we have already had over 400 percent inflation. That is why the government keeps changing the CPI (Consumer Price Index) or at least its starting point. They would rather that people not think about where our incredible debt is taking us. The government divides our massive debt into the whole population and it doesn't seem so bad when you do that, maybe $25,000 per person, but if you divide the debt only among those who are actually paying for it, the taxpayers, the figure becomes more like $200,000 per taxpayer! (Exact figures are almost impossible to calculate because the total true debt is so huge that it varies by trillions of dollars depending on which sources one uses. I have even seen the figure of $800,000 per taxpayer if you consider the total of everything for which the government is responsible).

Inflation was relatively negligible for the first 140 years of our country's history but since we stopped making our own money and have been paying the Federal Reserve Bank to do it for us inflation has been our constant companion, even more so since we stopped using gold and silver as our founding fathers assumed we would. That's why they put it into the Constitution, to keep a reign on ever-growing big government. That's also why that part of the Constitution is ignored. We can pretend that the Constitution speaks of the right to abortions and same sex marriages which it clearly says nothing about but it clearly says we shall use nothing for money but gold and silver.

No one knows how massive our debt can become before foreigners stop lending us the money to run the country. We already owe more money than any nation has owed in the history of the world. Yet we borrow over TWO THOUSAND MILLION dollars every day! Will we just give New Jersey to our creditors? I don't think so. They already own quite a bit of it. Are we going to file bankruptcy as a nation? I don't think so. That doesn't leave many options. The value of the dollar has been dropping faster than I can earn them. How about you? I read my first book on currency devaluation in 1979 and the dollar has lost about 70 percent of its value since then. It has lost 33 percent in the last six years. One of my sources say that the real rate of inflation is 8 percent, more than double the anemic figures provided by government which has a vested interest in seeing that the "official" rate of inflation is low.My very old fashioned suggestion is that we stop spending more than we take in (ha ha) and start to pay off our massive debt because a person or a nation that is in debt isn't really free. Unfortunately the debt is so big it may not be possible to pay it off. I see no evidence that any political party or any president has any real intention of reducing our debt. There are so many compelling reasons why we need to borrow more money. "We can afford it," I actually heard a citizen reply when he was informed that it was costing us more than one billion dollars per day, each and every day, just to cover the interest on our debt.

Whichever political party is in power when this ponzi scheme of deficit spending hit's the fan will likely bear the brunt of the blame much as Herbert Hoover was blamed for the Great Depression, over seventy years ago. There is blame enough to go around, however. As the cartoon character Pogo said years ago, "We have met the enemy and he is us!" The founding fathers of this great nation warned what would happen if the general population learned that they could vote themselves goodies out of the public treasury. We have not heeded their warning. "What kind of government have we?" an interested party asked Ben Franklin as he came out of the convention that fine day in Philadelphia well over two centuries ago. "You have a republic," Franklin replied, "if you can keep it." I do not believe that we will lose it in battle but we seem to be frittering it away.

20. A Yankee Salary: $2 an Hour

In the mid-1960's Dutchess County in the mid-Hudson Valley of Upstate New York was a rural county with hundreds of small farms and one small city, Poughkeepsie. Its rural nature, its scenic riverfront, its mountainous hills to the northeast, and its distance to New York City, less than two leisurely hours by car, made it an ideal place to live for the rich and the famous. Lowell Thomas, James Cagney, Norman Vincent Peale and quite a few others had homes in Dutchess County. The same is true today: James Earl Jones, Eddie Murphy, Mary Tyler Moore, Liam Neeson and James Gurney (author of the Dinothopia books) all live within 20 miles of me. Robert Di Nero has a place across the river and there are others who are able to live their lives far from the glitz and glitter and the phoniness of much that passes for being of celebrity status.

President Franklin Roosevelt had his home here and it is one of my favorites, especially his living room/library which is about as large as an average house. Today the home is open to the public with an accompanying museum which houses such interesting items as the letter Albert Einstein wrote about the possibility of building an atomic bomb and a huge aquamarine of 1200 carats. Roosevelt collected models of boats and ships and submarines and much of his collection, some models as big as six feet long, was on display the last time I visited. Some of these "boats" are truly works of art worthy of a visit by anyone with a nautical interest.

A little over a mile to the north but still in Hyde Park is the fabulous Vanderbilt Mansion and the estate that surrounds it. Once owned by George Washington's personal physician the grounds are beautiful with trees from various parts of the world. It is a great place to soak up some sunshine or share a picnic. I believe that it was Thomas Jefferson who said that it was worth a trip from Europe to see the view from the grounds of the Hudson River and the Catskill Mountains in the distance. I first visited the grounds in 1965 and I have been back at least a hundred times.

I once met an elderly gentleman there who had fought in the cavalry of the U.S. Army in the days of "Pancho Villa". We were both enjoying the magnificent vista of sun split clouds as they topped the tree frosted crests of the not-to-distant Catskill Mountains as the ever flowing Hudson glided gently to the sea. This former veteran was eighty years old at the time we talked and the stories he told were like an earlier version of Tom Brokaw's THE GREATEST GENERATION. His life story could easily have been a book or a movie and I was surprised that he was still searching for the meaning of life. "If he has not found it in 80 years what chance do you have?" I seemed to hear in my mind but I dismissed that thought because I believed that I would find what I was looking for even if I didn't quite know what it was.

My contract with IBM was extended once for an additional two months and I thought that perhaps I could work for IBM directly rather than through a sub-contractor. With two years of college under my belt the personnel department at IBM told me that I was over qualified to go into manufacturing (the only jobs available at the time). Ironically in the 1990's I worked at IBM in manufacturing alongside co-workers who had masters degrees and even PhD's and with some who were only high school graduates and we were all doing the same kind of work for the same money. Education is not quite what it used to be and unfortunately neither is the job market. Manufacturing lost another 25,000 jobs in January of 2005 and I was one of those who were "laid off" along with a hundred co-workers. We seem to be the only nation in the history of the world that is trying to build an economy on "service" rather than production or manufacturing. Will we be the first? I wouldn't count on it.

My job at IBM was ending and my friend with whom I had shared a mobile home was getting married so I decided to return to South Carolina. Once again I enrolled for a semester at the University of South Carolina in Columbia and once again after that semester I was out of money and had to find a job. I contacted the Employment Security Commission which is what the employment offices run by the state are called in South Carolina. When they asked about my previous job experiences I told them of the job that I had the year before working for the IBM Systems Development Lab where I earned IBM's beginning salary for hourly workers which was $2 per hour. "Well, that's a Yankee salary," I was told, "You can't expect to make that much here." Eventually I tired of finding dead end leads, or hearing that I was over-qualified or under-qualified. I did not have the confidence to just start knocking on doors and trying to find a job on my own (actually it didn't occur to me) so I contracted with an employment agency, the kind where you pay them to find you a job or if you are lucky enough they will find you an employer who will pay the fee to get you. The fee at the time was a month's salary.

At this agency I met a fine young woman who did succeed in placing me at Blue Cross Blue Shield. Patricia and I became friends. She was a little older than me, a divorcee with a daughter. I recall that she was dating someone who was older than she, a gentleman who was a member of the State Senate. What impressed me the most about Hugh was not that he grew watermelons but how many he grew, over 7,000 acres. That was over 10 square miles of watermelons! I did not know that such large plantations still existed, even in South Carolina.

One night Patricia's ex-husband decided to cause her some grief. In the late hours of the night when the lights were off and everyone was asleep he slipped into her driveway and poured sugar down the gas intake of her automobile. Starting up the engine was all it would take to suck the sugar into the carburetor and ruin the engine, costing perhaps a month's salary or more to fix. Fortunately Providence was shining on Pat and she noticed the white granules on the ground where her vindictive ex had spilled some of the sugar in his attempt to punish her. It looked like sugar and when Pat tasted it she knew that it was indeed sugar. She called her mechanic and he told her to absolutely NOT start the car under any circumstances. The gas tank was removed and the tank drained and flushed along with the intake pipe. It was a minor inconvenience but not the major expense that it could have been. "He couldn't even do that correctly," she told me. I decided not to ask what she might have been referring to as it was really none of my business.

One evening Pat invited me to stay for dinner and I was just about to say "Yes" when she pulled a loaf pan out of the oven and it was covered with tentacles. Now I have eaten fried grasshoppers, snails, frog legs, and alligator, and at least the snails and the alligator were delicious, but my adventuresome spirit suddenly left me when I saw the tentacles and I quickly said, "No thanks, I'm not hungry." At least I wasn't that hungry!

The people at Blue Cross Blue Shield had hired me because they liked me but they really did not have a position for me. I was assigned to read all the correspondence for the previous year and to design a number of form letters to be used by the correspondence department. At first I shared an office but eventually, as I needed more room, I was given an office of my own on the ground floor. Within a few months I put together a book of form letters and post-cards that answered about 95 percent of the inquiries that were received by the correspondence department. Such things today are undoubtedly done by computer. The correspondence pool consisted of over 40 typists and Natalie Contorno (Ilasi) was in charge and we became friends and so we remain to this day.

Natalie's husband had retired from the U.S. Army at the age of 45 and was in perfect health at the time but within two years he was dead of heart failure. His only job after retiring was to collect money from his automatic car wash business. It was not enough to keep him going. I was surprised to learn a few years later that the average life expectancy in this country was 2.7 years after you retire, regardless of the age at which you retire, if you have nothing else to do. Of course these statistics may have changed a little in the past 35 years but basically it seems to mean that we were created for meaningful activity and if we are not doing something that we perceive as worthwhile, be it a part-time job, a hobby, or even volunteer work, then we expire. Of course, exercise, diet, nutrition, and smoking history (or lack thereof) are all part of the equation. The human body and the human soul were not designed to "retire" and do nothing. The whole concept of "retirement" is a 20th (and now 21st) Century phenomena. I have read that one of the many differences between Heaven and Hell is that while there are many meaningful activities in Heaven there is absolutely nothing to do in Hell except remember what we have lost. Aside from the awful stench, the pain and the suffering, and the nightmarish demons, a person would die of boredom if it were possible to die there. Some interesting thoughts but I have no intention of trying to verify them firsthand.

I was supposed to be a manager-trainee at Blue Cross Blue Shield but after five months I had not decided what department I wanted to learn to manage so I was assigned to work with the people, mostly women, who handled the nuts and bolts of the claims work. I could not believe how much I hated it so after a few weeks I decided that it was time to quit and try for another semester at the University. Not long after that Natalie resigned and returned to Brooklyn. She found a job at Paramount Pictures in New York City and I returned to my classes.

One of my biggest problems was that I really did not know what I wanted to do with my life. I read about the merchant marine but I figured I probably would not have had the stamina necessary to do that kind of work even for a few years. I took tests designed to help me figure out what I'd be best at, tests designed to show what I was capable of doing, even tests designed to show how I compared with successful people in different fields (psychologist or minister, high probability, veterinarian, forget it) but none of them seemed to help. "Keep on keeping on" became one of my mottoes but it was not easy. If I had not had such a strong self-image, flawed though it was, I could easily have fallen into the drug culture, something to ease the pain and loneliness, but I valued my ability to think and reason much too much to experiment with something that could impair that ability. My one experience with marijuana was at a friends wedding party a couple of years later and it nearly did a number on me.The "weed" was about as common as cigarettes are today and I thank God that except for that wedding party I never got involved with either of them.

I had many intelligent professors at the university and a few who should have gone into research or better yet, therapy. From a major in psychology I switched to the school of education and took several courses. Although I liked kids well enough I soon realized that I did not want to teach them the rest of my life. Perhaps the whole idea of being locked into anything for the rest of my life was a little scary. I studied political science and acquired enough credits for a minor in the subject. I even took a course under Professor Albert Moreno who once instructed Fidel Castro when he was a student. It was fascinating to hear him tell how he and Castro had once stayed up most of the night arguing political theory until the wee hours and when they finally parted I believe Moreno said that he did not even return to his residence but left the country on the next flight out. That is why, I suppose, he was alive to teach me about the intricacies of Central American politics.

One night I was watching THE TONIGHT SHOW with Johnny Carson. I had purchased my first television, a 12 or 13 inch black and white TV for two weeks salary (televisions were much more expensive back then) in order to be able to watch the series Star Trek, the science fiction phenomena that has influenced so many in different ways. Just as Sidney Portier winning the Academy Award in 1964 for best actor in LILIES OF THE FIELD inspired young Oprah Winfrey so young "Whoppi" Goldberg called to her mother

to come see Star Trek, and was inspired by a TV show that presented a black woman who wasn't a maid. The first inter-racial kiss
ever seen on TV was on Star Trek, and when Nichelle Nickols wanted to quit her job as Uhura, the communications officer on board
the Starship Enterprise, none other than Dr. Martin Luther King
himself convinced her not to do so. The rest, as they say, is history. In my opinion the last Star Trek, ENTERPRISE, which ended
in 2005, was one of the best of all the sequels. In the late 1980's
Uhura (Nichelle Nickols) presented my brother-in-law Col. Mark
Stephen with the Military Engineer of the Year Award at a banquet
in Southern California.

However, that night as I watched my TV I noted that one of
Johnny Carson's guests was actor Steve McQueen. What was unusual about this night was that Steve McQueen, the guest, had brought
his own guest. That might have been a television first. I can't think
of a movie with Steve McQueen in it that I didn't enjoy at the time
although I might not have seen them all. As THE TONIGHT SHOW
progressed I discovered that Steve cared about the Navajo Indians.
He had taken a car full of medicines and vitamins out to the Navajo
Reservation. There he found a 10X50 foot trailer (we call them mobile homes today). This was home to Father Ian Mitchell, his wife
Caroline and their three children. I seem to remember they had a
young Navajo boy who lived with them as well.

When I first moved from South Carolina to Wappingers Falls,
New York, I shared a 10X50 foot mobile home with my air force
buddy and it was barely adequate for the two of us. I can't imagine 5 or 6 people crammed into one that size. That night on THE
TONIGHT SHOW Steve McQueen had brought Father Mitchell,
the Episcopalian minister from the trailer on the reservation as his
guest and both were actually the guests.

About a year later Fr. Mitchell and his wife Caroline gave a concert at the University of South Carolina. Fr. Mitchell was the one
who wrote the first guitar mass for the Episcopal Church and later
he wrote one for the Catholic Church. Today a folk mass using gui-
tars is not unusual but it was something brand new in the United
States at that time.

I really liked their music and after the concert I ended up talking
with Rev. Mitchell and his pretty wife Caroline. They had a problem that I was able to solve. We were all in the U.F.O. at the time,
Columbia's infamous coffeehouse. Rev. Mitchell sang a few songs
there and got a great reception. I overheard him say to his wife that

he was surprised that a place like this could exist in South Carolina. It was a place where blacks and whites could meet socially and on equal terms. Many of the people who went there were against the Vietnam War and that was almost considered treason at the time. Wars tend to be good for the economy and besides we were fighting the communists and who could be against that? The U.F.O. didn't survive to much longer after their visit because those who favored the Vietnam War were opposed to its existence, and those who hated long hair were against it, and those who saw it as a drug haven were against it, and those who saw it as a threat to the status quo were against it, and finally those who saw it as irreligious were against it. To sum it up, there were quite a few people opposed to the U.F.O. period. The powers that be had to find a reason to close it and drugs were the only thing they could think of as a reason. I always felt that if they were really interested in just controlling the drug traffic they would have left the place alone, staked it out with undercover agents and picked up any drug pushers or sellers who might have come there. By closing the U.F.O. any drug sellers who went there were forced to go underground and it seemed to me that it would require a lot more effort to keep track of what was going on. As I recall, however, no one was arrested on a drug charge. There was some sort of trial for being a public nuisance or something like that but the place was shut down which was the goal in the first place. One letter to the editor that was published spoke of the coffeehouse in terms of its influencing the minds of our emotionally immature soldiers. I felt like answering that one and saying that if our soldiers were so emotionally immature perhaps we'd be better off if we didn't draft them in the first place. I wrote a letter intended to be a letter to the editor but I never sent it. In it I compared the charges against the U.F.O. with the heresy and corruption of the minds of the young charge which the prosecution used in 399 B.C. against Socrates. A sentence was handed out, something like 6 years, which was incredibly long and designed, I thought, to tie the matter up in the courts for years to come. In any event even the people who ran the U.F.O. had to make a living and when it was closed they must have gone into something else. I never did here the end of the affair. But it was at the U.F.O. that I started a conversation with Fr. Mitchell and his wife Caroline.They had recently moved from the Western United States (from the reservation I think) to Westchester County, New York, but they had not yet gotten New York drivers licenses. They were in a bit of a quandary as they had two more concerts, one in

Waycross, Georgia, and the other in Douglas, Georgia, but no way
to get there. I offered to drive them there for the weekend in my
Volkswagen Bus because they would have had to cancel the concerts
otherwise. They were all set to accept until they saw my micro-bus
which ran better than it looked. I did not object when they counter-
offered to rent a nice new air-conditioned automobile that I drove
instead.

Consequently I was treated to two more of their concerts as I
ferried them through Georgia. I even purchased a 12 inch long playing record (LP) of their songs which I still have. CD's had not been
invented yet and I suppose that I should not be surprised that the
popular expression for over 60 years, "stuck like a needle on a record" has no meaning for today's young adults because they have
never heard a record much less one that had the needle stuck in a
groove, repeating the same phrase or line over and over.

The following year I got to visit the Mitchell Family once again as
they visited one of their friends, Jane Lachicott, on Pawley's Island,
S.C.While I was a student at the University of South Carolina I had
the opportunity to meet and talk with all kinds of interesting people
(author Pearl Buck, Ambassador John Kenneth Gilbraith. Robert
Short, the author of The Gospel According to Peanuts and others
I do not at the moment recall) but I remember Ian and Caroline
Mitchell as two of the nicest and most interesting people of all.

From political science and elementary education I changed my
major back to psychology, still trying to find out why I hurt so much,
why I couldn't find my niche, even why I couldn't keep a girlfriend.
I learned a lot but not enough. True to form my funds ran out after
the semester and it was necessary to find work to carry me through.
This time I accepted a job at a Nabisco warehouse packing cookies
in Nabisco trucks. I liked the hours, late afternoon until around
midnight, what the manufacturing industry called second shift until
they discovered that they could save millions by making everyone
work 12 hour shifts and eliminating weekend overtime. They call it
continuous production and even America's unions weren't powerful
enough to stop the change. What most Americans don't realize is
that on average we work 360 hours or nine weeks longer each year
than most Europeans. Of course, that is why we are so productive.
France moved from a 37.5 hour work week to a 35 hour work week
a few years ago and I believe they now have a 34.5 hour work week
currently.

At Nabisco, then on the outskirts of Columbia, I worked with just one other person. Scotty was a nice young man, small in stature, but a hard and consistent worker.Each night we filled five to seven trucks with all the Nabisco cookies and crackers that would be delivered to retailers throughout central South Carolina on the following day. We were not truck drivers although we had to move them around in order to fill them and on occasion we drove them a few blocks to a service station for a check up or an oil change. Not being truck drivers and being South Carolinians we did not feel that it was necessary to join the teamsters union. We were the only two who were not members. Imagine my surprise when I received a Christmas card that Christmas from Jimmy Hoffa who even from prison was trying to maintain his hold upon the union. It was a little scary.

Six months of packing trucks with cookies, even with all the free samples I could eat, was enough for me and then it was back to school for another semester. I know now why I was so sold on academic education. If my father had said that education is the key to success once he had said it or something like it many hundreds of times over the years. I believe that too, but I believe ones "real" education is the one you acquire on your own after you are finished with "the system". Some of the things taught in college now are things I studied in high school and my mother studied in the 8th grade. They call it the "dumming down" of education. Some people questioned after the September 11, 2001, attack on the World Trade Center, why we let so many hundreds of thousands of foreign students into our country and part of the answer besides needing their money is that we need them after they graduate. We are not training and teaching enough of our own citizens to become the scientists and engineers of tomorrow. Instead of teaching the basics, reading, writing, and arithmetic, the emphasis for the past thirty years has been on self-esteem. In that "the system" has succeeded. One recent study of a large number of rapists, murderers and criminals of various sorts showed that they all had high self-esteem, no self control, but high self esteem. What they and many do not have is self-love. The difference is crucial. You cannot love your neighbor as yourself if you do not love yourself. If all you possess is high self esteem based on your "feelings" then your neighbor becomes a "thing" to be used with no more feeling than many three year olds would feel at taking something they wanted from someone else.

If parents don't teach their children morality by example and many parents are "to busy," and if the church doesn't teach them because they don't attend, and if the school system believes it is not their responsibility, then the result is inevitable: overcrowded prisons housing more people than the entire population of some of the member nations of the United Nations. Put another way, we now have in the prisons of the United States more people than the combined populations of the states of Alaska, Delaware and Wyoming combined with the populations of all the major cities in South Carolina thrown in for good measure. That is a lot of people and the cost to the taxpayer is enormous. Of course most of these people are in prison because they used drugs to enhance their own self esteem so perhaps the "affiliation ethic" of the National Educational Association is not working as well as the old "work ethic" that we used to go by in the public schools, things like reading, writing and arithmetic. Some schools don't even want to grade their students because it might hurt their "self image". In real life we are graded all the time. If you don't make at least the equivalent of "C's" you don't keep your job very long. If you don't make "A's" or "B's" on your evaluations you don't get a raise. Real life is hard sometimes. Grading is not "on the curve" and you have to earn your self-esteem for a job well done. I do not envy today's public school teachers (the good ones that is) because the system is stacked against them. No wonder so many of them send their own children to private or parochial schools.

Courses in child psychology, abnormal psychology, social psychology, and developmental psychology were all under my belt when I accepted a temporary 6 month assignment at the South Carolina Employment Security Commission.Basically I was an interviewer helping people to obtain employment, matching jobs with those I thought were qualified for them. Even here I once inadvertently broke the rules by going to a client's home with a job offer that I thought was suitable. I had tried to reach this person by phone to no avail and I knew that this particular job would go fast.What I had yet to learn was that some people really didn't want to find work if they had worked before and were eligible for the six month payout of unemployment compensation. One of the relatives of the person I was trying to contact knew the system and how it could be worked. She complained of my visit and I got a lecture for my efforts from my boss, a retired Colonel. I never did more than I was required to do after that. At the end of six months I was offered a permanent position in a small town over an hours drive from Columbia. I thought that it would mean moving to the town which was near nothing but even smaller towns. The idea of commuting such a long distance which I did for many years to Connecticut in the 1980's did not occur to me. At that time I lived in New York and commuted over a hundred miles per day round-trip to where I worked for National Semi-Conductor in Connecticut and where my cousin Darlene is today head of social services for the entire state. I didn't think to pray about it. I just thought it over and decided to try for one more semester at the University and I turned the job down.

Being deprived of an automobile for all my teenage years I had developed an interest in autos more than most. I was not attracted to the huge horsepower cars of the day but I liked small little cars like the tiny two seater Messerschmidt that my neighbor had won when I was 13 or 14. I never saw another one of those, but little cars were also more likely to be within the range I could afford. Once I traveled all the way to New York City to purchase a used Citroen 2CV, the so-called "Ugly Duckling." This was I believe the very first car that was eliminated when the first laws on automobile safety were passed in 1967. I don't think it passed any of them. Very few of these were ever sold in this country to begin with but there is one I still see occasionally in Dutchess County.

In Europe where the governments believe that adults are mature enough to decide if they want to drive something really efficient and usually quite small they are allowed to do so. The same is true in Japan. Many cars sold in Japan and in the countries of Europe are forbidden in the United States. Some of these super efficient 50-70 mpg vehicles are sold in Mexico and Canada but not here. The small Citroen looked like an emaciated VW but when I saw the 2CV for sale in the automobile section of the NY Times I just knew I had to have it. It was a used vehicle that someone from overseas had brought with them and apparently left behind when they returned to France or Belgium. The car only had a 425cc two cylinder engine that was horizontally opposed like an ancient aircraft engine or perhaps a BMW motorcycle. The car was made out of sheet metal. It had four doors and canvas seats with about an inch of foam rubber on them. The roof was a high quality artificial canvas that slid back and clipped onto the rear of the vehicle making it into a convertible. I don't think I ever drove it with four people in it as that would have slowed it down considerably. As it was it took about a minute to get up to 60 mph if the wind wasn't blowing towards you.

The front wheels of the vehicle, besides turning like a normal car, also veered or angled like a motorcycle's front wheels. Once when I did a quick U-turn in front of one of the buildings in which I had a class several people came running up to me until they realized I was just quickly turning to grab a parking space and that the car was not turning over which it appeared to them to be doing. It was a fun car and got a lot of attention and more importantly about 60 mpg.

Once I had driven over to Drake's Restaurant near Providence Hospital for a hamburger and a delicious dessert they had, sort of a mini-custard pie with fresh strawberries. The desert alone was worth the trip but I also knew one of the waitresses there. After enjoying my meal I went out to the parking lot and a gentleman came over and asked me about the car. He remembered seeing me driving on the fairly new I-95 a few months before when I brought the car down from New York and he wanted to know about the vehicle. As we were talking two punks came up to us, one was even shirtless. The other held a zip gun, a home made pistol and they told us to follow them. The guy who I had been talking with moved a slight distance to my right and the one with the gun moved along with him. The other one stood in front of me and while looking quite menacing I couldn't tell for sure if he had a concealed weapon. My only thought was that I wasn't going anywhere. I had heard words between the two people to my right and then I heard a strange sound coming from the black teenager who looked to be about 20 years old. I looked to my right and saw the man I had been talking to running the 60 feet or so to the door of Drakes. As he was running I heard a shot ring out. Just as suddenly the punk in front of me took off running followed by the older one. About the same time other people came out of the restaurant. Within two minutes at least three police cars and maybe four were on the scene. I was told later that the reason they responded so quickly is that the state legislature often had lunch at Drakes and the person calling in had just said excitedly "robbery at Drakes Restaurant" and patrolmen had thought that the restaurant was being robbed. In any event one very large black officer was interested in every detail and as he took off in his car to search for the two would be robbers, one of the white officers came over and told me that a minister had followed the two into an alley and been robbed and shot just a few days earlier. The minister had survived but the bullet just missed his heart. The officer also told me that he'd have pity on the two young blacks if the black officer found them. "He really hates it when his people do something wrong," he told me. The person who had stopped to ask about my strange little car was actually an off-duty police officer and he told me that when he was talking with the punk with the gun he noticed the level of the gun was pointed down and he figured that if he was going to be shot he would rather be shot in the leg than in the torso. That was when he swung at the guy and knocked the gun out of his hand but couldn't see where on the ground it had fallen. That was when he took off running and the owner of the gun retrieved it and shot at him. I never thought to follow up on whether the two were ever caught or not. I was just grateful that everything had turned out alright for me and the other auto enthusiast who had wanted to know what kind of car I was driving. I drove by that intersection a few years ago and Drakes was no longer there. In its place was a fast food outlet, a sign of the times I guess.

21. Koscot Interplanetary, Inc.

Over the years I had accumulated about 4 years worth of college credits but they were still not enough to give me a degree in anything. Actually I only needed one course in statistics and two years of a foreign language and I would have qualified for a degree in psychology but I was learning to hate the school work because I could still not see where it was leading me. It seemed like I was going round and round. I envied people whose lives were all mapped out for them especially those who knew what they wanted. I could not see how I could contribute very much no matter what path I chose.

In my last semester at USC I went to a meeting at a Holiday Inn sponsored by a cosmetic company. One of the people I met there had been an instructor at USC. He had been working on his doctorate and gave it up to join the cosmetic company. I was told that he had earned in excess of four million dollars in the previous three years and the thought occurred to me that if I could do just ten percent of that it would be enough to do all I wanted to do (buy a medium sized new house with some acreage, buy a new car and a small aircraft and still have money in the bank). Today with the stealth-tax of inflation I could only buy the house with that amount of money.

The cosmetics, based on mink oil, were the finest ever made but what I did not fully realize was that the big money was in selling the distributorships. I was taken on an all expense paid trip to Florida where I toured an enormous plant that housed Koscot Inter- planetary, Inc. I discovered that the founder of the company, Glenn W. Turner, did not even have a high school diploma. He had made $100 million dollars in the previous 24 months and here I had just spent the better part of a decade trying to accumulate enough college credits to obtain a degree in anything so I could......but that's where the thought ended because I still had no idea.

So much of life revolves around money: earning it, saving it, investing it, and spending it. I remember once as a student when I was hungry and all I had was twenty cents, two thin dimes. I walked five blocks to the grocery store in the section called Five Points because five streets met there and I purchased a Kraft macaroni and cheese dinner for seventeen cents. I then walked back to the Thomas More Student Center on Green Street and in the student kitchen in the basement I prepared half of the package, carefully folding up the aluminum foil packet of cheese and saving half of it and enough macaroni for a second meal. Eight and a half cents is what my meal cost me. It is amazing how good something like that will taste when you are really hungry.

The trip to Florida and all I saw impressed me as did the camaraderie of the people. It was a fellowship, almost, but not quite, a community. Virtually all of the people I met expressed such a positive attitude as I had never before seen. I had read most of the books by Norman Vincent Peale on positive thinking and books by Dale Carnegie, Napolean Hill, and W. Clement Stone, but these Koscot people seemed to be really living their positive thinking and not just talking about it. Their enthusiasm was contagious and I wanted some of it, and the possibility of earning some real money, well that seemed too good to be true.

I managed to borrow the money from a friend to buy my way into a distributorship by Koscot Interplanetary, Inc. a company that was as audacious as its name. I attended many seminars and training sessions to learn how I could have such a positive outlook and how I could make the kind of money that some of the distributors were making. I was told to borrow even more money to purchase a Cadillac, necessary to impress prospective customers. That part seemed phony to me but I discovered that some people were impressed by fancy cars and hundred dollar bills. Since I was only marginally impressed by such things I couldn't quite convince myself. Besides, I thought that a new Mercedes would be much more impressive. It was pointed out to me that although I was impressed by a large Mercedes most people in the south at least (at that time) would be more impressed by a new Cadillac. I guess I was to practical or middle-class. I did go out on a limb and purchase a new car but it was a mid-range Toyota that was well built and economical but hardly sufficient to impress anyone except perhaps myself. Before Koscot I had never even considered buying a brand new car.

Lessons in a dynamic motivational course called "Dare to be Great!" became part of the companies operation and they taught many of the basic rules of salesmanship coupled together with positive thinking and success dynamics. Somehow I could not inculcate them into my thinking. Deep down I did not really believe that I was as worthy as everyone else, surely not as worthy as those who had achieved so much with their lives. I wanted to believe and I tried to believe. I even tried the suggestions that I attempt to brainwash myself into believing that I was a worthwhile person. Ironically, I have been told that as a child I had a positive and dynamic personality but I guess life, up to this point, had beaten it out of me. The company also taught me how to influence people in a way that I thought was unethical but it was pointed out to me that this was the American way of advertising and that all of advertising was an attempt to persuade people to part with some of their money.

I could see the good of it and the bad of it but try as I might I could not quite convince myself. Years before I had read Vance Packard's book "The Hidden Persuaders," about Madison Avenue's advertising gimmicks that were hidden from the conscious mind but designed to elicit the desired response: buy! I did learn one practical technique that almost always enabled me to find a parking place even in a crowded place like New York City but I was not able to utilize this to become the mature and financially independent person that I wanted to be.

The most recent hidden persuaders that I have found are that some advertisers are using distorted photographs of young models to sell their wares. These distortions are undoubtedly done by computer now that computer graphics has become so sophisticated that computer created people can be made virtually indistinguishable from live human actors. Soon they may be indistinguishable. Voice reproduction techniques are now so perfect that someday soon you may see a film of someone doing something and it will be a computer creation with a voice that is electronically an exact match for a real person. This is not science fiction. It already exists though fortunately not many have access to such technology. The photographic distortions I mentioned are just a much simpler version of this technique. They show already to-thin models made to look like starving refugees in a prison camp and pre-adolescent girls thinking that this is desirable and not realizing that no healthy person in real life looks like this are sometimes attempting suicide and to often are willing to undergo starvation to look like these models. On the other hand the problem of childhood obesity is growing very fast in this nation. A hundred years ago no skinny woman would have been considered "beautiful" and obesity was not the problem it is today. Perhaps the two are related. The other advertising extreme of our times is the youth-is-everything age-is-out syndrome. Now there is certainly nothing wrong with staying healthy and looking young but I heard one beautiful 17 year old model tell about being passed over for a series of fashion photographs because "she was too old." This insanity is what the Bible calls "the world" as in the expression, "The enemies of man are the world, the flesh and the devil." One credit card company in the mid-1990s was even advertising itself as "worldly" as if this were something desirable.

At the time it did not occur to me to question if the company I was supporting was worldly. Are cosmetics worldly? It all depends. I only knew that I wasn't succeeding in selling cosmetic distributorships in Columbia and a group of us moved to Augusta, Georgia, to hold meetings there. I moved to North Augusta, which is actually a town in South Carolina, but it made no difference. I recruited a few young women to sell cosmetics for me but my efforts were insufficient to warrant even a mediocre success.

There was a young woman (I'll call her Suzy) that I brought to the training sessions. With hindsight I think she was more interested in me than in the opportunity I was trying to sell. Suzy was a descendent of the many Irish immigrants who settled in that area long ago. She was a pretty girl as I recall and the attraction was somewhat mutual.

One night after the meeting ended most of us drove over to the International House of Pancakes as we usually did. I took Suzy along with me and a couple of the others from the meeting asked if she were my girl friend. It was well after midnight when I drove her back to her home. We sat in the front seat of my car talking for some time and eventually ended up in a passionate embrace. With a twist on the handle the seat reclined and then I really began to kiss her. We were both getting pretty excited when I stopped as quickly as if someone had thrown a bucket of cold water on me. "What's the matter, why did you stop?" Suzy asked. "I don't know," I told her, but actually I did. I hardly knew her. I wasn't in love with her, and I hadn't been raised this way. I wanted "it" alright but not like this. I was embarrassed and I decided that I'd better not see Suzy again. Avoid the temptations of sin and all that. Frankly I didn't trust myself to see her again. I wasn't proud of myself because I hadn't had sex with her and I wouldn't have been proud if I had. I just considered myself fortunate and let it go at that. Perhaps it would have been healthier for my self image if I had given the whole episode more thought but at the time I decided to forget it and move on.

And move on I did, although this time I went 900 miles north of North Augusta, back to Dutchess County and Poughkeepsie, N.Y.I was leaving South Carolina once again. I figured that maybe if I went to where people had more money perhaps I would be better able to sell my product to them. I did not realize that success is internal, if you don't have it in you, moving will not bring it to you. "As a man thinketh in his heart so is he," Jesus once said quoting the Book of Proverbs. The heart, however, is the deepest part of a person, so deep one often doesn't know what is there oneself. Why are we here? What is it all about? What is one's place in the Universe? What is important? What is not? These were questions I sought to answer but I did not find answers in New York, at least not right away.

During the years I had returned to South Carolina my friend Mikael (not his real name) had sold his trailer and purchased a house not far from the IBM plant where he worked. Unfortunately I arrived back in Poughkeepsie just in time to be a witness at his divorce. His wife whom he had dated since she was 15, married at 18, and who was now divorcing him at 22 had grown into an entirely different person. Part of her falling in love and getting married was undoubtedly motivated by a desire to leave her North Carolina home and prove her independence. She may even have wanted to "show" her parents a thing or two. When she left my friend she did the one thing that would most upset her southern parents, not her husband, who had grown up in international society (the Shah of Iran once gave my friend's dad a gold handled dagger as a gift and his aunt knew the Eisenhowers well enough to have three of the presidents somewhat primitive oil paintings hanging on the wall of her apartment when I visited. They were just signed DE for Dwight Eisenhower). My friend's former wife established a relationship with a person of "color". Inter-racial couples are not that unusual in the south today but 36 years ago that could not be said. I felt that there were all kinds of psychological undercurrents in what I was hearing but I could not see where I could do anything to help except to be a truthful witness.

I needed a place to stay and Mikael now had a small three bedroom house to share so I paid him a monthly rent and it was like old times. I traveled to Rockland County which is across the Hudson River and about 50 miles to the south. There I helped support the meetings that brought people into the business and earned money for some of the people but not for me. I can only surmise that I had a strong mental block, what Oprah Winfrey calls a "shadow belief," and that kept me from the financial freedom I desired. Try as I might I could not elicit anyone to buy a distributorship in Koscot. I was fast running out of money and had to find employment of some kind in order to survive. Christmas was coming and for three weeks I worked in the Poughkeepsie, N.Y. post office, sorting mail during the Christmas rush. This enabled me to keep going for another month and a half. I had only one problem while I was at the post office but it was a problem I had not encountered before although there was the incident when I was hitchhiking home around age 14.

Today, fortunately, we have sexual harassment laws to protect people in the workplace but then it was pretty much every man and woman for themselves. My problem was that one of the other workers, perhaps 10 or 15 years my senior, could not keep away from me. He kept reaching over me and around me and occasionally brushing against me as he put mail into the little boxes into which I was supposed to be sorting and distributing the mail. Ten years later I had a similar problem only this time it was a younger woman who was about 10 years my junior. Fortunately the law covers all sexes and forbids unwanted sexual advances from anyone. The law isn't perfect and is sometimes carried to extremes like the public school that suspended a five year old kindergarten student, a boy, who had kissed a five year old girl on the cheek. This, of course, told more about the repressed sexuality and emotional frigidity of the teacher or school administrator than it did about the little tyke who was undoubtedly from a loving happy home and only doing what he had seen done at home.

It is a sad commentary on this great country of ours that such laws are necessary to keep sexual predators at bay regardless of their preferences or orientation. In the words of Luiz Solimeo, "Immorality and amorality have reached unparalleled levels.Even ancient pagans had greater notions of modesty, fidelity, honor and honesty than men today." My discomfort in those pre-law days had quickly reached such a level as my co- worker harassed me that I was debating in my mind if the sentence I would get for stabbing him in the hand with the six inch nail like object that we occasionally used would be worth it to make him stop. Fortunately for both of us a supervisor who was certainly more street wise than I was told this character to back off and he did. This incident convinced me that these predators might indeed have a knack for selecting victims who are "nice" people, ones who for one reason or another won't make waves. So often we think that other people are like we are when in reality the world is full of every kind of person imaginable, from saints to monsters. Looking back I can only imagine that my need for a job and the money it provided was so great that I did not want to jeopardize it on the very first day.

For a few months in 1971 I worked in a clothes packing plant. Perhaps distribution center would be a more accurate description. The company was called Barclay Knitwear. It was located across the river, north of Poughkeepsie, in Port Ewen. There I helped sort and distribute new clothes as they arrived from the manufacturer. Dozens of women worked at sewing machines sewing labels into various items. I unpacked hundreds of sweaters, sweatshirts and other shirts and distributed them to these women who sewed a label into each and every item. The labels fascinated me. Some said "Sears" others said "Penny's" and some even said "Made exclusively for John's Tailor Shop" but the items were all identical. I had taken them all from the same box or crate and distributed them randomly. I had a new appreciation for some brand names after that experience.

At Barclay's I met a girl who had also left South Carolina. She was tall and thin and we had lunch together several times. I surprised her on her birthday (in February) by giving her an out-of-season watermelon, imported form Mexico or Chile, but she told me that she hated watermelon. It wasn't a very romantic gift I'll admit but I don't know if she said what she said because she was brutally honest or just insensitive. I could see that she had other problems and I did not pursue that relationship any further. I had other dead end, short term or temporary jobs that kept me from going hungry or being homeless. Unfortunately my relationships with the opposite sex weren't much better than the jobs I found.

22. NATPAC

Mikael had a friend at Vassar College that I got to know. Ester (also not her real name) was from the mid-west and the daughter of a wealthy businessman. Early one evening we drove down to New York City to pick her up at Kennedy Airport and bring her back to Poughkeepsie. She looked exhausted and almost fell asleep in my arms in the back seat of the car. What kept her from a true peaceful sleep was some kind of recurring nightmare. "No, no, keep away from me," I heard her mutter just loud enough for me to hear. I didn't know what to do for her so I just prayed for her. The nightmare seemed to recede and Ester seemed to rest more soundly. I found out that she seldom slept more than an hour per night which I thought to be impossible. One night I was visiting Ester in her dorm at Vassar and she was working on a term paper. We talked as she wrote. It was around three in the morning and I could not keep my eyes open any longer. I put my head down on the desk and fell asleep. When I awoke two hours later at 5 a.m. Ester was still at her desk writing where I had seen her last.She said that she had slept for an hour but you couldn't prove that by me.

Ester had these nightmares often and I discovered that she had more than one psychiatrist back home that she could phone at any time for help. I was in her room once and heard some of her side of one of the conversations with one of the psychiatrists. "No, no, of course, I know they are not real," she said. I was not so certain. Today, of course, I know that they were very real indeed but I also could have prevented them from bothering her and keeping her awake all night, had I known then what I know now. Ester graduated from Vassar and as far as I know returned to the mid-western city from whence she had come. I never saw her again. Later when I began to understand a little of what Christianity is really all about and how it is our responsibility to push back the darkness, whenever and wherever we can, I thought of Ester from time to time and said a silent prayer for her. She was a brilliant person and as nice as she was troubled.

Mikael, always a hard worker, received many promotions and eventually moved to the IBM plant that was in Manassas, Virginia, at that time. I found a tiny apartment with a semi-private bathroom for $20 per week. It was located on Church Street, a beautiful tree lined street of older homes running in an east-west direction through the City of Poughkeepsie.I guess calling it an apartment was stretching it a little bit. All it consisted of was a small room with a single bed, a desk and chair and a tiny sink and an antique two burner gas stove with a tiny oven at the far end of the room. There was also a semi-private bathroom. The heat provided was inadequate for the poorly insulated house. One burner of that little antique stove on low, however, was enough to keep the winter chill away.

The other inhabitant of the upstairs of this house on Church Street was an elementary school teacher. Tony was a friendly middle-aged guy with a terrible self image. His apartment consisted of a large bedroom with a sofa and a double bed, a private kitchen, and a small porch. We shared the bathroom and neither of us had a living room. Tony was an alcoholic who had once spent some time in the Foreign Service. I believe he started drinking when the love of his life turned down his proposal for marriage a few decades before I met him. Tony never got over the rejection. He had spent some time in Washington, D.C. and also in at least one Mid-Eastern country. While in that country he had the same Arab driver for quite some time and they became friends. One night the two of them drove far out into the desert to secretly witness a ceremony that no Westerner was supposedly ever to have seen. After leaving the car they proceeded on foot for a good distance before climbing up a rocky outcropping. Even before being able to see anything the two of them could hear drums and chanting. The last few yards were traversed by crawling on their stomachs. Below them were about 40 shirtless men chanting to the sound of the drums and at the same time whipping themselves on their backs. Years later I had a déjà vu experience when the Indiana Jones movies came out and I remembered Tony's account of his adventure.

Several fires were burning and all the men were facing diagonally away from Tony and his Arab driver and towards the man who was obviously their leader. Although the lighting was poor it was enough for Tony to see streams of blood coming down the backs of some of the men. During a momentary pause in the chanting Tony coughed a cough which might have been over-looked in the moments before but now in the eerie silence caused several of the men to look in Tony's direction and with a shout grab for their swords. They had seen two heads on the bluff above them and instantly decided to sever them from the rest of their bodies.

"Run! Run!" the driver shouted, "Or you will die." Tony was fearful but the poor driver was terrified and upon reaching the car drove it faster than Tony thought it could go. Whether or not any of the cult members had automobiles the driver did not know but he had no intention of finding out. Apparently he knew what his fate would be if they got caught.

I knew nothing of alcoholism at the time and I remember foolishly telling Tony he shouldn't drink so much. He drank the hard stuff, not beer or wine. All of it can kill you but 90-proof seems to do the job quicker. Once, when I found out how much money Tony paid for a single bottle I facetiously said, "You spend so much for a single bottle, why don't you buy it wholesale by the case?" I regretted what I had said later when I found an entire case of Gin or Vodka in Tony's apartment.

That case of booze reminded me of something that happened years before in Columbia. A veterinarian and friend of the family, Dr. Vandergrift (the father of the girl I had a crush on when I was in summer camp at age ten) had a radio show that covered central South Carolina. People would call in with questions about their pets but the emphasis was on placing unwanted pets with new owners. Someone called in and said that they had heard that a home was being sought for an old crow. Dr. Vandergrift replied that the only Old Crow he knew of came in a bottle. Apparently the local distributor of Old Crow, a popular whiskey, was listening and he sent Dr. Vandergrift a case of Old Crow in appreciation for mentioning his product on the radio. It seemed like a very southern thing to do and I wondered if the program was in the north and a northern distributor had heard the joke whether a similar case would have been sent.

The rent was due and I did not have a job - again - so I purchased a copy of the Poughkeepsie Journal, New York State's oldest newspaper (since 1785). I was desperate and had to find employment. I had even prayed for help and the distinct thought that I seemed to hear in my mind or spirit was, "Take the next job you are offered." That sounded great to me but of all the job offerings in the paper there was only one that I felt I was qualified for and so I shaved, dressed up, and headed for McDonald's. I had never worked in fast food before but I was desperate. It was only a half mile drive to

McDonald's from my tiny apartment or room. I could easily have walked but as it was I never got there.

As I drove the few blocks to the restaurant I noticed a large sign on the side of a building that said NATPAC. It was just a block from McDonald's on Main Street. I didn't even know what kind of company it was but I seemed to remember seeing an ad for employment there in a previous newspaper. My appointment was not until 3 p.m. and I still had half an hour so I pulled into the skimpy parking lot in front of NATPAC.

"Just what kind of company is this?" I asked Gene who turned out to be the sales manager. My quick visit became a two hour informal interview. Gene liked me and I thought he would be a reasonable person to work for although I knew nothing about home food services at the time. Within days I was in an intensive week long school in Hohokus, New Jersey, learning about meats, home food services, freezers, and sale techniques. I was issued a black leather sales case and all the forms, contracts, and answers to overcome objections that I would need to make it as a sales professional. Basically the plan was tailored to each family and was heavy in meats and skimpy in other areas. The meat was top notch Choice aged American beef and completely guaranteed with home delivery as one of the main selling points. If a family did not have a freezer one would be provided, but for an additional twelve or fourteen dollars per month a family could purchase a brand new upright commercial freezer. The actual cost of the new freezer was more than the twelve or fourteen dollars but the customer received a reduction in the monthly cost of their food to offset the cost of the freezer. Soon the company was making stainless steel microwave ovens available and I sold those as well. I worked 60 hour weeks on average, usually six days and often seven. I covered a seven county area although I tried to keep it down to four. There was a great deal of driving involved, so much so that the IRS audited my income tax return my very first year. Fortunately, I had kept all my receipts for gasoline and toll bridges and a mileage log as I had been instructed to do. The gentleman at the IRS was a pleasant person and all went well. Of course, I suppose if I had been a crook things might not have been so cordial.

Within six months I had moved out of my tiny one room apartment and into the entire upstairs of the house next door. The house was a two family house and I rented the upper half of it, a two bedroom apartment with a large living room, eat-in kitchen, private bath and a front and side porch. The rent cost me $150 per month and I immediately set about to find a room mate to share the place with me. I had a succession of room mates, some excellent, some not quite what I wanted. I ran an ad in the Poughkeepsie Journal once and a nice chap from Washington, D.C. answered. He was on temporary assignment to IBM and had a doctorate degree in mathematics. He only worked for them on occasion when they had a problem that his expertise could solve.

Mike didn't take the room the first time he saw it but called me back the following evening. Initially he thought that the idea of commuting almost 18 miles to work was a bit much but during his first lunch break some of his co-workers took him to lunch in Danbury, Connecticut. I think they went to Rosy Tomorrow's an attractive multi-leveled restaurant that I frequent myself on occasion. In any event Mike decided that if driving 50 miles round trip to another state for lunch wasn't considered unusual in this part of the country then commuting 35 miles round trip to work wasn't out of the ordinary either.

In March of 1973 Tony, now my next door neighbor invited me to dinner at the Holiday Inn on South Road in Poughkeepsie. I knew he was doing it because it was my birthday but I was quite surprised when a procession of waiters and waitresses came out carrying a birthday cake and singing "Happy Birthday!" to me. In December of that year I went home to South Carolina for Christmas and I was shocked to discover when I returned that Tony had died suddenly of a stroke or heart attack and was already buried. As I recall Mike had been one of the last people to see him alive but on that detail I am not absolutely certain.

My life wasn't as miserable as Tony's (it just seemed that way) but my drug of choice was not alcohol but work. Some weeks I worked 70 hours. I was surprised one quarter (three month sales period) when at a company meeting in Ozone Park on Long Island it was announced that I was runner-up for salesman of the quarter for the entire multi-state company. I had my pick of electronic toys and at first picked a television set which I did not have but then traded it back for a Panasonic Cassette stereo system which I thought I would probably get more use out of than the TV. I did too, until a burglar stole it. Actually I was glad that I was only runner up because the winner was going to get a night on the town and even though the town was New York City I really had no interest in doing that. If I'd had a wife or girlfriend it would have been different but going to a bunch of night clubs with a bunch of guys seemed a lot less desirable than a new stereo.

In the course of my going into private homes in the Mid- Hudson Valley I analyzed the eating habits of many hundreds of people. I also met many fascinating people from all walks of life. Some of these people lived in apartments and others lived in mansions. I remember one mansion that had such a huge living room that a life size painting of a horse which hung on one wall did not seem out of place or to big. I was not successful in selling the service to every perspective client but I did get to meet all kinds of interesting people.

One night I had an appointment to meet a family in eastern Westchester County. Although I never made it to their house I did meet a pretty damsel in distress and was able to render some assistance.

The directions to the house I was going to required me to drive east on I-84 towards Connecticut and then turn south on I-684. It was the month of March, quite cold but not freezing, at least not in Poughkeepsie. Flowers would be blooming or at least beginning to in South Carolina but spring was still six weeks away in the Mid-Hudson Valley. I had driven about 40 miles and then turned south onto I-684 and had driven several more miles in the direction of my prospects home. A bitter cold rain was falling. The number of cars and trucks on the road was nothing out of the ordinary until I drove up a long sloping hill and as I mounted its crest I could see cars and trucks stopped on the highway as far as the eye could see which because of a curve in the road was about ¾ of a mile. I immediately slowed down figuring that there must be some horrible accident ahead of me, beyond my view, for this many vehicles to be stopped on an Interstate Highway. The truth was that there were dozens of accidents as I discovered when I brought my vehicle to a stop. The road was impassable. I couldn't see beyond the tractor trailers in front of me once I stopped so I got out of my car and grabbed onto the open door just in time to keep myself from falling. The entire road was covered with a sheet of ice perhaps a quarter of an inch thick. I walked very slowly so as not to fall until I heard someone yell, "Lookout for the truck!" I looked to my right just in time to avert an accident as a parked and apparently driverless vehicle was silently sliding sideways towards the tractor trailer that was partially off the road and to my left and with me in between them. No engines were running and there was very little sound of any kind until the pick-up truck sliding on that icy road slammed sideways into the much larger truck about where I would have been walking if a stranger had not yelled out a warning about the silently moving vehicle. There was no sound at all and then "crunch" as the metal buckled under the impact. Well over 125 vehicles were bumper to bumper and quite a few of them had minor damage.

About an hour passed and vehicles slowly began to move, some under their own power, others being pulled by tow trucks. The ice had begun to melt as the temperature of the rain rose a few degrees, but it was another half hour before I was able to drive a quarter mile to the nearest intersection, turn left, and stop at a service station to use their outside pay phone. I called the family that had been expecting me over an hour before and explained to them all that had happened and why I was late. They told me that it was to late for them to have me come at that time and I was never able to re-schedule the appointment to explain our food service and how it might work for them.

As I hung up the phone at the otherwise closed service station I noticed a young woman who looked perplexed as a couple of men stood by talking to her. Her car had been hit by several vehicles, and although the damage was not severe, in both the front and the back, on the driver's side of the vehicle, metal was pushing against the tires. A couple of men who had been trying to hammer out the damage were having no luck and were apologizing because they had to leave. I started talking with the young woman who was just a few years younger than I was and she told me that she had a "gig" at a night club in Danbury, Connecticut, which was less than 20 miles away. Apparently she had sung there before and she was supposed to have sung there that night. She had used the same phone to call the night club manager and tell him what happened to her. She had said that she had someone working on her car and that she wouldn't need help. Now she was not so sure. I told her that I had a chain in my trunk with a steel hook on it and that maybe if I tried to pull her vehicle sideways with my car I could pull the metal away from her tires which were incapable of turning in their present condition. I had never done anything like that before but she agreed to let me try. It took several attempts but we eventually succeeded. The tires did not look damaged but I was concerned that internal damage might have been done to them. I offered the suggestion that since I now had nothing to do for the rest of the night that I follow her to the club to make sure that she did not have a blow-out on the way,

or at least to be there if she did. It was only 12 miles or so out of
my way. Once we headed north the road was clear of ice and traffic
and we had no trouble getting onto 1-84 and east to Connecticut,
Danbury, and the night club.

We went into the club together and after introducing me to the
manager she talked with him for about 5 minutes and then joined
me at the table where I had been waiting for her. I didn't drink,
maybe 4 or 5 beers a year, so I just had a cup or two of coffee. We
talked for about 45 minutes and I was surprised at how much faith
she had in God.

"He sent me you," she said matter-of-factly, "and you solved my
problem." She was convinced that God looked after her and I felt
that she had greater faith in God's day-to-day guidance than I did.
We exchanged addresses and I drove the 48 miles back home.

We wrote to each other a time or two and she did a tour of some
kind in Europe, singing her way across the continent. When she
returned she invited me to be her guest at a very classy French restaurant on West 57th Street in New York City. She asked me if I had
ever eaten snails before and I admitted that I had not. "They really
know how to fix them here," she told me. I was still a little reluctant
to make a meal of them in case I didn't like them. "You order them
and I'll try some of yours," I told her. She was right. They were delicious and I knew the difference the next time I ordered them a few
years later at a place up-state where they were only so-so. From this
experience I learned to only try something totally new or different at
a place that really knows how to fix the item. That way if you don't
like it it's because you don't like it, not because it wasn't prepared
properly. I waited years to try alligator and I am glad I did. When
my brother-in-law, Col. Mark Stephen and my sister Anne invited
me to dinner at a way-off-the-beaten-track restaurant outside of
Tampa, Florida, years later, I finally had the opportunity to try alligator and I was pleasantly surprised again. It, too, was delicious.

However, that night in the French restaurant I told my friend
that I was concerned about all the solo travel she did, a beautiful 28
year old singer, traveling the world, singing in night clubs, some of
which I was pretty sure were owned and operated by the mob, but
she told me that she knew that God had a plan for her life and in His
time she would find it. I knew, intellectually at least, that He had a
plan for my life too. Only it seemed to me to be so well hidden that
I wondered if I would ever find it.

23. The Charismatic Renewal

It was autumn of the year 1973 and I had an appointment with a family that lived in a fine home, not quite a mansion, but a huge home in a really nice neighborhood. The owner was an upper level executive at IBM and they had had dinner guests. I arrived just as they were finishing their after dinner coffee and I caught part of a conversation about a mutual acquaintance who had what the doctors had said was terminal cancer, beyond the scope of science. This person, however, had gone to something called a Charismatic Prayer Meeting at a church I was familiar with, St. Columba, in the town of Hopewell Junction. It wasn't really a church in the contemporary sense because there was no building. It was actually a Catholic elementary school and on Sundays services were held in the school cafeteria. I don't remember much of what was said that night at the IBM executive's home but I remember what I said when I heard that this man's cancer disappeared after being prayed over. It still sounds odd when I think about it and I'm not sure now why I said it then but my reply at the time was, "Wouldn't you have to be awfully emotional to believe in something like that?" The executive and his associates, the dinner guests, assured me that their friend, who was now free of cancer, was a very down to earth, scientifically minded person, and not in the least bit overly emotional.

I did not know what to think. I believed in healing. It is part of the Catholic tradition of Christianity that over the centuries there have been special people who were so close to God that His healing power flowed through them and that people who sought them out for a healing miracle sometimes had their prayers answered. I was, however, somewhat dubious that this was happening in the latter part of the 20th Century and just down the street so to speak. I made a mental note to investigate but time passed and I was working a very busy schedule of six and seven nights per week.

The other reason I didn't rush to go to a "prayer meeting" or even a "Bible study" was that I imagined it might be rather dull and uninteresting. When I was a student back at Carolina I had attended a Bible Study in the home of the pastor of one of the most famous churches in South Carolina. Matthew Brady, the famous pioneer photographer photographed Trinity Episcopal Church in 1865 and General Sherman's Troops used it as a hospital. It was one of the few buildings that were not destroyed in the burning of Columbia during the War Between the States. Southern legend has it that Sherman's officers thought that it was a Catholic Church and therefore saved it.

In any event Reverend Sterling was the pastor of Trinity Episcopal Church and it was at his home that I attended a Bible Study on Thursday afternoons.The people were nice, sincere, and I enjoyed it for a while. After several weeks someone asked me if I was a member of Saint John's Episcopal Church since no one there had seen me at Trinity and there was no little astonishment when I mentioned that I attended the Catholic Church. "But Catholics aren't supposed to..." someone started to say and trailed off in disbelief. At that time I had not even heard of a Bible Study in my church but the Catholic Church has never claimed to be founded on just the Bible. Fortunately there are Bible Studies in many Catholic Churches today and there is a hunger among many nominal Christians for a deeper understanding of God and the Universe. As the world grows less predictable I believe this may continue.

There was a portrait in Rev. Sterling's home that always fascinated me. It was old, perhaps two centuries, and was meticulously done. It was I suppose, a beautiful young woman of about 30. It was truly unique and I had never seen anything like it before. The view was of the back of her head. The natural tendency was to walk past it into the kitchen in an attempt to see the other side but that was all there was to it, the back of her head. I also seem to remember a magnificent but faded rug with the date it was made in the center of the rug, 1500 A.D., and all sorts of figures and scenes around the date. I wondered it that rug had once hung on a castle wall somewhere.

The fellowship of the group was appealing but after a few months I drifted away. I could read the Bible on my own I rationalized, although I didn't do so, and besides I had other "more important" things to do. Confronted with another Bible Study or something like it, well I didn't rush to go down and check it out. How much time passed before I ran into another family who told me of the incredible "happenings" going on at St. Columba's I do not remember. I was still quite curious and although I wasn't aware that I needed a healing of any kind the idea of seeing a demonstration of God's power was appealing. Finally I placed a phone call to the rectory to inquire when these prayer meetings were held. It was the second week in the month of May in 1974 when I attended one for the first time in my life.

I needn't have worried about the meeting being dull or uninteresting. It was different from any other kind of church function or meeting I had ever attended. It was also strangely beautiful. I discovered that although the people were using a Catholic facility they weren't all Catholics. There were Baptists and Lutherans and Methodists and Presbyterians and Pentecostals and even some members of the Jewish faith. Most, however, were Catholic, and they talked about Jesus as if He were their best friend in all the world. The vast majority of these people were completely sincere and they talked about Jesus with a familiarity that made it seem to me like He had been their dinner guest sometime within the previous week. That bothered me somewhat but these people had almost a glow about them, a joy and an enthusiasm that was the most genuine I had ever seen, far surpassing what I had experienced at the Koscot meetings a few years back.

After the meeting I hung around and asked a few questions but I really did not know what to ask so I determined to return the following week and continue my investigation. Someone gave me a pamphlet. When I got back to my apartment I read it in its entirety. The pamphlet answered some of my questions but now I had a lot more. The week seemed to pass slowly and I was anxious to attend the next get-together. The second meeting was pretty similar to the first. People talked about what they had experienced during the week and how they felt God had helped them in one way or another. Some shared their stories or testimony about how God or Jesus had saved them from alcoholism or drugs. It was pretty evident that something had happened in their lives. Again there was the singing. They called it praying in "tongues" but it sounded like a breeze in a forest that quickly increases to a real wind (but a melodious wind) and then, after a few minutes, disappears. I have walked in a forest and heard and felt such a wind. This, like that, was somehow strangely beautiful.

Just before the meeting ended someone asked for prayers for a six month old baby. We were told that the baby was born with some kind of speech defect and that the baby had never cried or ever uttered a sound since it was born. I was about 30 feet away from the baby as those in front prayed to Jesus that God heal this baby's vocal cords. Those in charge of the group placed their hands on the baby. The baby was certainly not making any sound at the time. The people behind the group leaders placed their hands on the shoulder of the person nearest to them and this continued until rather quickly all 300 of the people present were in physical contact with the baby as they prayed for a healing. It seemed the right thing to do so I placed my hand on the back of the person in front of me and prayed, along with everyone else, that God would heal that baby. Now I do not know what was wrong with the baby and I cannot absolutely say what transpired but shortly after all of us prayed that God would heal that baby's vocal box I heard that baby cry.I wondered if the power of the love of all those people had done it. I felt quite joyful myself and decided I had to know more.

At the third meeting someone explained about the blood sacrifices of the Hebrew Old Testament and how that was a precursor to the blood that Jesus shed for the sins of the world. Further explanation made it sound like silently claiming the blood of Jesus as a protection was like calling forth a force field of some kind though which a bullet could penetrate but not evil. It all seemed fascinating to me. I was hearing things I had never heard before and I was seeing things I had never seen before. I had always considered myself a Christian but someone showed me a passage in the Gospels where Jesus said that His followers would pray in new languages and that they would lay their hands upon the sick and they would recover. If I was a Christian how come I had never done either?

It was at that third prayer meeting in the month of May in the year that President Nixon resigned that I decided that I wanted what these people had. Again I stayed after the large meeting broke up and decided to attend one of the smaller meetings that were held in the various classrooms. I went to the workshop that seemed most appropriate. As a Christian I knew that I already had the Holy Spirit within my spirit but I had not received the Baptism of the Holy Spirit, the Baptism that John the Baptist mentioned when he spoke of Jesus saying, "I baptize with water but there is one who will come after me who will baptize with fire and the Holy Spirit." I wasn't sure what a baptism of fire meant but since no one mentioned it or looked burned I guessed that it was figurative language. I also asked a few questions as I observed a few individuals being prayed over. Someone said something that prompted me to ask, "What about re-incarnation?" "Oh!" "That's demonic!" someone else answered. "Do you believe in it?" I was asked.

Over the course of my lifetime I have had several dreams, all different from each other and different from any of the symbolic dreams I usually have. These dreams seemed to be little bits and pieces of something that was of a different order than ordinary dreams which can be pretty weird in themselves. In one I was a soldier attacking a village 3,000 years ago. In another I was sitting under a tree on top of a bluff overlooking a river. It was a beautiful place, a place I would certainly visit today if it were nearby. In my dream, however, I was an oriental and I was amazed, absolutely stunned, when a couple of ships sailed up the river. In my dream I could not even imagine what kind of ships these were. They looked as if they had come from another world. Of course, upon awakening, I, the dreamer, knew that the ships were typical European sailing vessels of a few centuries ago. This dream, especially, had a depth to it that I knew made it more than just a dream but I had no idea what until I read several books about Edgar Cayce, America's so-called sleeping prophet. The best of the lot was a book by James Bjornstad called TWENTIETH CENTURY PROPHECY and published by Bethany Fellowship. I even visited the organization in Virginia Beach that was founded to promote the teachings of Edgar Cayce. Needless to say Dr. Bjornstad was not convinced of the possibility of re-incarnation but I was. I have heard a major Christian preacher/writer say that a belief in Jesus and a belief in re-incarnation were incompatible but it certainly did not seem that way to me. God is Supreme. Even the dictionary says that. Being supreme He can do a lot more than man gives Him credit for doing. If He can give us the opportunity to fulfill some long desired goal or accomplishment then, in my experience, He is magnanimous enough to do so.I recall a Christian from a rather strict church asking me how I could believe in something as ridiculous as re-incarnation and I answered that it was no more ridiculous to believe in life before birth than it was to believe in life after death. The physical world and the spiritual world may intertwine but they are distinctly different. In the physical world it took close to seven years for the European Space Union to send a small robotic craft to Saturn's moon Titan but in the spiritual dimension such a trip would only take a fraction of a second as we count time.

In any event I answered truthfully that I did indeed believe that re-incarnation was a possibility and that we may indeed have more than one life experience. Several people were visibly upset by my answer. Someone suggested that I might have a demon affecting me or my thinking. They asked if they could pray over me (to drive it out I presumed). Since I certainly didn't want anything to do with a demon I agreed.They gathered around me. One person placed their hand on my head, as another hand went on my right shoulder and a third on my left shoulder and they all began praying, some in English and some in other languages that I had come to recognize as "tongues". All of a sudden I became a little apprehensive over the whole affair. Having learned in the previous meeting about the power of the blood of Jesus to protect me from evil, I claimed that protection from anything not of God that might be going on, including the prayers that were being said for me. The fear left and I felt good but I was not aware of any other change. I made a point of not mentioning re-incarnation again. The Catholic Church doesn't believe in re-incarnation nor does any Christian church for that matter. There are verses in the Bible that appealed to me in reference to what we call re-incarnation: "As you sow, so shall you reap," and "he who kills with a sword will be killed with a sword," and a few others. I felt that this was more than figurative language. What if it were actually true? We explain away so much in the Bible because it doesn't fit in with our mindset. Jesus told His own disciples that He had much to share with them but that they couldn't bear it yet. That has been explained by pointing out the terrible deaths that all but one of them had but what if He was referring to something else? Well, there is no need to speculate. We are all responsible for our own beliefs and actions. I believe those Muslim clerics in Afghanistan who have called for the death of the Muslim man who became a Christian 16 years ago are condemning themselves to the same fate. They are reminding us once again of their true colors. Their religion is one of hatred and death, murder and retribution. They, and only they, have the "truth" and everyone else must die. The god they worship is nothing like the God of Christians and Jews who said, "Come, and let us reason together." Their god is not the God who created the Universe or a God of Love. Their god says "worship me or my followers will kill you!" and that is why they are so filled with hatred for Christians and Jews. They are the "dark side of the force" as the movie STAR WARS would have it. Now, I'm not saying that every single one of the people who follow this god (because that is what they were born into) are evil, but some unquestionably are, and if we ever forget that fact or pretend it doesn't matter what "god" one worships, then WWIII is all but assured.

I have met only a few Christians who truly believe that Jesus is the Lord and who also believe in re-incarnation. A belief in re-incarnation, however, or a lack of belief in it is not going to keep anyone out of heaven whereas a sincere wholehearted rejection of Jesus and all He stands for will do so. I believe that as you sow so shall you reap! Jesus taught us not to even wish evil on our enemies, just the opposite of those who want to kill all who don't worship the god of the ancient Bedouin Arabs. The difference is the same as difference between what Jesus said, "Turn the other cheek," and what the leader of the popular cult followed by many Hollywood types has said, "We will destroy you" to some who have opposed his teachings.

I thanked those who prayed for me and I asked them how I could go about receiving the Baptism of the Holy Spirit. I was told that the way this group operated was to have a five week seminar, some biblical background and teaching in what this power was and basically what to expect. A new "Life in the Spirit" seminar was beginning the following week. Five more weeks! I wanted it then! I had already been coming for three weeks. A woman spoke up and suggested that I might want to consider the group that met in St. Mary's Church in Wappingers Falls. This was a much smaller group, about 25 people, led by a born-again Christian Catholic who was an engineer from IBM.

The group that met at St. Mary's at that time met on a different night than the group that met at St. Columba's, and I had made tentative plans to be elsewhere that night. For several months I'd been hearing about the value of meditation, that there was more to it than hippies sitting in a circle, burning incense, and chanting "OM." Some major corporations were even teaching their employees to meditate. Meditation has been proven to be healthy but at the time I did not know that Transcendental Mediation was actually a religion. I had, however, finally made contact with a group that was offering a free introductory lesson or seminar on TM on Friday night, June 4, 1974, at a local motel. I had missed the previous TM lecture a few months earlier and I really wanted to catch this one to see if it was something that could help me. However, I could not attend both the prayer meeting at St. Mary's and the lecture so I decided to do something that I did not usually do back then and that was to pray for specific direction and guidance. I don't remember how I got an answer but it was clear to me that the prayer meeting

was where I should go and that was where I went. It was one of the
best decisions of my life.

The group that met in St. Mary's Church was similar to the one I
had been attending at St. Columba's but considerably smaller. The
format of the meeting was similar as well.

People shared how they felt God was working with them or what
He was teaching them. They sang and they prayed in the different
languages that each of them had received when they were baptized
in the Holy Spirit. Personally I thought that the idea of receiving a
prayer language was great. I had studied Latin and Spanish in high
school and French in college and the idea of receiving a pray language that I didn't have to study appealed to me. Actually I didn't
do very well in any of the languages I attempted to study and because I enjoyed the company of my Chinese friends at the university
I thought that maybe Chinese would be more interesting. I was
responsible for convincing the authorities at the University of South
Carolina to establish the first "non-credit" course that they had ever
offered in Chinese. I even had to recruit an elderly retired Chinese
couple to teach the course. The wife was the daughter of a famous
Chinese educator and when she was a teenage student she had been
sort of an assistant to the famous American educator John Dewey. I
remember her telling me that Dewey would occasionally get an idea
or inspiration and get excited and run to a portable typewriter of
some sort and make a big production out of having to get it down on
paper quickly before he forgot it. The way she remembered Dewey
and the way she told the story, even with her heavy accent, was quite
humorous.

I dropped the course. Spanish and Latin were a cinch by comparison. I have been told that from that small beginning at USC,
however, has grown a complete department of Chinese studies.
Still, the idea that I could acquire a language, any language, with
which to pray - well, I was all for the idea. I even said a silent prayer
that I would get Chinese. I wouldn't know what I was praying when
I used my prayer language but I wouldn't have to worry about it
because the Bible says it would be God's Spirit praying through me
when I prayed. And I thought that the ability to pray in Chinese
might impress my Chinese friends! Of course it doesn't quite work
that way but I didn't know that then. I had picked up a copy of the
international best seller, PRISON TO PRAISE, (translated into 53
languages and with more than 90 printings), and that explained a

lot about the dimension of spirit in general and the ago old conflict between good and evil specifically.

This book and what I had seen in the last three and a half weeks had convinced me that there was a dimension to Christianity of which I was only dimly aware.

God has a tremendous sense of humor and that night in June when I was praying along with two dozen others, standing next to an Italian woman who was praying in an oriental dialect, and without anyone laying hands on me (the traditional and biblical method to receive the impartation of the Holy Spirit) I received my own Pentecostal experience or Baptism in the Holy Spirit. The experience goes by many names but for me it was very similar to what is mentioned in the Book of Acts (the first section of the Bible right after the gospels). I did not see tongues of fire come out of the sky but a light more brilliant than any I could imagine seemed to descend upon me and envelope me with what I, today, can say was pure love and pure joy and pure acceptance. I could not have said that at the time because I had no frame of reference with which to compare what I had just experienced. I only realized that I had been crying profusely when I observed how wet my hands were and that was exceeded by puzzlement over the fact that my hands were over my lips and it was then that I realized that I, too, was singing and praying in a spiritual language that I had never heard before. It was as if God had reached down and touched me, a speck of dust, on a planet that is a speck of dust, in a solar system that is relatively insignificant, in a galaxy of medium size, in a universe that is so large, with billions of other galaxies, as to be almost beyond belief and certainly beyond comprehension. If I had opened my eyes and suddenly found that I was no longer in the 20th Century but in the 30th it would have seemed completely normal. Instead when I opened my eyes I found that everyone was still singing and praying and I thought, "Well, if they can do it so can I," and I began praying again in my new prayer language. I had never felt so joyful in my entire life. I was shocked to hear myself say, "I know what she's saying" in the silence that followed the burst of prayer and praise that had just transpired. The Italian woman next to me smiled and the engineer who was not only the leader of the group but also the woman's husband said, "Oh, tell us, we've always wanted to know" or words to that effect. I opened my mouth to tell them but I had no words. I "felt" that Terry had been praying for me but whatever I thought I knew was gone. I felt so foolish that I didn't say anything else for the rest of the night and for those who knew me then, and how much I used to talk, that must have been a record.

For some reason I really wanted to read the Bible, and I read it, all 2,000 pages of it. More important was the fact that I understood much of what I had not understood before. I read a number of books about the experiences of others who had had a similar spiritual experience to my own. There were subtle changes in my behavior. I didn't talk as much. I listened more. Defending my ego became far less important. I did not realize how much I had changed until I, once again, visited South Carolina.

I was at my folk's home in Darlington and I called a friend on the telephone. Her husband had been our family lawyer for many years and it was he who answered the phone. When I told Benny that I had called to see if I could drop by for a visit he told me that his wife, Jeannyne, was not feeling well but he asked me to wait a minute while he consulted her. I could barely hear a conversation in the background and it seemed like more of a lengthy discussion but finally Benny returned to the phone and said I could drop by but that I might have to leave within 15 minutes because of the way Jeannyne was feeling. I agreed and drove over to their home, about a mile east of the town square and the courthouse which is often in the center of many small southern and mid-western towns that have been mostly by-passed by interstate highways and mass urbanization. The courthouse in Darlington is the fifth one to stand there in center of town.

Someone else was visiting the Greers at the time and we all had a wonderful visit that lasted not 15 minutes but well over two hours. Jeannyne had not seen me since I had received the Baptism of the Holy Spirit. In the final minutes before I departed she told me that when Benny first told her that it was me visiting my parents for a few days and that I wanted to drop by for a visit her first reaction, because of a long and exhausting day, was, "Oh no, I don't think I could put up with Richard tonight." She had relented but with the provision that I might have to leave after a very brief visit. "But praise God!" she added, "He is really working with you." It was true and we had all enjoyed the visit.

After visiting my parents I left South Carolina again but this time I was headed for Ohio, to visit my cousin Darlene who lived on a farm outside Kenton and who with her husband Bill operated a pet shop in Mansfield. The other reason my younger brother Francis and I were going to Ohio was because mom was treating us to a spiritual retreat at a Catholic retreat center in western Ohio. We enjoyed visiting our cousin and then we drove to the retreat center. There we learned some ancient Christian ways of meditative prayer that were far more effective than TM could ever be.In one I had sort of a vision quest and I experienced what might be called a waking dream. The spiritual director guided us just so far and then he let God and our subconscious mind take over. I was physically sitting in a chair with my eyes closed in a small conference room on an estate in a very flat section of western Ohio but suddenly my consciousness was by the shores of a beautiful lake surrounded by tall mountains. In a clearing not far from the shore I noticed a tent. I stuck my head inside and a young man in his thirties in flowing white robes was brewing some tea. I instantly knew it was Jesus and He invited me to have some tea. I accepted His offer. The flavor and delicacy of the tea was exquisite. "This is delicious," I exclaimed. Why I was so surprised at how good it was I do not know. "Why shouldn't it be?" Jesus replied, "I made it."

There should have been a thousand things on my mind, I thought later, from age old philosophical questions to personal "whys" but no thought surfaced to my head, my heart or my lips. I was thoroughly absorbed in the moment. I just sat there around the fire drinking this incredible tea and soaking it all in. Finally Jesus spoke again and said, "Come here often." And suddenly, as quickly as everything had appeared, it disappeared. I saw only what anyone would see if they closed their eyes, the inside of their eyeballs or nothing. I opened my eyes and found myself sitting in my chair at the retreat center near the Indiana border. Around me some participants were sitting quietly eyes wide open. One or two were quietly crying. Some were still in silent prayer or meditation but all had a story to tell, although some chose not to tell it, of where they had been and what they had seen. Many had seen Jesus and spoken to Him as I had.

Alas, I must confess, the next time I meditated on this beautiful place I pictured a magnificent log home across the water's inlet from where I had first seen Jesus in the tent. The house was mine but it caught fire and burned to the ground. The imagery frightened me and it was years before I visualized that place again. Today I think that the log home represented my ego, that part of us that must be burned away before we can find ultimate spiritual fulfillment. No wonder I was frightened. At the time I thought of the beautiful log home and the fire and I marveled at my audacity in imagining that I had a beautiful home while Jesus had only a tent. At the time I did not know or remember that God has said that he would not deny us any good thing, even a log home, if that is our hearts desire.

For years I lived in an attic apartment on Taylor Avenue in the City of Poughkeepsie that had as it major source of heat six fire-bricks elevated over one burner of a gas stove. On top of the fire-bricks was a large pan of water with a lid on it that provided just the right amount of humidity to balance the heat. This was a somewhat primitive arrangement and probably some would consider it dangerous but we were always careful and never had a problem. The landlord did not charge us as much for the apartment as most rooms rented for and I lived there for years. Over that period of time there were four successive owners of the building and the last one to purchase the building liked the apartment so much that he decided that he wanted to live there himself and we had to move. Of course this was in a section of Poughkeepsie that was close to more undesirable areas and sometimes in the stillness of the night I could hear occasional gunfire from the criminal element. One day I purchased the Poughkeepsie Journal and there on the front page was a grisly murder that had taken place right on Taylor Avenue (Avenue was somewhat of a pretentious name as the street was a dead end street and only two blocks long). I continued to read until I got to the address and then, somewhat in shock, said out loud to no one but me, "THAT'S WHERE I LIVE!" Denise, who had lived on the ground floor, had been murdered by her live-in boy friend. I had offered her a ride just the day before. Apparently they both had been taking drugs and she was wearing a fashionable tie and the argument began over who was the man of the house and it escalated from there. The same guy who kindly offered to bury my dog when she was hit by the pick-up truck also tried to bury Denise in the same place. I didn't know all the facts of the case, only what I read in the paper. I was sound asleep on the third floor at the time and hadn't heard a thing. I did find some literature from one of America's largest religious cults on top of a pile of trash when Denise's apartment was being cleaned out and I wondered if the evil associated with that had been a factor. Eventually I had to move and I wanted to have more than a tent and more than a log home but I would learn to be grateful for whatever I had. The idea of any kind of house that was my own seemed rather appealing after having to leave my place of residence after so many years. I even had to change my phone number and I had had the same number for 25 years.

Back in Ohio, in addition to visiting my cousin Darlene and experiencing the spiritual retreat, I had another fascinating experience. During my time there I had one of the most dramatic encounters that I have ever had with the "dark side."We stayed at my cousin's farmhouse outside Kenton for a few days and while in town we had heard talk of a group that sounded Christian from some sources and more like a cult from others. Since the group was supposed to have been Catholic in origin I wanted to ascertain that it was sound and that the town's people were not being conned "in the name of the Lord." Since I had heard both good and bad reports on this group I decided that the local newspaper ought to have the facts on the situation.I have found that while I don't always agree with the interpretation or the slant of the news by the media that some journalists are more interested in the "facts" than in an unstated agenda and I found one of these. The information on the place that I will call "the farm" (the may have called it that too) that I obtained from the local press gave me the impetus to continue my search for the truth.

Miles from town, out in the country, we located "the farm." We had heard that a number of Catholics who desired a more spiritual life had joined together, sold their homes, and as a group, had purchased a large farm. Across the country a number of communities like this had formed and some wonderful life-changing events were happening to their members and to those who were exposed to them. Perhaps this group was similar and the negative reports were merely jealousy. I intended to find out.

My brother Francis was with me when we located this perfectly manicured, impeccably clean farm. The cold was biting like the invisible scorpions in the Book of Revelation that plague the planet earth before the end of time. It was late autumn but I wondered if the cold was something more than just the temperature falling.

The farmhouse looked deserted. I looked in one room that I could see into and there did not appear to be any furniture of any kind. We knocked on the door to no avail. Then we walked around the big farmhouse toward the buildings in back of it. Nothing physical was out of place. I had never seen a working farm, if this was one, as clean as this.

I yelled out "hello" a couple of times but the only answer was the wind as it charged through the nearby trees on its eternal journey to nowhere. "Well, I guess no one's here," I said to my brother and turned to leave. I think we were both surprised to find a woman who appeared to be in her 40's walking towards us from the direction of what had appeared to be an empty house.

Who spoke first I do not remember but I introduced myself and my brother. "What is this place?" I asked. The woman said that she was sister so-and-so and gave me an answer that was not quite an answer. Like Saint-Exupery's Little Prince, I wouldn't let go of it and upon further questioning I was told a story similar to what I had heard in town: a group of Catholics who had experienced the same touch of God as the 120 in the upper room in the Book of Acts had joined together and purchased this place to live close to God and the good earth. It sounded "ok" but there was still something...I couldn't put my finger on it. This former nun, or so she said, told me that they (I saw no physical evidence of any others) provided free baby sitting, a sort of day camp, for the harried residents of Lima, Ohio, and other nearby communities. As she added that the children often played in a wooded grove that I could see in the distance, the hair stood up on the back of my neck. A cold blast of air blew through me and I had the instantaneous thought "Indian Burial Grounds." It was such an incredible off-the-wall thought to come from nowhere that I knew that it had not come from nowhere. My intuition (make that Intuition with a capital "I") was telling me the source of what some might call the negative energy I was feeling. Others would just plain call it evil.

I knew enough from history to know that not all the Native American tribes were composed of just, honest, people. Some of them were unquestionably evil even to the practice of human sacrifice. Still, there was something else. Being a relatively new Christian I enthusiastically said something about Jesus. As I said His name warmth that was noticeable welled up within me. Immediately the woman's voice changed. Gone was the pleasant smile. Gone was the friendliness.

"You must go beyond Jesus," she shouted at me. Now as a Christian I believe what Jesus told his own apostles, "He who sees me, sees the Father, for I am in Him and He is in me." A bucket full of ocean water is the same biologically, chemically, and physically, as the ocean itself and Jesus spoke of Himself as Living Water that He would give to all who thirst for truth and righteousness, if they humbled themselves enough to ask. It was not automatic. I was so surprised at the now distorted ugliness on the face of the woman who was now shouting at me I meekly asked, "What's beyond Jesus?" Now she was really screaming at me, "The Father!"

I could feel a love within me, more than my own, for this poor messed up woman. A rage beyond anything I had ever seen except in a few movies about patients in a mental hospital now filled her. Her eyes were filled with a blackness that could have frozen a birdsong. I was at peace yet I was experiencing one of the strangest sensations of my life. If someone had asked me before that cold autumn afternoon, "Can you feel words?" I would have answered, "No, of course not!" Words can affect your feelings and make you happy or sad depending on who says them and what is said but you cannot feel them or so I believed at the time. Yet standing in front of me was a wild-eyed raving woman screaming at me as loud as she could and I could feel her words bouncing off of me. These words (I remember only nine of them) weren't hitting me exactly but I could feel them. They were being deflected by an invisible shield of some sort that was six or eight inches in front of my physical body. They weren't hurting me but I could feel each and every word as they bounced off a sort of "extended" me that was six or eight inches in front of the "me" that I could see. I could only surmise that it was something like a spiritual "force field" and I would not want to know what it felt like without that shield in front of me (actually I do know).

An hour later if I had been a "fair witness" as in the classic science fiction novel, "Stranger in a Strange Land," in a court of law I could not have repeated or remembered even the gist of all this woman was yelling at me, so surprised was I at being able to "feel" her verbal attack. Then she shouted nine words at me that I will never forget. With a ghastly face, twisted in ugliness, I heard this poor unfortunate creature scream, "I don't know whether you're the Christ or not!"

I was dumbfounded. I could almost hear Rod Serling say, "You have now entered The Twilight Zone." Actually I'd been there for 15 minutes, now it was time to leave. Another blast of cold wind brought with it the thought that a cup of coffee and a piece of pie would sure seem mighty good. Didn't I see a crossroads diner about three miles back?

As I began to think these thoughts the woman in front of me quieted down until she was pleasantly standing before me once again. I was still as I had been a few minutes before minus the loving warmth and concern I had for her but the transformation of this misguided cult member was so tremendous that I have wished more than once that I could have gotten it all on film: from pleasant, to raving maniac, to pleasant again, all in 10 or 15 minutes.

"Well, we have to leave," I told her.

"Do come again sometime," she replied with a pleasant smile on her face, seemingly oblivious to her behavior of the previous few minutes.

"Not likely!" I thought to myself.

It was my first wide-awake encounter with what I believe was an evil spirit, demon, fallen angel, alien, or whatever noun you are most familiar with in this regard. It was not my last. As I began to write the above words about this time and place in my life all of a sudden I experienced a piercing headache, much as I get when I eat aged cheese and chocolate on the same day (I enjoy both items and can eat them with no difficulty but not in the same day or I experience an excruciating headache that time alone will diminish). It was perhaps the fourth time in 25 years that this particular and fortunately rare type of headache tried to literally attach itself to me. Recognizing it for what it was I mentally or spiritually demanded that "in the name of Jesus, leave" and as suddenly as the pain flared up, it left. I wish it were possible to get rid of every headache so easily.

Before I left the area I was able to warn some members of the local Catholic Church that under no circumstances should they let their children go out to the "farm," free babysitting or no free baby sitting.

While visiting there in Kenton, Ohio, I noticed a sign that appealed to me and I decided to attend the church service that the sign advertised. It was a pleasant and decidedly Christian congregation and after singing and praying and towards the end of the meeting someone asked if there was anyone in attendance that had not been there before. I raised my hand and some of the people were genuinely amazed that a Catholic would set foot in their church. I explained that like them I had received the Baptism of the Holy Spirit, Jesus had set me free, and that I no longer felt bound by man-made restrictions as to denominations. If God were present in a church or group of people His eternal and now internal witness would make me aware of it. They were my brothers and sisters by whatever name.

The minister of the church shared with me how he had been a Methodist and having become convinced that the Baptism of the Holy Spirit was meant for always, not just for the early church centuries ago, sought this blessing and power, received it, and was promptly asked to leave because at the time his denomination did not accept this teaching as part of their theology. A few years after that I met a Catholic priest who told me that he received the Baptism of the Holy Spirit in 1941, but he said, "Back then you didn't tell anyone!"

I believe it was from the people in the church in Kenton that I learned that the cult at the farm had been founded by a defrocked priest who one night told his congregation that henceforth they must follow him! Over half the people left that night never to return. Others who sought to follow Jesus left soon thereafter leaving behind all their earthly wealth which had been converted into the farm itself. Years later someone told me that those who left, although they had lost all their worldly goods, had with God's help, formed a true Christian community, and that it was thriving.

24. The X-Files

I left Ohio and headed back to New York. I still had (and have) much to learn. I continued in my sales job at the home food service and I continued to attend the large prayer meeting at St. Columba's as well as the smaller one at St. Mary's.I learned much but I could not quite fit into the fundamentalist mold that many of these wonderful people embraced. I had learned that Jesus was who He said He was, and I had seen first hand the power of evil. I have had run-ins with members of most of the major cults in America, the largest of which are listed in the current edition of revised classic "The Kingdom of the Cults." I discovered that the United States has become the breeding ground for religious cults. There are well over 3,000 separate groups and hundreds of people claiming to be "the chosen one," or the "Messiah" or "Christ for this age."This, of course, is one of the signs that Jesus said would happen before the end of the world, (others claiming to be Him). I have been in the presence of evil and I have listened to the experiences of others.

One night I had an appointment to explain the home food service to a high-ranking official in Federal Law Enforcement. This man and his associates had cracked some big international cases and I had read about some of his amazing exploits, which were reported in the major newspapers. He was sort of an Elliot Ness or Melvin Purvis of the 1970's. He was a Christian but he had not experienced the Baptism of the Holy Spirit himself. He told me that his mother had received this great blessing and that she was praying for him (thank God for praying mothers). We talked more that night about spiritual meat than the kind I was paid for selling. Although the food service did not fit their family's lifestyle, I enjoyed my visit. At one point, I mentioned the reality of evil and the agent who was as nice a person as you would want to meet told me of one of his experiences that was not in the newspapers. The experience could easily have fit into the "X-Files." Perhaps his experience was part of the inspiration for the "X-Files."

The exact details I do not remember but that is just as well. What I do remember is that this agent and his men had been working on a case for 2 years. He was only 24 hours away from making an arrest in an international drug case when his superior blew up at him, called him incompetent (which he most assuredly was not), and ordered him off the case. Whether the operation was to be shut down or someone else was to take over the case I do not remember. The next day, however, the agent told me, he was called back into his superior's office where he received an apology. His boss apologized and said, "I don't know what came over me."

As I drank my coffee, I could see that the agent in front of me was still as surprised to have received the apology as he had been at being railed at on the previous day. "Neither I nor any of my men had done anything to deserve such a condemnation," and then he added, "and it's unheard of that a Washington bureaucrat would apologize to some one under him."

The operation continued as planned and an arrest was made. "I've arrested a lot of men in my day," the agent told me, "all of them criminals, but this arrest was different. This felon was the most evil person I had ever encountered." The agent proceeded to tell me that the indictments on this individual were such that if convicted he would be in prison for the rest of his life. I seem to recall that some of the crimes this individual was suspected of having committed were truly horrendous and to hideous to repeat here. The criminal was placed in a secure prison. Three locked doors and at least two armed guards had to be crossed in order to reach this criminal (there may have been three guards).

"When we went to get this guy we found his cell empty. There was no evidence of an escape. All the doors were locked. The armed guards saw nothing and heard nothing. The only thing we found in his cell was evidence of a satanic ceremony."

I thought of what is called spontaneous human combustion, which has been known about for centuries but which has never been entirely explained to my satisfaction, but I was told that there was not even evidence of that, just some voodoo paraphernalia and nothing else.

"The people in Washington don't want to hear about anything like this," the agent told me, "They want answers."

I could see where the obvious answer would be unpalatable to those who took down the Ten Commandments from the walls of elementary and public high schools across the nation. We wink at pornography and wonder why so many women and children are raped. Even the Supreme Court, supposedly the wisest judges in the land, says that child pornography is ok as long as it is only life-like computer graphics and not real children, and then we wonder at the FBI statistics that show that thousands of children are abducted each year in these United States. Only occasionally does a high profile case catch the medias attention like Elizabeth Smart, a case that drove me to pray, but there are many more. We are in a real war with evil and so often evil wins because we do not even recognize it for what it is. Hard core pornography is one of the biggest industries in the United States, bringing in more money each year ($57 Billion) than the combined revenues of ABC, CBS, NBC and all of the professional football, baseball and basketball franchises combined. This hard-core pornography doesn't even include mainstream movies or advertising that features semi-naked men and women. Addiction to pornography is one of the major causes of divorce in this country, how many millions I do not recall, but the percentages are staggering.

When God created the world and all that is in it He said that it was good! At least that is what is recorded in the Bible, which I happen to believe is really the inspired word of God and not just history or poetry or even mythology, as some believe. Therefore, there is nothing wrong with creation. The fault must lie within the human heart. Mankind has been rejecting God since Adam and Eve. When the ancient Israelites continued to reject God even after all that God did for them through Moses God sent them prophets. I was always taught that many of them were killed by the very people they were sent to help. As a lesson, the Israelites were without a nation for twenty-seven hundred years but God promised that He would not abandon them and that He would gather them together again as a nation. "Whoever heard of such a thing," said the prophet Isaiah 27 centuries ago, "a nation born in a day?" That day was May 15, 1948, when in one day a nation that had not existed in almost three millennia suddenly came to life again. In my lifetime, this and three dozen other ancient promises in the Bible have been fulfilled for the first time since they were written. The mathematical probability of all of them happening in one lifetime is off the scale. We are living in the times that the Bible spoke of so long ago. This century should be the most incredible one yet!

Although modern Israel is only 58 years old, there are those who have dedicated their lives to its destruction. In doing so, they are fighting God Himself. They cannot win. This does not mean that every action or decision by the Jews in Israel today is good or just or even the best one for those involved but it does mean that those who are fighting Jews or opposing them just because they are Jews are ultimately on the losing side.

I do not know the solution to the on-going problem that exists between the sons of Hagar and the sons of Sarah. I do feel that if a tribe of Native Americans decided they wanted New Jersey back (New Jersey is of similar proportions to Israel in size and shape, just slightly smaller) and they started blowing up pizza parlors, shopping malls, and wedding parties, that we would not tolerate it. At least I don't think we would. God, besides being a God of Love, is a God of Justice. The only thing He hates is evil. The random killing of civilians is evil no matter who does it and ultimately is useless and counter-productive. The only thing that I can do is pray for both the Palestinians and the Israelis. God is no respecter of persons. All who seek Truth, Justice, and His will are pleasing to Him. God created mankind and He is for us all. His heart rejoiced as did mine at the would-be suicide bomber (a young woman) who couldn't go through with her task because she began to identify with the young mothers and children who would be killed if she killed herself and them with the bomb she was carrying into Israel in the spring of 2002. This young woman was someone special, someone more spiritually mature than those around her. She was beginning to understand. I prayed for her also. Although it is little comfort to those whose loved ones have been killed by suicide bombers the persons doing the killing are condemning themselves. The law of the Universe is that they must then experience all the horror they are inflicting on others. Why do you think Jesus said to bless your enemies, not curse them? You might have to kill them if they are trying to kill you but don't curse them or hate them.

Two generations ago Jesus told a woman in England (He spoke to her inner mind or spirit when she was praying to Him) that when she saw how wonderfully her prayers had been answered, that she would deeply regret, that she did not pray more (GOD CALLING edited by A.J. Russell). Who can read the daily newspaper or watch the nightly news broadcast without praying if they understand the power of prayer. It has been my experience that anything that concerns us concerns God even more because He loves us.

"You are trivializing God," a Hindu Brahman told me once after I had mentioned that I had prayed and asked God to help me with my hobby. "Then why did He answer my prayer?" I replied, but my friends hands shot up to cover his ears. He did not want to hear more because it conflicted with his worldview. I had only seen that once before, a person actually holding their ears so that they would not be able to hear what I was saying about Jesus. A woman I had worked with in IBM once told me that eventually she would be God. When I heard that, I was truly speechless.I could not think of a single thing to say. I had no idea that she thought so highly of herself and it suddenly dawned on me why I had such a difficult time getting along with her. I had tried to share with her on a couple of occasions, how in answer to prayer, I had been led to go to a distant city and how I had materially benefited by making the trip. Since she had apparently never experienced anything like that, she simply could not believe it.I have met others who worship Deepak Chopra of Hollywood and believe that he is God. I noticed with interest that when he was on Larry King Live in 2005 he was espousing the idea that the age of nations (invented by God according to the Bible) is past and that we need to unite into a one-world government to save the environment. Many Christians believe that this will be the battle cry of that wonderfully charismatic problem solver who will prove to be the most evil man the world has ever known, the Anti-Christ. Working to stop polluting the world is worthwhile but not at the expense of freedom. This sounds good on paper but don't fall for it. There will be no room for any individual rights in a one-world government. Of course, before that happens we will need a worldwide financial crisis to pave the way for a new world currency or at least some kind of worldwide money to replace the disgraced dollar but I'm getting ahead of myself. We still have some time left before all this happens, years or decades I do not know. It is going to be interesting and I do not say such things to scare people but to prepare them.

Most people who believe in God believe he is concerned with only big things.Why would he bother to help me find a fine wine or a rare die variety? For the same reason that he does the big God-like things, strange, as it may seem, unreasonable as it is, simply put, He loves us!

Those of us who have been blessed with faith in God know that He loves us. If you do not have such faith - pray - ask for it and keep on praying, no matter how long it takes, until you have it. Most people who believe in God believe that He resides up in heaven somewhere but Christians also believe that God lives within their spirit. I have no special power. There are those who are smarter than I am, those who are more educated, and those who are better looking. I made the decision, however, to ask the same Spirit that Jesus promised His followers nearly two thousand years ago that He would send to those who asked, to come and live in my spirit. That gives me an access to God that even some who believe in His existence do not know they can have. That does not make me "good." Jesus, Himself, objected when people called Him "good." "There is One who is good," He said, "our Father in Heaven." I believe it was that Spirit within me that so inflamed the woman in Ohio, even though, ultimately, God was her Father as well, even if she chose not to follow Him.

Forgive me for being old-fashioned (if that is what it is) but I cannot accustom myself to thinking of God as He/She anymore than I can the "new" term B.C.E. in place of B.C. For more than a thousand years, the Western World has divided time by the birth of Jesus Christ, A.D. (Anno Domini) meaning in the year of Our Lord, and B.C. (meaning Before Christ). Only in the last two decades as we move towards a more Godless society and substitute man as the measure of all things has B.C. been changed to B.C.E. (Before the Common Era). What is common today and for the last two thousand years that was not common before the birth and sacrifice of Jesus, is grace, the forgiveness of sins, the fact that all men and women can now have a personal relationship with the Living God, who is God and not a pretender, that through the acceptance of God's great gift of Life we can have Eternal Life and not just eternal existence, or worse yet, eternal death, well, that is all true but I don't think that is what the inventors of the term B.C.E. had in mind.

I believe that God in all His glory is beyond our comprehension. I believe He created the vastness of the Universe and all that is in it. That, too, is beyond our comprehension.

God is neither male nor female. He is pure Spirit. However, if God chooses to call Himself, "Our Father" then who am I to deny "Him" the right to do so. Is God politically incorrect? He is God, the Supreme Being. I am not! Neither is my former co-worker, nor any other who walks the face of the earth, though many claim to be.

It is true that the Bible says that when we see God as He is we will be like Him, but being like someone and being that someone are two entirely different things. I once went to a traveling concert and one singer particularly caught my eye. I kept thinking that I knew her but since this group was from another state I knew that to be highly unlikely. Still she seemed so familiar. I must know her from somewhere, but where? The music was truly inspirational, Christian songs from different cultures from around the world. Suddenly it dawned on me that this person was a dead ringer for Jennifer Love Hewitt one of my favorite movie stars. I inquired and found out that this person was considered somewhat of a snob by those who knew her because she did indeed look like Miss Hewitt. Now as far as I can tell, never having met her in person, Miss Hewitt is one of the least snobbish of all the people in Hollywood. Miss Hewitt's appearance is an asset to her. To the person who looked so much like her that she could have made television commercials, it was a hindrance. The point is that being like someone is not being that person. In South America there is a distinguished psychiatrist who is of the opinion that the most common mental illness is the delusion that we human beings can be God. Sorry, but that job is already taken! That we have the potential to become like God through the power of Jesus and His Holy Spirit, well, that is what Christianity is supposed to be all about.For Christians that is the goal, to be like Jesus, to have His Love, to show His compassion, to share His Joy, to be His brothers and sisters, "adopted" into the Kingdom of God, but we are not supposed to be trying to do this on our own, using only our own abilities and power or through rituals and rules. That is what the cults do.

The Bible is fascinating, for what it says and for what it does not say, for what it hints at and for what it loudly proclaims. "God is Love!" Jesus said once (He probably said it many times), and "No one who turns to Me will I ever turn away!" That even includes an axe murderer like Karla Faye Tucker of Texas. Stoned on drugs she killed an adulteress when she was a teenager. Over the decades she spent in prison she had a true conversion (one of my brothers is a corrections officer and he tells me that there are some who "get religion" hoping it will get them an earlier parole). The first woman to be executed in Texas in over a hundred years was a changed woman. I could see this in her spirit. So could my Hindu Brahman friend. She wasn't even a Catholic but the Pope could see it. So did Rev. Billy Graham. Both pleaded for her to continue her life in prison but to no avail. She would have been a wonderful asset to the Texas prison system but "an eye for an eye," it says in the Old Testament, and that is apparently still the law in Texas.

Karla Faye Tucker had no fear of dying. She didn't believe that she had been forgiven; she knew it! She had discovered God's great

Love. The State of Texas didn't forgive her, but God did. What a wonderful world this would be if more ordinary people of every race, creed, and denomination, and party, could also discover the great truth that Karla Faye Tucker discovered (without having to go to prison, of course).

25. Friends

I did my best to share what I had discovered with my dearest friends. Many of them became interested enough to seek out this seemingly new but actually very old experience of Christianity, some right away, some over the years. It is my nature to share the good things I've discovered with others, whether it be a good book, a really funny cartoon or an excellent movie. How could I not tell my best friends that God was knowable, not just the disinterested source of the ancient organic molecules in space from which life may have arisen but a Father who loves us dearly and cares about our day-to-day lives, and that we can know Him and have a personal relationship with Him.

I shared what Christians call the "Good News" with Edouard and Sabine, two French nationals, and among my dearest friends. They had lived in Africa for many years and returned to the United States in 1973 when their daughter Quitterie was born. They lived inside the Washington, D.C. beltway off of Connecticut Avenue where they rented the home of a Major General while he was stationed in Europe. I had visited them there several times and when I experienced my own spiritual awakening I wanted to share with them what I had learned, although in actual fact, it was not that much. I felt, as I often do, that a good book could say it better, so while I was at the religious retreat in Ohio, I looked for a book that might better explain the nature of this spiritual experience.

There were many excellent books on the subject and after praying about picking out a good one I selected one that told about the beginnings of the Charismatic Renewal within the Catholic Church since my friends are Catholic. The book told about lives that were changed for the better when ordinary Catholics, hungry for a deeper relationship with God, sought out this age old experience of God's power. I purchased two copies of the book, one for myself. I did not wait but sent one of the books to my friends as soon as I could. It was the first time in my life that I ever sent someone a book that I myself had not read. When I finally read the book I thought it was good, but not that good. Based on reading it I would never have chosen it on my own. It seemed to lack the dramatic fire of a book like PRISON TO PRAISE which has helped millions but the book I had sent my friends was just what was needed to spark an interest in what God was doing in some of His people.

I had met Sabine for the first time nine years before at the Thomas More Center on Green Street just two doors down from the campus at the University of South Carolina.

She was a graduate student who taught French while working on her Master's Degree. Her future husband was studying hydrology at the University of Arizona and the following year they were married in that very same Catholic Student Center or rather the chapel behind it. Sabine read the book I gave her and I was greatly relieved that it was more meaningful to her than it had been to me. When I asked her what she thought of the book I distinctly remember that she said, "It sounds wonderful, if it's true!"

Sabine started to attend a weekly prayer meeting in Gaithersburg, Maryland, where she enrolled in one of the first five-week-long "Life-In-The-Spirit-Seminars" that were held there. After the seminar the participant was "prayed over" with an actual "laying on of hands" as was done over nineteen centuries ago. Prayers were said and the person wishing to receive the "fullness of the spirit" acknowledged that they were a sinner (only one person who ever walked the face of this planet wasn't) and they asked God to forgive their sins, believing He would do so if they asked. The participants also acknowledged that Jesus was the One specifically sent by God to take the penalty for their sins upon Himself and that His death on the cross fully paid for those sins if they accepted Him as God's Messiah. They also asked God to fill them with His Precious Holy Spirit. The proof of the acceptance of this great gift of the Holy Spirit was usually, but not always, indicated by the newfound ability to pray in a new language that the recipient did not possess previously. This is all mentioned in several places in the New Testament but it is usually explained away or simply not believed.

My friend went through the "Life-In-The-Spirit-Seminar" up to the very finale and experienced exactly nothing. Sabine was, to say the least, disappointed. Shortly after the seminar, together with her husband and children, they all went on a family vacation to the ocean. The moon was high in the sky. It was late at night and everyone was fast asleep in the tent except Sabine. The campfires ashes had long since grown cold but the fire of the Spirit burned in her heart. The temperature was neither warm nor cool but pleasantly unnoticeable. Sabine left the tent and went for a solitary walk along the eastern shore. The only other sound was the constant beat of the waves crashing against the coastline.

Wondering why she had not received what the New Testament calls the "gift" of praying in tongues, when others at the seminar had, when many others in the book I had sent her had, when I had, Sabine prayed. "God," she said, "I want the Baptism of the Holy Spirit with the gift of tongues." Again she prayed, "I really want this experience that Richard brought to my attention and which you have blessed him with."

In the Bible it says that God can give us more than we can ask though this may take some time to see. That is what He did for my friend and she did not have to wait another night. I had had a glorious life changing experience in the months before but it had lasted perhaps a minute or two, certainly no more than three or four as we count time. It was a glimpse of eternity, a few seconds in the presence of God's great Love, a short non-physical journey outside of time as we know it, a momentary visit into a state of timelessness, but the truth of the matter was that no more than a few minutes passed when I received this blessing from God like millions of others before me. Sabine also had a glorious experience, beyond the space-time-continuum, beyond the ability of mere words to convey. God touched her in the same way as He has touched millions now living but when her consciousness returned to its normal resting place and she became aware again of days and hours and minutes, and earth and sky, she was quite surprised to discover that she was praising God in a previously unknown language and that the brightness of the moon had been superseded by the rising sun on the eastern horizon. Six hours, as we count time, had passed.

Some people experience very little. Some quiet individuals who have been Christians for a long time in a denomination that hasn't taught them about the possibility of having their own Pentecostal experience have on occasion just started praying with a new joy and in a new language when they are prayed over. God is not as obtrusive as some of His people and He would not violate the personality of anyone. Of course, there are others who have such an outstanding experience that I could no more explain it with words than the astronomer portrayed by actress Jodie Foster could explain what she saw and felt in the movie CONTACT as she traveled beyond space and time for what was less than a minute in one reality and 18 hours in another.

I was not aware of any great change in my friend after her spiritual experience. There was more of a sparkle in her eye and she had more patience but I have noticed these two traits in many who have been blessed by the Holy Spirit in this way, me included.

In 1975 I attended the third Catholic Charismatic Conference in Atlantic City, N.J. This was before the gambling casinos moved in and changed the nature of the area which had been a family vacation spot much like Myrtle Beach, S.C. is today. It was an awesome experience to be surrounded by tens of thousands of born-again baptized in the Holy Spirit Catholics. Just their normal conversation sounded like the roar of a mighty river. One of the guest speakers was Ruth Carter Stapleton of Fayetteville, N.C. She spoke on the subject of inner healing (emotional or spiritual healing) versus the more obvious physical healing. I was quite impressed with her and purchased her book on the subject. I liked it so much I wrote and told her so. We began a correspondence, an exchange of half a dozen letters over the following year. In one handwritten letter Ruth wrote, "I also had the opportunity to help my brother, Jimmy, in his campaign. Long ago I promised him I'd do all I could to help him in his efforts in the political life to which he has been called. This is an emotionally demanding activity as well as often physically exhausting. Please pray that I may have the strength needed for the activities that lie immediately before me." Of course I did pray for her and for him and Ruth's activities, her ministry, was beyond what most people would have been capable of doing in the days and months ahead. From that point on her letters were typed and the newspapers kept me informed about her incredibly busy activities.

I recall, especially, when I read the letter mentioned above, that I thought, "How sweet, her brother is probably running for mayor of Fayetteville." Imagine my surprise when someone told me that her brother was Jimmy Carter, who of course, was running for the office of president of the United States! I did not make the connection because Ruth always signed her letters just "Ruth" and her printed envelopes, personal in size, were from Ruth Stapleton and not Ruth Carter Stapleton. It was because of Ruth that I voted for her brother, and I am sure that there were others who voted for him because they were impressed with her. Before Ruth's brother was even elected president her first book on inner healing had already gone through three printings. Her workshops on inner healing carried her to Florida, Tennessee, Alabama, and New Jersey. After President Carter's election Ruth's ministry carried her around the world. She was quite concerned over Christians who were daily being murdered by communists, Muslim extremists, and others. Even today in the 21st Century, in the neighborhood of a thousand Christians per day are being killed for their faith in Jesus. From China to Arabia, East Timor to Africa, more people are dying for their faith in Jesus than were ever killed by lions in Rome's arenas. The forces of evil don't care what God you worship as long as it's not the God of Judaism or Christianity. The so-called veneer of civilization is very thin indeed.

I have wondered if the "emotionally demanding" and "physically exhausting" schedule of which Ruth spoke were a contributing factor to the cancer that claimed her life. I was shocked to discover that the cancer had killed her but I had yet to learn that one of God's answers to prayer is "No." I also had little grasp of the fact that although God might bless us with a token of His love He is more concerned with the big picture which He alone can see.

It was because I needed inner healing, the accumulated scars of a lifetime, that I was attracted to Ruth Stapleton's ministry. In addition to her books on the subject I read similar books by others like Francis McNutt. Such books went beyond psychiatry because they dealt with the spirit, a dimension that psychiatry ignores to its own detriment. I know I was changed for the better but it would be difficult, even today, to be more specific. I began to see things that I had not seen before. I discovered that behind most of anger is fear and even Christians are frequently affected by fear, seeing it as an ally and not recognizing that it is really an enemy. Perhaps hellfire and brimstone worked well in Jonathan Edwards's day in Colonial times but today it often turns off the lonely and the sick and the dispossessed. Some people simply could not believe in a hell worse than what they are already living. Try telling the suicide bombers who believe that their god is going to reward them for the atrocities they commit and that what really awaits them will be far worse than what they leave behind and they will simply dismiss it out of hand. Those who use fear to attract people to God seldom succeed.

One night in the winter of 1975-1976 after the prayer meeting in St. Columba's I looked across the crowded hallway and saw someone I had never seen before yet someone I seemed to instantly recognize. At least a dozen people stood between me and Diana (not her real name) and yet she stood out as clearly as if a spotlight were shining on her. So intense was my feeling of recognition that I pushed through the crowd and somehow thought of something to say. We hit it off right away and it was as if we had known each other for years. We were a lot alike, even our birthdays were the same, although we were born in different years. Our personalities clicked in a way I had not experienced before. Once I had an odd dream in which we were twins during the Roman Empire.

Diana told me that she was separated from her husband so I did not think of her in a romantic way, at least not at first. She came from what had been a good sized family but tragedy had befallen several of her brothers and they had all died from accidents, murder or other unusual causes. Diana even had to identify the bodies of a couple of her brothers when her parents were unable to go to a distant state to do so. She had been married but her husband preferred to find his sexual fulfillment outside of marriage and no woman should have to endure that, not Karen Blixen, who wrote her memoir, "Out of Africa" under the name of Isak Dinesen, nor my newfound friend. A movie was made from that memoir, and it was excellent.

Dinesen's ne'er-do-well husband Bror Blixen-Fineche had given her syphilis from which she suffered the rest of her life but Diana was not in danger of this as the beings her husband chose to consort with were not physical. Being a student of psychology I had heard of people who thought that they were having sex with non-physical beings, aliens from UFOs and such like, but it never occurred to me that it could actually happen. "He has sex with demons, evil spirits" Diana bluntly told me once when I asked her for about the third time why she had left her husband. I certainly could not fault her for wanting to get away from a situation like that. Her problem was beyond my range of experience. I was not a psychiatrist, not even a psychologist. I could think of little to suggest except to recommend that Diana pray for her husband and she was already doing that. I never met him but it came as no surprise when they eventually divorced. I recently read that over a third of all divorces in this country involve internet pornography and that is only about one step removed from having sex with aliens.

Diana and I enjoyed each others company and we spent a lot of time together. She was a really fine person and it was difficult for me to fathom how she had come through so much tragedy with such a kind and gentle spirit. She was so normal that she was a living testimony to God's love and healing power. I'm sure we ate out together but I don't remember doing so. I do remember some very long talks and few day trips where Diana actually came along with me on my sales presentations, once all the way to Matamoras, Pennsylvania (about 60 miles). Diana told me that she had once gone flying in a sailplane that was launched from an airfield not far from there and that, like hot-air ballooning, is something I've always wanted to try. We took some scenic day trips and the truth was by that time I had a crush on her but I was not emotionally mature enough to have a successful long term relationship with her. I was over 30 years old and certainly should have been emotionally mature by that age but I was not. If the saying that all families are dysfunctional to greater or lesser extent is true then the dysfunction in my family was in the area of emotional growth. I have a brother who remembers a childhood that never was and a sister whose fears have been substantial. For many years I wondered where my own fears came from but I was so close to the problem that I couldn't see that I had learned them or absorbed them from childhood on. Fear is such an insidious enemy of mankind that even when I was told I was fearful I couldn't see it. I'd been held up at gun-point in Columbia and didn't even get nervous. I'd crawled out (or was carried) from three different auto accidents, two in which the vehicle was totally demolished and I was unconscious from minutes to days. I was at death's door and never flinched. How could I be fearful? In the book of Job in the Old Testament Job says, "The things that I have feared have come upon me." Was it possible that by fearing something I was bringing it upon myself? Were my fears, sub-conscious as they were, causing me havoc with the opposite sex as well? When Diana finally told me that she did not want to see me any more it was a blow I should have anticipated based on prior experience but I did not. It had been 15 years since the Air Force Colonel had told me that my problem was that I didn't think my problems were problems, but time and circumstances had at least taught me to recognize that I had problems. What exactly they were and how I might eradicate them was an entirely different subject.

"Muddle through" was a saying I had often heard. "Keep on keeping on" was another. "They also serve who only stand and wait." I seemed to believe that time alone would make me the better person I wanted to be and since I was trying to grow the passage of time did help. I had begun to understand, ever so slightly, the real power of prayer. Some aspects of prayer can be taught but some can only be discovered. I am still in the discovery process.

Diana's departure from my life was traumatic but I endured as I always do. "When the going gets tough, the tough get going." The slogans seemed unending but they seemed to help. I had recited them for years like American mantras. What I desired more than all else was a wife and family of my own and financial independence but as objective and common as those goals were they seemed beyond my grasp. Only by the grace of God did I endure.

My ability to sell freezers and microwave ovens and home food delivery diminished greatly or rather the desire to succeed by selling them was no longer there. Eventually I was closing no sales at all. My heart wasn't in it and my income, a draw against commissions, shrank to where it did not pay for the gas to drive to my prospects homes. A successful four year sales career was finally finished. I did not seek another sales job. I didn't seek a job at all.

The weekly prayer group I had faithfully attended at St. Columba's, over 300 strong, had broken up. I remember the night the group leaders announced that the meetings would no longer be held there, that the group was splitting into two and leaving St. Columba. I was stunned! In the silence of awe and almost disbelief I suddenly heard in my spirit, "I know what I'm doing!"What was God doing? If it was His will that the group split into two groups and move on I could not object although I certainly did not understand why. I did not even know what He was trying to accomplish in my own life. I had come to depend on the spiritual uplift that I had received from the group and maybe that was the problem, instead of bringing to the group I was taking from it. Maybe God wanted us to grow up and not depend on a group but on Him. I did not know but I accepted the decision. When the "Promise of Life" broke into two smaller groups, I did not join either. Occasionally I attended a similar group that met in Newburgh, N.Y. but I did not feel the same about the group or the people, nice as they were. Oftentimes I have been invited to join this group or that church but I have declined.

A couple I had recently met, both smokers, had both been diagnosed with terminal cancer and they were only in their thirties. I had always been somewhat fascinated by the mystery of cancer since the whispers I'd heard over the death of Mr. Peters when I was seven or eight years old. Now I knew people who were dying from it. I became intrigued with the disease. What were the real causes of cancer? I had an acquaintance in college who died from cancer of her blood but I did not know Karen very well. Now I seemed to be meeting people everywhere who were getting cancer, had had it, or who had relatives or friends who had one or more of the 200 diseases we call cancer. Perhaps it was fear again, this time of the unknown, that spurred me onward, but I made what turned out to be a two year study of the avoidable causes of cancer. I spent most of my time in the library and corresponding with scientists. I seemed to remember writing to Dr. Elizabeth Whelan, the mother of epidemiology (the study of health statistics). I don't remember what she told me but I added it to all that I was gleaming from science journals and even scientists who were writing for the popular press. Some of what I read was clearly over my head as I was not even a medical student but gradually knowledge replaced fear as I became convinced that cancer was 85 percent preventable. Smoking, exposure to radioactive materials, asbestos, and carcinogenic chemicals (a very small percentage of the more than four million known chemical compounds) and over-exposure to sunlight were all causes of cancer. The biggest cause however, seemed to be what we Americans ate and drank or what we didn't eat and drink. The most serious deficiency seemed to be the lack of whole grains and raw nuts in our diet and the fact that we eat to much animal fats. We don't drink enough water to flush out the overabundance of salts in our daily fare. I discovered that we were the only mammal on the planet that ate more sodium than potassium (a situation somewhat remedied by America's most popular fruit, the banana). We eat too much processed food devoid of vitamins and minerals that are essential to optimum health. We also don't eat enough salt water fish. I decided that a book needed to be written to bring these facts to the public and I began to write one, documenting my sources as I wrote.About two years passed and I must have had a few odd jobs to survive but the only one I recall was again working at the post office, this time in Wappingers Falls, N.Y.My book looked more like a college thesis than a book and by the time it reached 120 pages or so my interest waned and so it remains unfinished to this day. Over the next 20 years what I had studied and learned gradually became public knowledge but I still do not think that the citizenry take it seriously enough. People still smoke though a pack of cigarettes today costs more than a carton did when I started college. Of course people still get lung cancer, bladder cancer, breast cancer, and all the other cancers associated with smoking.People still eat more junk food than is healthy and then they try to make up for their over-indulgence with supermarket vitamins and synthetic fat free foods. We don't get the balance that the human body needs and we are always craving more, just as a young child who is deficient in certain minerals will sometimes eat sand in an attempt to satisfy that need.

Vitamins and minerals were something that I had been taking for years but I began to search for what was the best and the healthiest. I discovered that of all the vitamins sold in the United States very few were so pure and so natural that they qualified as food.I wanted to take what was worth taking, something that might make a difference in my health over time.Although they are not sold in stores Shaklee supplements are sold in every city in America and I have been taking "Vita-Lea" for over twenty years as do some of our Olympic champions. Although I have never sold Shaklee products, over the years I have convinced most of my closest friends and relatives to try Vita-Lea and with time and experience most of them have been using it for years as well. One friend is a frequent world traveler and he never leaves the country without his.

I have been told that some people whose body is seriously deficient in one or more of the necessary vitamins, minerals or trace elements and who suddenly start getting all they need will have a troubling reaction. One of my friends was not told that like a new car there needed to be a gradual "break-in" period. She was not told to only take one green tablet of Vita-Lea for a full week with her biggest meal before beginning to take the normal two tablets per day. She told me that she had an adverse reaction the one time she tried the supplement. Try as I might I could not get her to try them again gradually, the way that she should have tried them. "I'm allergic to all vitamins," she told me. When, years later, she developed breast cancer I felt somewhat guilty at first that I had not tried harder to convince her to take them. She is in fact the only friend of more than 20 years who has never smoked who has gotten cancer. My friend chose the conventional route of surgery followed by chemotherapy and other drugs which are sometimes successful and always expensive. Two years after her cancer was removed it reappeared, this time in her lungs and bones. Since one of the drugs she was taking was also reducing the calcium in her bones I started to tell her how Shaklee scientists had discovered that when a person took alfalfa with calcium their bodies absorbed it 400 percent more effectively. I had been using alfalfa for years (even Wal-Mart sells alfalfa tablets now) but my friend stated categorically "I will never take Shaklee!" Suddenly I had a flashback of a Kuwaiti woman being interviewed by a television crew at the end of the Desert Storm War.

The Kuwaiti woman's brother had been killed by the invading Iraqis and her comment was, "I will never forgive them!" Both statements were said with such finality that I felt equally sorry for the Kuwaiti woman years before as I did now for my friend.It struck me as odd how I had a flashback to a war scene from the previous decade when we were discussing cancer but the fight against cancer is a war and I now think the two attitudes were somehow related. Somehow I seemed to see that her attitude, although she is a beautiful person otherwise and filled with much love, had a part in the cancer that had taken hold of her. In any event unless God intervened in a miraculous way my friend would not be long for this world. Of course I said nothing to her about any of this and unless she reads these words she will never even know that I felt guilty over not trying harder to convince her.

Of course no one can guarantee that a person will not get cancer but the number of cases would be greatly diminished if we all took advantage of all that is known about preventing it. Instead we expect the Federal government to do something. If the country were not in debt we could afford to pay for everyone's lack of knowledge or lack of discretion. As it is the government is responsible for 43 to 48 TRILLION dollars in obligations, not the 9 Trillion you will be reading about in the paper within a year.

As my interest in the avoidable causes of cancer waned somewhat my appetite for spiritual growth increased. In the summer of 1978 I heard of a four day conference that was being held in Chicago by an organization known as World Evangelism. Two years earlier in our bicentennial year a former news reporter had taken me to a meeting in Brooklyn, N.Y. and I was convinced that this group of people had God's blessing upon them. That night in Brooklyn I saw many interesting things but the one I remember the most was a small five year old boy on crutches. His crutches were the smallest I had ever seen. The gentleman in charge of the meeting was a Christian Evangelist named Morris Cerullo. He taught for a while about Jesus, who He really was, and what Christianity was supposed to be. He spoke on healing and then he mentioned that he could somehow see into the spiritual dimension and that he saw God's anointing was on several people in the audience, sort of like rays of sunshine, invisible to the rest of us, or in any event to me. Those people were called forward and asked to come up on the platform to be prayed over for whatever they needed. There were only a few and some came up gladly and some reluctantly. One of these was this little child on crutches.

Now such an event is certainly open to charlatanism in addition to which there are certain diseases that are psychosomatic in origin and can be affected by the appropriate stimulus, whatever that might be. There are also people who want to be healed so much that they can work themselves up into an emotional state where they can convince themselves that they have been healed, even when they have not experienced any manifestation of a healing. We adults can play games in our minds even when we don't know that we are playing games, but five year olds seldom, if ever, have the sophistication to play serious mind games. They call a spade a spade. Things are black and white to them, not the many shades of gray with which many adults have learned to live.

The crutches were taken away from the little boy and he was told that he could walk. He just stood there and the look on his face clearly said, "You've got to be kidding!"

"Jesus has healed you. You don't need the crutches anymore," we all heard. "Just put one foot in front of the other one. You can do it," he was told. I still don't think he believed it but now several people, all adults, were encouraging him to try. Ever so slowly the youngster moved one foot in front of the other. It worked! Then he moved the other one. It worked too! Back and forth he walked across the raised floor completely oblivious to the 3,000 others in the audience or those around him.He kept staring at his legs as he walked back and forth. He was not laughing or crying as an adult might have been but the look on his face was one of sincere awe. His legs worked! They didn't work before and now they did. An adult could fake such a thing, even convincingly, but not a five year old child. I had tears in my eyes.

Two years later, when presented with the opportunity to spend four days in Chicago learning from Morris Cerullo about God's love for the world and for me personally, I decided to go. I drove my Volkswagen bus from New York to Ohio where I spent the night at the home of my cousin's in-laws outside of Kenton and the next day I continued on to Chicago. As I drove across Indiana I was amazed at all the corn that grew there. I must have driven past well over one hundred and fifty miles of corn fields. It was Labor Day weekend, 1978, the year that Cale Yarborough won the Southern 500 NASCAR Race in Darlington, S.C. for the fourth time. I arrived in Chicago for the very first time and drove along Lakeshore Drive more for sight-seeing than for necessity.

There were a couple of thousand people attending the conference. I sat about two thirds of the way down from the front, close but not to close, to whatever might be going on. I had not yet read the amazing life story of Morris Cerullo, a man whose life was once threatened by 300 witch doctors but who escaped much as the prophet of God had escaped from Jezebel's several hundred false prophets in the days of ancient Israel. I had only heard Morris Cerullo speak once before at the college in Brooklyn. His parents had been Russian Jews who came to America before WWII and were killed in an auto accident when Morris was a youngster. In the House of Miriam in the state of New Jersey a rebellious teenager named Morris experienced God in an awesome encounter that certainly rivals that of St. Paul.He was 15 when he had a life changing experience in some respects similar to Saul of Tarsus. Both had apparently had been taken up to the third heaven where they had an encounter with the living God. Saul changed his name to Paul and became one of the great founders of Christianity. Morris did not feel the necessity of changing his name but the result of that encounter is the internationally known World Evangelism whose goal is to reach every living person on the planet with the gospel message, that God loves us and that we can know Him.

There were dozens of different denominations represented in the conference. I shared my room with a scientist whose PhD was in some earth science but three Catholic nuns in their old fashioned habits, clothes from the 15th Century, are the ones I remember the most. Morris, besides teaching, shared with us about his own life. He reminded us that we could shop in any store we chose or we could leave the hotel and eat in any restaurant that appealed to us or simply take a stroll if we wanted to do so. He, however, when the sessions were over had to return to his room where he was registered under an assumed name. For security reasons he could not leave the hotel. He could not even eat with his friends in the hotel's dining room but had to eat all his meals in his room. All this because mobs of people would congregate around him just to touch him or be touched by him in the hopes of receiving a healing. At the time I probably would have been one of them although my hurts were not physical ones. The rewards of being one of God's prophets were certainly not earthly ones but any reader of the Old Testament knew that.

Brother Cerullo told us that he had been praying, asking God for direction in what amount of money to ask for at this conference. People often criticize evangelists for their frequent appeals for money. In some cases such criticism is warranted but I ask, "What is the money being used for?" If the evangelist drives an expensive foreign car and lives in a house three times as big as the average American home he does not get any of my money. As far as I know there has never been an organization on earth, no church or denomination, certainly no one individual, who has ever sought to reach the entire planet and every individual on it with the gospel message in one lifetime, and that is the goal of Morris Cerullo World Evangelism. People can reject the life giving power of Jesus if they have a choice but in much of the world there is certainly no such thing as freedom of religion. Even in supposedly "friendly" Saudi Arabia where most of the 9/11 terrorists came from, it has been a capital crime to tell people about the Jesus that Christians believe in (Muslims believe that Jesus existed and that he had a virgin birth, but that he was merely one of God's prophets, and that he certainly did not die on a cross to become the saviour). The things we put up with for the sake of oil. And look at Abdul Rahman; he became a Christian in Afghanistan 16 years ago and was just recently found out. The punishment in that Islamic country for accepting Jesus as your Lord is DEATH! Fortunately someone spread the word and heads of state in many countries pulled strings to get him out of the country and to freedom in March of 2006. And we think we are going to make the mid-east into a democratic society! Well maybe, after Islam disappears. I think Mohammed said that would happen after the year 3,000 or so.

Anyway, as Dr. Cerullo prayed in his room for guidance on how much to ask for in this conference the telephone rang. This was a bit unusual because for security purposes the phone number was always unlisted. "Is this Morris Cerullo?" the voice said with a distinctive southwestern drawl. "Yes, yes it is," Morris replied, somewhat surprised. "Well, this is so-and-so from the _____ (major city), Texas, police department and I wanted to make a donation to your work!" Still surprised that even a Texas police officer had gotten through on a secure line Dr. Cerullo asked the officer how he had gotten the phone number. "Well, I was praying and the Holy Spirit gave me your number," the officer replied.

There are no secrets from God, no facts not known, no prayer unheard. Suddenly it dawned on God's number one prophet of the

20th Century that one of his prayers was being answered. "How much do you want to give?" the officer was asked. "One thousand dollars" was the reply and that is the amount that we were asked to give. I did not know how I could give that much since I was not even working at the time but I felt led to raise my hand when we were asked to do so if we would donate that amount. The three Catholic nuns raised their hands as well and I am sure that, like me, they wondered how they would fulfill their promise. I did though and I'll bet they did too.

Surrounded by God's people from so many different creeds and denominations I felt led to pray for my friends, my family, and my country, even myself. I'm sure I prayed more than I remember but I distinctively remember praying to meet someone special. I was tired of being single. Several of my younger brothers and sisters were married and I was already an uncle five times over. I didn't even have a girl friend but that was quick to change.

The return trip to New York was uneventful and I quickly slipped back into my routine of whatever it was that was my routine. I had been thinking about returning to one of the prayer meetings at the Oblate Fathers Retreat Center in Newburgh, N.Y. just two miles north of where General Washington had his headquarters during the Revolutionary War. I had attended a couple of meetings there after the Promise of Life group broke up and I thought it would be a good idea to go back. Something interfered with my plans and I missed the first time I planned to attend but I made a firm resolve that I would attend the next one. I was not exactly sure of the hours and was late for the first session which was held in the chapel but early for the prayer meeting which, then, was a separate meeting in the former school cafeteria. It was an early autumn day. The leaves were still green on the trees and only a few vines, poison and otherwise, had begun to acquire some color caused by a change in the photosynthesis which in turn was caused by the shortened hours of daylight. I walked through the main door of this former school and immediately saw someone walking down the hallway. When I asked about the prayer meeting I was told that it would begin shortly and the person pointed in the direction of the cafeteria.

As soon as I entered the former auditorium/cafeteria I could see and hear the musicians warming up. I walked over towards them and sat down in the second row although the seats were arranged somewhat in a semi-circle around the musicians. I had enjoyed the music for a few minutes when the door opened from the long hallway and a pretty young woman entered. She looked younger than her 23 years and her name was Sharon. She walked over and sat down in the second row with one empty seat between us. She, too, had been late but felt led at the very last minute to leave her home in Goshen, N.Y. and drive the 20 plus miles to the prayer meeting. It was one of the few times in her life that she has ever been late for anything. Only three weeks had passed since I had prayed the prayer in Chicago amid all God's people "to meet someone." During a break in the songs we began talking and thus began a relationship that continues to this day. Five years later we were married and although we live in the Mid-Hudson Valley of New York we have visited South Carolina many times and have had some interesting adventures together, but that is another story.

26. The Day after Tomorrow

Thank you for reading this book. I hope you have found it worthwhile. If I were to write another book it would have to be on the coming financial crisis that will soon affect us all but I am a very slow writer and this World-Wide depression, if that is what they eventually call it, might be here before I ever finished. Consequently, I have included these final thoughts, this free "extra chapter" in the hopes that you might be persuaded to begin preparing for the financial storm that is fast approaching our shores and will soon engulf us all. This storm is not as unpredictable as the one in the movie "The Day After Tomorrow" but just as the politicians in that movie thought it "might" happen in "the future" and it happened much, much sooner, so no one can predict exactly when our "financial" storm will happen, only that it is inevitable, and that it is not far off. I have even read Think Tank projections that say we have an 80 percent chance of it happening in 2006. Being optimistic I hope we have a few more years until we feel its full fury!

As you have already read there is much amiss about the financial situation in this country. It has gotten out of control. This began long ago when Congress decided they didn't want to be bothered with their Constitutional duty of being responsible for the money of the country and turned that duty over to the newly formed privately owned corporation called the Federal Reserve Bank. As far as I know all countries now have such banks. Since this super bank was now lending us the money to run the country we also had to invent income tax to pay them for this "service." Banks do provide a function of course. They loan money at a profit and this enables business to borrow and build and for people to buy houses, things like that. Banks are not evil per se although I know there are those who would disagree with that. Neither are bankers per se. It's just the way things are. Nevertheless the Constitution says that we shall only use gold and silver for money and we have forsaken this basic principle and substituted paper. In the 6,000 year history of this civilization no nation that has ever tried eliminating gold and silver and substituting something else and calling it money has ever succeeded. Will we be the first?

Even the Old Testament of the Bible speaks of gold and silver. They are the only "real" money that exists. In the words of South African Investment Advisor Peter George, "Through the centuries, gold has lived up to its God-given Biblical role as man's most reliable store of value. No paper currency can match it. The Bible calls replicas 'dishonest weights and measures.'"

In my old college dictionary from the 1960s there are seven definitions given for money. The first two words of the first definition begin with "Gold, Silver..." A few years ago I purchased one of those big dictionaries that they use in libraries and this dictionary has twenty definitions of money. The first begins, "Any circulating medium of exchange..." Imagine that, ANY circulating medium of exchange! How about watermelon seeds? I know some South Carolinians who would be rich if we could get watermelon seeds circulating. The second definition says "see paper money." Gold and silver are there but they have slipped to third place. Neither dictionary says that money is a store of value because that hasn't been true since we ditched gold and silver. Few want to save what we call money (cotton and paper) when it is worth less and less each year. Indeed, the savings rate for Americans reached negative territory for the entire year of 2005. The last time this happened for an entire year was in the 1930s when Americans needed all they had just to buy food and fuel in the midst of the last great depression. These days we are using all we have to buy "stuff" from the Orient. Not only do we save nothing, zero, zilch, we borrow to spend what we don't even have. Being hopelessly in debt is the new American way!

I knew of an engineer from South America who worked for IBM in Brazil and he was assigned to a temporary job in East Fishkill, New York, for several months. When he received his first American paycheck he wanted to go out on his lunch break and cash it right then. He was accustomed to the money being worth less in his own country if he waited just 24 hours. His fellow IBMers prevailed upon him that it would still be worth the same the next day and he didn't have to rush to the bank and cash the check or lose money. The value of his check wouldn't change in 24 hours in the United States. Of course this was over a dozen years ago but perhaps this is akin to the mindset that has engulfed the population in the United States today now that the dollar is losing value more quickly than it ever has before. In Brazil the engineer could not buy gold to protect himself. Only the government could own gold. I should point out that liberals do not like gold and that socialists positively hate it, and while I am concerned about tomorrow it is "the day after tomorrow" that is going to affect us all financially.

In 1966 Alan Greenspan (the recently retired former chairman of the Federal Reserve Bank) wrote an essay entitled "Gold and Economic Freedom." In it he wrote, "In the absence of the gold standard, there is no way to protect savings from confiscation through inflation...Deficit spending is simply a scheme for the 'hidden' confiscation of wealth." At the time gold was valued at around $35 an ounce as it had been for thirty years. Less than a decade later America was completely off the gold standard, the serious inflation had begun and gold was close to $100. Another decade passed and Alan Greenspan was appointed Chairman of the Federal Reserve and gold averaged around $300. While many don't like the things he did while running the economy of the country (as if anyone could "run the economy") many forget that even he had a boss (the owners of the Federal Reserve Bank). We don't seem to mind inflation when it is in stocks or houses or things we own but when it is in food and fuel and new cars we don't like it. How foolish! Inflation is inflation! President Nixon was so upset with 4 percent inflation back in the 1970s that he inaugurated price controls which never seem to work. The important point to realize here is that we actually have well OVER 4 percent inflation right now. Although the official figure is something like 3.5 percent anyone who has kept track of their grocery bill, and heating bill, and gasoline bill, and...well, you get the picture! Some believe that the actual inflation rate is between 8 and 9 percent but it is very difficult to tell any more because so much is hidden from us. I know that a gallon of distilled water in Wal-Mart has gone up 10 percent in the past year and my favorite all butter raisin oatmeal cookies have gone up 24 percent. The propane I heat with has gone up 33 percent, etc.

Now imagine if you will that back in 1931 your grandparents (or your great grandparents) had saved two weeks salary to go on vacation. They had a $20 gold piece containing .96750 of an ounce of gold and a $20 Federal Reserve Note. Seventy-five years ago they were worth virtually the same, a full ounce of gold being worth almost $21. Well, a $20 gold piece from 1931 would buy the same things today that it would have bought in 1931, maybe even more. I have read that this is true even if your great-great-great-grandfather had that same ounce of gold when Washington was president or even if you had an ancient ancestor who owned a single ounce of gold before the New World was discovered. After all these centuries you could still buy just as much, if not more, as your ancestor could buy. If, however, your grandparents in 1931 had kept the paper $20 bill rather than the $20 gold coin, today you could only buy what any $20 bill will buy, about one 25th of what the gold would have bought. In a few years it will only buy one 50th of what the gold will buy. Even if they had put that $20 bill in the bank and collected interest all these years, even with all the interest, they still could not buy what the same amount of gold would buy. Actually if they had kept a $20 gold piece for you dated 1931 today you could buy a good used car with it as the coin itself is rare and worth over $7,000 although the gold in the coin is only worth around $500 as I write this. Alas, I had no relatives who left me either one.

More recently those who have really lost out are those who have had their money in the bank for the last five years or so. Even with the interest they are getting their dollars will not buy anywhere near what it would have bought when they purchased the Certificate of Deposit just five years ago. The same is true with government bonds. Many have realized this and spent the money investing it in condo's and second homes and things that seem to be going up, up, up, just like the stock market did a few years ago. I'll let you in on a big secret: Nothing goes up forever. Even predictions I have read of gold reaching $40,000 an ounce are not saying that gold is the best investment in the world. One source has even said he would not be surprised to see gold go to $80,000 an ounce.What these people are really saying, of course, is that the dollar could fall to levels that most cannot even imagine. I don't think it will fall to zero and I don't think we will see gold at $40,000 an ounce but I have no doubt that I will see it at well over $1700 an ounce and $7 gasoline and $8 a loaf bread in the years ahead. I only hope it will not be worse.

Some people do not know that the New Testament of the Bible warns of a time that is coming when no one, not even a king, will be able to buy or sell without a mark in their hand or in their forehead. For nearly two thousand years this prophecy in Revelation 13:16-17 was considered preposterous by atheists but it is likely to be fulfilled within the lifetime of some reading this book. The older versions of the Bible like the King James and the Douey-Rheims translate this as a "mark in the right hand" but some newer American versions get cute and translate this as a "tattoo on" the hand or forehead, but the

original scriptures say mark "IN" the right hand or "IN" the forehead. The mark is likely to be a micro-chip, or if this doesn't happen
for another 20 years, a microcomputer which will be implanted "IN"
or under the skin, not on it. This technology is already being used
for purposes other than finance.

Cryptically the ancient Book of Revelation speaks of sky high inflation but it uses words and concepts that are alien to all but scholars. "A measure of wheat for a denarii or three measures of barley..."
translates in modern terms to "a days wage for a day's food" as a
measure of wheat was enough to make the bread that one would eat
in a day and a denarii was the standard daily wage in ancient times.
That reference, however, was to a time far in the future. Could it
be the next few decades? As a youngster I had always thought that
this might happen in other countries but not here. We were the
United States of America; we loved God and followed his simple
commandments for a good and meaningful life. We even had His
10 Commandments posted in the Supreme Court and in most of the
courthouses around the country.

The thought occurs to me that if we are so hated by those who
hate freedom and democracy now, imagine how they are going to
love us when the fall of the dollar brings them down as well? All nations are inflating their currencies so it is not just the United States.
All governments are now addicted to spending what they don't have.
Of course, it is possible that it will not be a "crash" of the dollar but
an increasingly fast drop in its value. In the last 6 years the dollar has lost one third of its value, not officially of course, but go to
your library and look up a newspaper from Spring of 2000 and price
something like a new Hyundai Accent and price one in a newspaper
from the Spring of 2006 and you will see how much the dollar has
dropped in value. Perhaps the dollar will just lose another third of
its value in the next 4 years and then again another third in the following 2 years, and so on; not exactly a crash but not something
to look forward to if all you own is paper assets and nothing real.
Regardless of the form the crisis takes it is going to take a lot more
paper dollars to buy anything in the not-to-distant future.

As our grandparents lives were vastly different than our lives so
also will the lives of our grandchildren be vastly different than ours.
My grandparents had electricity until the Great Depression and after they lost their city home they moved to their country cabin some
twenty miles away. The young teenage girl who was to become my
future mother had to learn how to adapt to a home without elec-

tricity and how to use a hand pump for water. Today's seemingly "spoiled generation" may have a much harder time because many of them have never had to do without and such radical changes may be more than they can handle. They may not have to go without electricity or water but families may have to double up and rooms may have to be shared and cable vision may be to expensive for all but basic and a hundred other things I could only guess at. Somewhere in the Bible it says, "My people perish for lack of knowledge." Well, at least after reading this book you can never say that you did not know, that you did not hear, that no one ever told you.

Our grandchildren's lives will be so different from ours that future generations may not even be able to speed up to avoid an auto accident if experiments in Canada are successful. The same technology using satellites that allowed police to track down a stolen vehicle in Florida a few years ago and to find it in a garage in Virginia are being used to see if satellite monitoring can track speeders or even prevent them from speeding. While 85 percent of people find no problem going 5 to 10 miles over the posted speed limits in most places, believing as Jesus said, that the law was made for man's benefit and not the other way around, future vehicles may have more sophisticated computers than they now have, that are actually informed by satellite when you enter a slower (or faster) highway and the computer will either keep track of your speed or actually prevent you from going over that speed. Indeed our grandchildren are going to live in a brave new world unrecognizable from the one many of us grew up in. Even the world of 2016 will be as different from today as 2006 is different from 1996, those simple days when our biggest concern was whether the president was lying about his sex life. In a previous generation this would have been no ones business but his. Today, everything is everybody's business and there are few lasting secrets of any kind although figures from the Federal Information Security Oversight Office indicate that the government continues to manufacture well over 15 million new "secrets" every year. It's true that such secrecy in government keeps the public from knowing what is going on, but worse, it often keeps the left arm of government from knowing what the right arm is doing. Such secrecy may well have contributed to the failure of intelligence that led to the deaths of thousands in the September 11th attack on the World Trade Center and the failure to find the weapons of mass destruction that even some Iraqis thought they had. However, if you recall, just a decade ago, times were quite good in this country, millionaires were being made (over 3,000,000 last I heard with a couple of hundred billionaires on top of that). The stock market was going up, up, up, and even though hundreds of factories had closed and moved overseas, money was abundant. It can be abundant when it is only paper or cotton.

In 1929 much of our money was still real but following the boom time of the 20s the ratio of debt-to-GDP (Gross Domestic Product) in this country was around 260% and following the stock market crash and over the next several years of the Great Depression it worsened to around 350%. Our CURRENT debt-to-GDP ratio is now fast approaching that same 350%, THE SAME RATIO AS DURING THE MIDST OF THE GREAT DEPRESSION and yet the majority of citizens live as if everything is normal and no financial disaster is awaiting us around a future corner. Many are not even aware that if something happened tomorrow to affect our GDP, say a major earthquake in Tokyo (a distinct possibility) we would be immediately affected. Anything that caused a small but significant drop in our GDP could well cause us to slip first into a recession and then as things got worse, an all out depression. Even the Bank of Japan increasing the rate of interest they charge on the yen could do us in as investors have borrowed yen for years at zero percent and then used the money to purchase American bonds that pay three percent.

Since no one knows what will trigger our house of cards (or in this case paper dollars) to come tumbling down it could be at an even greater ratio thereby guaranteeing an even greater and longer depression. THE BIBLE CODE clearly implies a high probability of a major attack against Jerusalem this year, 2006. This could easily trigger a dramatic increase in the price of gold, the beginning of the end for the dollar, and possibly even the beginning of a World War. In any event the ratio of debt to GDP continues to grow at every turn as deeper and deeper into debt we go. If the crisis began tomorrow the result would already be worse than the Great Depression. Congress has increased the national debt about fifty times in the last forty years (or is it the other way around)? Does it even matter anymore? In the words of one financial analyst who has a sense of humor that not all can appreciate, "we are doomed!" Well, not yet, but in January 2006, the Treasury actually spent over the legally and congressionally mandated debt limit, so I guess we are not even pretending to be balancing the books anymore. As the ratio of debt increases this all but guarantees it will be a far worse depression than it was 75 years ago. It is therefore not much of a stretch to say that what is coming may be called "The Greater Depression" by future historians or to say as Christian evangelist and prophet Morris Cerullo has said, that the coming World-Wide financial crisis will make "the Great Depression seem like a walk in the park." Financial writer Richard Daughty is convinced that it will be "far far worse." The most famous octogenarian economist in the world has said, "There is no way out!" It is, of course, unlikely that the financial storm that is coming will be exactly the same as the Great Depression. Whatever it is called and whatever form it takes it will last longer and it will be more severe. Some who are millionaires today will be impoverished.

Yet, as recently as a decade ago, good jobs were so abundant that they were attracting millions of illegal aliens, even as the factories continued to move to Asia, lured by cheap labor and tax benefits provided by our Congress. Illegal immigration, of course, is continuing on an unprecedented scale and the number of illegal aliens has so over-whelmed some communities in the southwest that they have had to close their hospitals, bankrupted by the unpaid bills of those who have no money. In Los Angeles over 300,000 illegal aliens live in garages and according to one study done in California the average illegal alien costs the taxpayer $56,000 over his life time. The government admits that there are 11,000,000 undocumented illegal aliens in this country but I have seen figures as high as 21,000,000 and some even higher than that. Some who have sneaked into this country illegally are decent folks seeking a better life and they have gotten good jobs and hold to the old work ethic of another generation. I have mixed feelings about the fact that some in the mid-west have actually been able to borrow mortgage funds from banks and buy houses. Just being an illegal alien was not enough of a reason to withhold mortgage funds. Bankers look at the ability to pay, not where you came from or who you are. No one seems to really care about the growing number of illegal Hispanics who have already replaced blacks as the major minority. Both parties give the problem lip service. They hold meetings and the debate and come up with unrealistic solutions, all of which are costly. Many of these aliens are good hardworking people but thousands are wanted for rape and murder in their home countries south of the border. In fact in 2005 there were over 870 illegal aliens arrested in just one state (New Jersey) who were wanted criminals in their own countries. Some have continued to rape and murder here as well. Just this past month an illegal alien was arrested not far from here in the rape and torture murder of a young wife. Fortunately he spared her two very young children. Illegal immigration has become like fiat money, a problem no one wants to really face. We give it lip service and propose shipping all 11,000,000 back to where they came from even though we allowed them in and hired many of them. We would have to go into debt several more BILLIONS of DOLLARS to round them up and then spend over $6 BILLION to send them back. Instead of dealing with things as they are we are dealing with them the way we want them to be, a sure recipe for failure, no matter whether the problem is the war in the middle east or illegal aliens. Since we won't reinforce the border and stop the migration then we are all responsible. If it is not stopped than we will join the rest of the third world countries and I have seen estimates of a 15 year time frame on this. Mexico even prints pamphlets on how to sneak into the United States. They know that we apparently want the labor force. The humane thing, it seems to me, would be to require all to register and since we did not keep them out that they be given the opportunity to earn their citizenship, really earn it, along with lessons in English. This would cost no more than breaking up families and disrupting the economy by trying to find over 11,000,000 people all over the country and shipping them back to dozens of different countries south of the border. Criminals should be returned of course. I say include English lessons because this is an English speaking country and those who never learn the language will always be second class citizens. While it is undoubtedly politically incorrect to say that, it is also the truth! Our Congress has never had the guts to make English the official language of our country. They are so fearful of being politically incorrect and not being re-elected. It seems to me that there are forces in this country whose sole purpose is the destruction of the American way of life. When America ceases to be the light she once was as a beacon of freedom to the world I believe it will just be a matter of time until the most charismatic human the world has ever seen will step up to the plate to become the greatest problem solver of all time, until he controls the world economy and then demands to be worshiped as the living God. The Bible calls him "the Anti-Christ."

In any event it should never have come to this as far as illegal immigration is concerned but neither party has done much, if anything, to really secure our borders. No solution to the problem of so many illegal aliens in this country will work until we stop them from coming in illegally! Our very porous border needs to be sealed now or we are just fooling ourselves and Homeland Security will be just another government boondoggle. Many Americans are getting fed up with Congress for their lack of concern about the country they are supposed to govern and some in the southwest are fearful when they here talk of civil war and the future attempt to take back Texas to Colorado west to California and incorporate them into a larger Mexico. Impossible and ridiculous you say? Maybe, put from what I have seen in my lifetime I would not bet on it either way. Sadly, most Americans are not even aware that illegal aliens have killed just as many Americans in this country as the terrorists did at the WTC, just not all at once.

It is possible that the term "illegal alien" may, in time, change. As something becomes more and more accepted the social stigma or negative connotations attached to it becomes more neutral, if not down right positive. For instance, terrorists (not those in Iraq but in other countries) are often called "freedom fighters" in the media and the term "bastard" although common when this country was founded, is now seldom used except as a curse word. It meant a person whose mother was unwed. The term used forty years ago to refer to such persons was "an illegitimate child." So many "father-less children" are being born that I don't even know the most current legal term for such children. Although the "children of unwed mothers" cannot be members of at least one organization I know of, there is little stigma attached these days to the origin of any particular child although foreign born citizens still cannot be president of the USA according to the Constitution. Of course the Supreme Court could re-interpret that to mean something else and anything is possible when you abandon the laws of the land, regardless if they are the Ten Commandments or the Constitution. Science fiction writers have often written of future societies in which all children are the products of special laboratories, sex is either illegal or totally promiscuous and the natural has become unnatural. How far will society go before it collapses with new theories and practices that do not consider 6,000 years of what is tried and true? Are we really ready for a new enlightened "dark age?"

Unfortunately even as we have been experimenting with newer ways of living we have also been experimenting with newer ways of finance, fiat money, glorious, unlimited paper and cotton, backed by nothing at all but faith in the Federal Reserve Bank, Congress, and the bankers at the Treasury Department. We criticize the French but they have been there and done that! The French printed so many assignats that after 210 years it is still possible to obtain them. The same is true with marks from the Weimar Republic in Germany 83 years ago. One TRILLION were worth 23.8 cents worth of gold.

For six thousand years gold and silver were used as money with a little copper for small items and it worked well. Governments, however, have always want to spend more than they have but they cannot print gold. On the other hand it is quite easy to make money if it's only made of paper and not backed by anything but promises. Few people would trade a chunk of gold for a new CD stereo or two big handfuls for a new car and fiat paper money, backed by nothing but trust in the issuer, has truly been the law of the land since President Nixon took us off the gold standard over three decades ago. That's when the gradual inflation that had ever so slowly been creeping upwards for the previous 40 years began to get serious. Up until Nixon took us completely off the gold standard foreigners who had dollars could exchange them for gold from the U. S. Treasury. Of course it was Franklin Roosevelt who took gold out of the pockets of widows and working men and replaced it with paper in 1933. On the other hand if Nixon had not stopped the drain of gold from the treasury the country would have become bankrupt long ago. Considering the magnitude of the crisis that is coming that might not have been so bad.

From 1933 until 1975 American citizens were like the citizens of Brazil or Russia, we could not own gold other than jewelry. I have read that Roosevelt did not like the idea personally but that he was convinced by the bankers at the Treasury Department that such a course of action was best for the country. The simple days of "real" money are gone. Bankers who control so much of our lives have so much power that I do not believe they are likely to ever allow us to return to "real money" unless the population is decimated by WWIII or a comet does hit the earth or something of equal importance. Then food may become money. Some believe that a return to sound money (gold) will be the result of the joblessness and near starvation that some may suffer in the future but I, for one, do not think that even the coming crisis will bring us back to real money. Not when the 1900 year old prophecy in the Bible speaks of the "Mark of the Beast" that will one day be required of all in order to buy or sell. To me that sounds like just another extension of good old fiat money controlled by big bankers and governments working together for the control of every aspect of our lives but using computers and micro-chips. I hope that this is still a long ways off but I honestly don't have any idea how soon it will happen, only that it will.

Unfortunately the simple days of the 1990's are gone forever. Some of my sources believe that the stock market is going to really crash, down to 4,000, or even less. Government buying may have kept it from crashing so far but how long can this continue when the money is all borrowed. Stocks are overvalued, bonds are overvalued, houses and condos are overvalued. About the only thing that is still cheap is the oldest form of money in the world, gold, black gold (oil), uranium, and perhaps farmland. At $500 an ounce for gold (in 2006 dollars) that is only about $235 an ounce in 1980 dollars. Gold is no longer very cheap but it is still cheap! Oil at $68 a barrel is half of what it is likely to be in five years and if Iran can pull out all the stops it could double in less time than that.

Admittedly, gold is old fashioned, like marriage (a covenant of association between a man and a woman that was meant to last a life time). That concept, too, has been thrown out and serial marriages and other experiments in social behavior are abundant. Ford Motor Company and Allstate Insurance both contribute money big time to homosexual causes including the promotion of gay marriage between two men or two women. If we allow this then why not polygamy? While I have never heard of any ancient culture that allowed homosexual "marriages" polygamy was an accepted practice three thousand years ago and is still practiced in some mid-eastern countries and in the American Southwest. However the Bible says that homosexuality will increase before the world is finally completely destroyed so I guess it's just a sign of the times and we should not be too surprised at what we see happening. Six thousand years of civilization should have taught us many lessons but not if we are unwilling to learn them. The decline of the United States, as a super-power, is being compared by some to the decline of the Roman Empire. Just as they could not protect their borders so we seem unable or unwilling to do so. The Romans debased their currency too. They added copper to the gold and silver coins and continued to do this until there was no silver or gold left. How much easier is this to do when there is no gold or silver to begin with and all our money is made on printing presses or in mainframe computers? By the time the majority realize what is happening it will be too late to prepare. Even now we need to borrow about ONE HUNDRED MILLION DOLLARS per HOUR just to keep operating! We are now spending so much on war and other things that even if we all turned

over our entire income to the government we would still run a deficit
(when I started this book 80 percent income tax would have been
enough for us to get by, now 100 percent is not enough). The Asian
countries have so many of our dollars (about 2.5 trillion) from all
the TV's we no longer manufacture and all the other stuff we buy
from them, from tractors to trucks, and from cars to computers,
that if it were possible to buy all the gold that has ever been mined
since civilization began, they have enough dollars to do so (if gold
were only $500 an ounce). It may be that they have started to do
so already. At least that is one reason given by some for the recent
price increase in gold. It is going to get even worse when Chinese
cars, cheaper than Korean ones are sold in the US, maybe even causing GM and Ford to restructure, if not go out of business entirely.
Perhaps those to whom we owe so much will just buy GM or Ford.
They could afford it now that they have so many US dollars. Toyota
recently manufactured their 15,000,000[th] car here in the U.S. The
Korean's manufacture cars here now, along with the Japanese and
Germans as it is cheaper to do it here than in their home countries.

Many have not heard that in the summer of 2004 the Chinese
purchased the largest nickel and copper mine on earth (in Canada)
for mere pocket change of 5 BILLION and 700 MILLION dollars
cash. Sixty five years ago the Japanese attacked Hawaii. When
they failed to capture it because they lost the war they simply saved
enough dollars from stuff we purchased from them after the war and
they bought it, or much of it. Like the Chinese they, too, are pretty
smart, and they save a lot more than we do. Of course since we are
now saving NOTHING that can be said of anyone anywhere who
does save some of what they earn. Then again why save that which
is worth less each year? While it does matter who gets elected president or senator it seems not to matter when it comes to financial
matters. Both parties seem determined to spend us into oblivion.
They only differ in how fast and on what. Financial affairs really are
more important than the other kind that held the public interest for
so long in the previous decade.

Would you believe that there is actually a shortage of gold in the
world and an even greater shortage of gold coins? The gold fields
of South Africa are not exhausted yet but they are getting less gold
out of the ground this year than they did last year or the year before
or than they did 75 years ago. The same is true in other countries.
The cost of finding new gold and mining it is getting very high. The
environmental cost is even higher. This is also true for black gold

(oil). No new major oil fields have been found in 35 years yet the demand is the highest it has ever been.

According to the International Energy Agency global oil demand will increase a little over two percent in 2006. Last year, however, China alone had a 15 percent increase in oil consumption. In the last five years they have had a 100 percent increase in demand. Since current production is only slightly above demand 2006 or 2007 may actually be the first year where demand actually exceeds supply. The Asian countries, with far more than a "fistful of dollars," are having a booming market in cars and the price of oil is going to increase no matter what we do, and still we don't manufacture any truly efficient vehicles in this country.

Hurricane Katrina was actually just a Category 3 storm but the damage it did in the gulf caused gasoline prices to jump more than 40 cents at the pump. Only a few percent of the thousands of oil rigs in the Gulf of Mexico were affected. A true Category 5 storm could still sweep the gulf coast. If that happened the number of oil rigs affected could easily be ten times as many and that could, possibly, drive up prices at the pump ten times as much and truly disrupt our economy.

While over 200,000 people died from the tsunami on Dec. 26, 2004, off the coast of Indonesia, a tsunami is possible in the gulf coast emanating from the Desoto Canyon High, a place where three tectonic plates meet in the northern gulf coast off the western coast of Florida. While I could only guess at the number of deaths this would cause it could disrupt our oil supplies on a scale never before seen. While this will undoubtedly happen someday a more likely cause of increasing prices will be the fact that China has been sewing up oil deals with Brazil, Canada, Egypt, Gabon, Libya, Nigeria, Venezuela and a dozen other countries. If we don't get serious about developing our own oil fields and developing an alternative to oil, most likely ethanol or hydrogen, then our grandchildren will only be driving a private vehicle if they are very rich.

Although Mercedes has built an experimental 3 passenger diesel car that can go over 115 miles an hour and which gets over 70 miles per gallon there are no plans to put it into production. The German Loremo (Low Resistance Mobile) is supposed to be available in Germany within 36 months. The LS model will only use 1.5 liters per 100km or 150 mpg using a small turbo-diesel. The larger GT model will carry four passengers but it will require 2.7 liters per 100km or 96 mpg. Canadians and Mexicans have for years been able to buy the "smartcar" that gets 56 to 72 mpg depending on whether they have gasoline or diesel engines. I have read that the diminutive "smartcar" which is owned by Mercedes has proven as safe as the Mercedes 300 in crash tests but for political reasons it has been kept out of this country. For some reason we seem prejudiced in this country against small diesels which get phenomenal mileage. Since most of the European countries have signed the Kyoto agreement and we have not you would think that we could buy these highly efficient vehicles. Now I'm not saying we should or shouldn't sign the agreement. I don't know enough to have a truly informed opinion on the subject but why won't the EPA let Americans buy these vehicles that get 60 and 70 mpg? The only thing that I can think of is that the oil companies don't want them here. Since Mobil-Exxon replaced Wal-Mart last year as the number one profit maker in the county the oil companies need not worry. The little bit that we might save is not going to cut into their profits. I've recently heard that the "smartcar" which sells in France for less than $14,000 will be available in this country in 2008 but it will be sold as a status item with a restricted number of just 20,000 so it will probably sell for twice as much over here. If you really want to save then you have to pay! The Toyota Aygo, sold in Europe, carries four people and gets well over 50 mpg but that is not the American way. We want big, bigger, and biggest, and as a result we are going to experience what may be the biggest financial crisis in world history. I found it interesting that the dictionary I used in school in the 1960's doesn't even list the term "Great Depression." Of course, my newer one does.

The Federal Reserve Bank will not allow a recession to happen to let things normalize so a depression far worse than our grandparents knew is just waiting for the right trigger to set it off. I wish I had the ability to convey what I and others see to the citizens of America to prepare them. It is only my opinion but I believe that if you do not have gold, silver, platinum, farmland, or something real other than paper to leave your children they will be among America's new poor, the former Middle Class. Of course, I do not believe that gold alone will solve all our problems. We are going to need God's individual guidance to be where we need to be and when we need to be. Nothing can replace that and even the Bible says that there is a time to buy AND a time to sell.

The night is far gone and the dawn may well bring a financial tsunami of unbelievable proportions, a perfect financial storm that sinks not only our ship of state but others as well. Because of our tremendous trade deficit the United States needs to attract over TWO BILLION dollars in foreign capital each and every day to keep the dollar from falling further in value. These foreign investors are all that is keeping us from experiencing inflation the likes of which native born Americans have never experienced. We have to keep buying imported goods putting more Americans out of work to give foreign nations the money to loan to the US so that the government can pay off the owners of the Federal Reserve Bank and keep operating. I even read that one of the owners of the Federal Reserve Bank gave their employees a half million dollar Christmas bonus last year. I'm not talking about those who work for the Federal Reserve Bank but those who own it. Well, if you own something you can do what you want with it until Congress decides otherwise. However if Asia or Europe start to offer higher interest rates do you really think those investors who buy our bonds to keep us going will not dump them and switch to whoever pays the most?

In the February 2006 issue of a popular investment magazine someone wrote in to ask advice since the $10,000 they had invested 6 years previously in the stock market was only worth $10,500 after 6 years. The person wanted to know if they should sell and put the money in the bank. I had to laugh when I read that the person asking the question was basically told not to worry, that stocks are a long term investment! I have heard all my life that one should never have more money in the stock market than one can afford to lose and yet, most pension plans and 401K plans have all their money in overpriced stocks or in over-inflated real estate trusts or worse yet in derivatives and options. And it is derivatives, fancy investment vehicles used by banks and major corporations to speculate on options upon options that may truly destroy the world economy as they have already destroyed some of the biggest and oldest banks in the world. Chris Laird, editor of the Prudent Squirrel has said as recently as March 2006 that "There is an unprecedented derivatives atom bomb just waiting...the derivatives outstanding according to the Bank of International Settlements (BIS) has grown from roughly $20 trillion of value in the early 1990's to about $300 TRILLION (emphasis mine) now...Warren Buffet has stated that derivatives are weapons of financial mass destruction, due to their incredible leverage. Every year now, we hear of old time banks and new ones going broke in a day or two when a derivatives trade goes south for them...What would happen if there were a real interlinked derivatives domino collapse and not just one affecting two or three

banks only? A financial catastrophe of unimaginable scope...ALL
OF THESE DOMINOES ARE GOING TO CRASH TOGETHER
IN A PERIOD OF LESS THAN A YEAR OF EACH OTHER AND
PERHAPS EVEN WITHIN 3 MONTHS OF EACH OTHER...The issue at hand about the world stock, bond, and real estate bubbles is
that they are all peaking together. They are all at historic highs. And
they are all peaking at the same time in every nation on earth...when
any one of these lets go, it will cascade into the other like markets
around the world. That cascade...will lead to stampedes out of the
other bubble markets as well. Then we will see a massive financial collapse with all the synchronized bubbles world wide, real estate, bonds, stocks collapsing in one fell swoop. THIS WILL NOT
BE JUST A NATIONAL OR REGIONAL COLLAPSE, IT WILL BE A
TOTAL WORLD ECONOMIC COLLAPSE BECAUSE ALL THESE
BUBBLES ARE NOW SYNCHRONIZED (emphasis mine)."

Another person in the same issue of the magazine I mentioned
earlier asked about gold and was told that they should have "5%" of
their holdings in gold as insurance against whatever might happen,
advice that is 50 years old. None of my sources seem to think that
one should have anything less than 25% in gold and some of them
have all their money in cash and gold and farmland. If you ask "why
farmland?" consider that China has 24 percent of the worlds population but only 7 percent of its farmland.

Another way to look at the situation our nation is in: think of
it this way: if you owe too much on your credit cards you will not
be able to buy that new hybrid-SUV you want. Deficits DO matter to individuals so how can they NOT MATTER to our country as
a whole regardless of what anyone says to the contrary. Common
sense isn't too common any more but it will tell you that it is better to be debt free than head over heals in debt. In just one week
in November of 2005, Congress increased the national debt to the
extent of $207 for every non-governmentally employed American
in the country - IN JUST ONE WEEK! From the fall of 2004 to
January 2006 the debt increased at the average rate of 50 BILLION
dollars per month each and every month. No one really knows the
actual amount of the total national debt (all that the government
is responsible for) but figures I have seen range from $200,000 to
$800,000 per taxpayer! According to official government figures
we only went into the hole for $319 BILLION DOLLARS in 2005
but if one included Social Security and Medicare obligations and
were required to figure things the way a business does then the

actual deficit was around THREE THOUSAND FIVE HUNDRED
BILLION DOLLARS or THREE AND A HALF MILLION MILLION
DOLLARS. It is beyond ridiculous in my opinion. When are the foreigners who keep us afloat by buying our bonds and giving us the
money to run everything from the military to social security going
to catch on that having dollars is a losing proposition? Guess what?
They already know! At one recent treasury auction of government
bonds only 21 percent of those available sold. What if no one showed
up to buy them?

The dollar has lost well over 95 percent of its value since the
Congress turned that part of their duties over to the Federal Reserve
Bank in 1913. Spend! Spend! Spend! It's the new American way.
Argentina recently upset the World Bankers by buying 40 tons of
gold to add to their treasury. Russia has decided that they need to
double what they have. The Arab countries have always preferred
gold. In fact in when I was a child the government had to mint special
larger than half dollar sized gold coins that were equal to four British
gold sovereigns in order to buy their oil. Back then they wouldn't
take our paper money. Americans couldn't own such "coins" until 1975 and these gold pieces are, today, valuable collector's items.
I've only seen pictures of them. The people of India have always
used gold and it is the major gift that is given there at weddings and
other occasions. They, too, are buying. The Chinese who save over
30 percent of their income have recently been allowed to buy gold
for the first time since the communists took over in 1949 and they
are even encouraged to do so by their government which realizes
that their paper money is as worthless as everyone else's. Of course
if the Chinese buy all the gold in the world, unlikely as that is, who
do you think will control the world in 25 years or so? There are some
who believe that the gold in Fort Knox has been "loaned out" by
the Federal Reserve Bank and that the country doesn't actually own
what's left. I cannot verify this but find it interesting and possibly
still another reason why gold will soon skyrocket in price, two steps
forward and one step back, until $400 and $500 and $600 gold
will seem like a give-away price. In any event it is still a lot cheaper
than it is going to be in a couple of years. And then there is the
book "Unrestricted War: China's Master Plan to Destroy America"
by People's Liberation Army, Colonels Liang and Xiangsui? Here
is an interesting quote from that book, "Financial war is a form of
nonmilitary warfare which is just as terribly destructive as bloody
wars, but in which no blood is actually shed...when people revise the

history books...the section on financial warfare will command the reader's utmost attention." IT SHOULD BE COMMANDING OUR UTMOST ATTENTION NOW! We are losing in a war that we don't seem to realize is even being fought and Chinese cars will soon be selling in America. Buy one if you like but I'll ride a bicycle before I'll buy a Chinese car unless it gets better than 60 mpg, a car we could make but won't.

It came to light recently that a state-owned business in the United Arab Emirates had purchased the British Company that had been running our shipping operations (ports in the states of New York, New Jersey, Pennsylvania, Maryland, Florida and Louisiana). I guess when you have enough money you can buy almost anything. I don't like the idea that Chinese Communist soldiers are unloading ships in California, and it's bad enough that foreigners own so much of the United States, but turning over the operation of the major east coast seaports of our country over to a foreign government struck me as the most insane thing I had heard in 50 years. I felt I couldn't be alone in feeling like this and was not surprised that 93% of 284,000 respondents in one survey said that they were "very concerned" about port security. Of course when a country owes as great a debt as the United States owes I guess we don't have as much choice or say in the matter. It's all about profit to the big corporations. Funny, I thought "homeland security" was all about our homeland. I have read that we only check 5% of all the containers coming into the country now as it is (over a million a year in Miami alone). Remember the movie, "The Sum of All Fears" with Morgan Freeman? It was about terrorists who brought a nuclear weapon into Baltimore and set it off. It was a very descriptive, violent, and suspenseful movie with even a little humor and I would have said "good" except for its wishy-washy politically correct villain. I think Gov. Robert Ehrlich of Maryland might have seen it. I read that he was upset (as I would be) that he was given no prior warning about this. Baltimore is one of the cities over which he governs. Fortunately enough Americans heard about this in time and the furor created caused the deal to be rescinded. This would never have come about if we were not so greatly in debt and I suspect that it is only going to get worse in the future as more and more of the United States and its business operations, mines and mortgages are purchased by those foreigners who have so many of our dollars and nothing to buy with them because we don't make it anymore. Many hundreds of plants and factories all over the country are already foreign owned. "Owe no man any debt but the debt of love," it says in the Bible, but that's almost un-American these days.

Many Americans still think of the Chinese as poor and, of course, many of them are poor (just as many Americans are poor). However, an example of the new wealth that exists in China might be the life size rose that was available on Valentine's Day, 2006, in Beijing's Guohua Shopping Center. The rose was priced at 199,999 Yuan ($24,691) and was made from over 8 ounces of pure platinum. I could imagine Audrey Hepburn admiring this rose or even Jennifer Love Hewitt, but even I have a hard time picturing a Chinese "Breakfast at Tiffany's."

One wonders if those same Chinese who are interested in "Financial Warfare" are the ones who are trying to develop a bio-bomb, a genetically engineered weapon that would only kill Caucasians. My thought when I first heard about this was "I wonder who they test it on?" Such technology may not be possible for another 20 years but it just shows where the world is heading. "Wars and rumors of wars, famines and epidemics (bird flu or man-made diseases?), earthquakes in many places, and this is not yet the end, just the beginning," said the person almost 2,000 years ago (who became the worlds most influential citizen) when his followers asked what signs would precede the end of the world. If you don't believe that this person became the most influential person to walk the face of the earth then why are books still being written trying to disparage His character and why is Hollywood still making movies trying to reduce His influence? I understand human nature enough not to be surprised when someone like James Frey exaggerates his life story a bit to make it a best seller (A Million Little Pieces) but there are only two reasons why Sony Corporation would make a fictional movie that pretends to be factual and blasphemes the life of Christ; the first is money and the second is that they know they can get away with it. Such a movie about Jews would bring an unbelievably strong protest and if Sony made such a blasphemous movie as The Da Vinci Code about Mohammed, Sony factories and offices around the world would be in danger of being destroyed. It will be interest-ing to see if Sony sales drop even five percent because of this insult to the followers of Jesus. Sony Pictures hired damage control special-ists Sitrick & Co. one of the nations leading public relations firms to handle the controversy about this blasphemous movie and to steer the debate away from what the movie is really all about. I don't plan to destroy my Sony electronic equipment (DVD recorders, CD players, etc.) as a protest but call me old fashioned because you won't find me buying anything with that brand name on it again. Sony knew before they even finished the movie that they were insulting hundreds of millions of Christians, and indeed Christians from the Philippines to the Island of Malta are protesting it. These days, however, it's all about the bottom line and American Christians generally make pretty wimpy protests when they are insulted. I had no doubt that this movie would be produced but I was surprised at the people involved with it. So many in Hollywood (not all of course) seem determined to prove the scripture that "...in the last days men will prefer to believe a lie." (According to the real code discovered in the Bible by brilliant Israeli scientists using supercomputers, the beginning of the "last days" started in the last decade. Whether they will last a generation [what many Christians believe], a century or a millennium is unknown to me). In any event The Da Vinci Code would be better named The Da Vinci Hoax and indeed there is a book by author and journalist Carl Olson and Sandra Miesel with that very name. James Frey knew he was exaggerating to promote his book but if anyone on national TV has been criticizing Dan Brown the author of The Da Vinci Code for passing off his work of fiction as real I must have missed it. Maybe it's not considered a lie if you believe it is true, or if you are criticizing Jesus Christ. I've often thought that the Da Vinci Code was the devils answer to The Bible Code, the latter illuminating truth and the former promoting doubt and disbelief. I'm reminded of the person who heard one of the builders bragging that the Titanic was a ship "that God Himself couldn't sink." Well, some people survived that too!

Hollywood might survive. I've never seen a chart of the earthquake faults in the area and there are undoubtedly faults presently unknown to science that won't be revealed until the "big one" hits. Of course if Hollywood is destroyed in the next five years in the big LA earthquake I'm sure that there will be those who will say that its destruction was just a coincidence. Coincidence, now that's a word and a half!

In the best Star Trek movie, Star Trek IV, Spock is faced with a situation that is beyond his logic. "That's extraordinary!" says Admiral Kirk when Spock tells him that he has to make an unprecedented "guess." "I don't think he understands," Spock says to Dr. McCoy who is standing nearby. "Bones" assures Spock that the captain (excuse me, admiral) is behind him all the way by saying, "He has more confidence in one of your guesses than in most men's facts," or words to that effect. Spock, after being reassured that this is a good thing, replies something like, "Then I will try to make the best guess possible." No one can be absolutely sure about all that I have written about and revealed to you in this book about the coming financial disaster but where I have had to make educated guess's, I too, have tried to make the best guess possible. Unfortunately the coming financial crisis is not a guess. It is inevitable.

What is coming is not likely to be the end of the world but it will surely be the end of the world as we have known it. All I can hope is that you will start thinking about this and then begin in some small or large way to get ready. In April 2006 I received a nice note from a friend in California. Robert wrote, "Back in 2003 when you were writing me on the future value of gold and that I should start to invest in it, I had no idea how important those emails would be to me today. If it were not for you softly prodding me to take an active look at buying gold, I would have missed out on such a grand opportunity that I'd be kicking myself for not listening to you. For this I truly thank you. It took a while, but it finally sunk in and I bought my first lot of gold...I bought when gold was $340/oz. and I don't think we'll ever see...prices like that ever again...From then on it's been an upward trek which stands today at a 70% return on investment. Thank you for not giving up on touting gold to me three years ago!" Such responses as this make all my efforts worthwhile. The more people who are prepared for the coming financial storm the better off I believe society will be and even $600 gold will seem cheap when it is selling for $1600 in the not-to-distant future. I'm certainly not trying to tell people how to get rich. If I knew that I'd be rich myself but I am trying to persuade them to prepare for the greatest disaster this nation has ever faced.

Some people always look to government to bail them out in times of disaster but I do not believe that the government is going to be able to help much in the future. It will barely be able to help itself. Look at the way things fell apart immediately following Hurricane Katrina in September 2005. The citizens of New Orleans have known for centuries that their city was below sea level but they depended on government to keep the sea back. The barrier protecting them from the sea was insufficient and that too has been known about for decades. Monies to strengthen it were spent instead on other "more important" things, like a bridge to a big casino; after all there will always be another day. Remember the police who supposedly abandoned their posts during the hurricane? Well it turns out they were "phantom police" who had never really been hired in the first place. Some $40 million dollars allotted for that purpose was used for other things too. I have also read that the crime rate in New Orleans is one of the highest in the nation. "Politics is God's punishment to mankind for sin" said a holy man over a thousand years ago. Sadly, very little has changed. The citizens of New Orleans discovered the hard way that there will NOT always be another day. Some feel that giving Billions to rebuild New Orleans and not having a strict accounting for the money spent would be just like the monies given to hire the "phantom police." I suppose we can just print more money. The major definition of inflation, by the way, happens to be too much money chasing too few goods, meaning the more we print the more it takes to buy something. The way the government throws money around you would not know that the dollar is dropping in value and that some who have money are fleeing the country trying to preserve what they have.

The citizens of Los Angeles, California, know that a major earthquake, the "big one" is overdue, but few have moved out of harms way. There will always be another day, right? Some say we can't afford to rebuild New Orleans but if we can't afford it how will we ever be able to rebuild Los Angeles in a few years. The death and destruction there will make the death and destruction in New Orleans seem almost insignificant. I will not be surprised to see 25 times as many deaths in LA and the cost of rebuilding Southern California will be incredibly more expensive if it is even done in our lifetime.Some have questioned if it is really the Federal government's responsibility to rebuild. Who will loan us the money to do it? We are already the biggest debtor nation on earth. How can FEMA or anyone even prepare for something the magnitude of the "big one" that is coming to LACALIF in the Hebrew year 5770 (Sept. 2010 - Aug. 2011)? Perhaps FEMA could begin by moving all the trailers that they purchased and did not use for Katrina victims to the Arizona desert, the graveyard of aircraft, or some other GSA site and keep them for the victims of the future LA quake. At least it would be a beginning.

What nations cannot do, individuals can. I know of those who have moved out of Los Angeles County to avoid the coming destruction and there are those who have moved to Australia and Panama and South Africa and at least one I know who has moved to Thailand in the hopes of a more normal life in the future. Who can be sure, though, that another government will be better and another country will be safer. I am convinced that the financial storm that is coming will cover the earth, not just half of it as the storm did in the movie "The Day After Tomorrow."Everyone will be affected. What we all can do, however, if we have a mind to do so, is to not follow the herd that is running off the cliff. Get out of debt, buy only what you need and then buy the best so it will last a long time. All the foreign goods we buy are simply enabling the US Government, addicted to debt like a heroin addict is addicted to drugs, to borrow more of that money from those foreigners and getting us deeper and deeper into debt until we awake from our long sleep and find, as Thomas Jefferson warned us long ago would happen if we borrowed from foreigners, that we are slaves in our own country. A new book is coming out this year entitled "I...SLAVE" by Alex Wallenwein on this very subject.

What our nation may no longer be able to do, we can do.Like marriage, it's an old fashioned idea, but my suggestion would be to get out of debt as fast as you can. Forsake the 52 inch plasma projection TV and the condo in Brussels or Miami. Sell your big overpriced house and build a smaller more efficient one. That's what the founder of Wal-Mart did years ago when his house burned down. Of course he was a billionaire, not someone pretending to be one.

Another suggestion would be not to cancel your vacation, but only take one you can afford. In a few short years the Jones will be envying you as they get ulcers trying to figure out how to pay their over-due bills which have all been converted to variable loans "to save the country" and newer laws forbid them from filing bankruptcy. There is a freedom in being debt free that many will never know. There is a little time left to prepare, a few years I hope. Spend time with your children and loved ones. If they don't live nearby it is unlikely that you will be visiting each other as often in a few years when gas is $7 a gallon and it costs a thousand dollars to fly across the country on an economy flight. In October of 2005, Dr. Jim Willie, statistical analyst in marketing research and retail forecasting said it this way, "It is painfully clear that there is no solution to the US Economic woes...This nation is in big time trouble," Remember the gentleman who said, "Barring a comet hitting the earth, or an alien invasion, it will happen!"

Learn all you can about food storage. Food is more important than gold or silver. If you are fortunate enough to live outside the city you might even be able to have a garden. In a few years you may need it. During World War II they were called Victory Gardens. The vegetables my dad and I planted and ate when I was a youngster were truly healthy and nutritious. Most Americans would be shocked to discover that our vegetables have no where near the vitamin and mineral content they once had. Between 1963 and 2000, according to a comparison of pamphlets put out by the United States Department of Agriculture, spinach has lost 42% of its vitamin C content, 17% of its vitamin A and 10% of its magnesium. Today's spinach wouldn't even satisfy Popeye! During the same period of time corn has lost almost 42% of its vitamin C, 30% of its vitamin A and one third of its calcium. Today's corn has less than 80% of the magnesium that the corn had that we grew and ate back when I was a kid. No one seems willing to say why our vegetables are becoming less nutritious. Thank God for Shaklee's Vita-Lea!

Nearly half the vitamin A and calcium in broccoli have vanished since 1963. Collard greens, good for strengthening the eyes and popular in South Carolina have lost over 60% of their vitamin C, over 40% of their vitamin A, over half of their potassium, 84% of their magnesium as well as over a quarter of their calcium. Whether this is because of washed out soils that are deficient in minerals, genetic manipulation of the plants, cheap non-organic growing methods, or from some other cause, no one seems willing to say. I believe it could be all of the above but that is just my opinion. I am grateful though that I learned about Shaklee's Vita-Lea over 20 years ago and have been taking it twice daily since then. (No, I do not sell it, so I have nothing to gain if you become convinced that what you are getting from your food alone is not sufficient for optimum health or you are using something else - I'm concerned with those who are using common synthetic vitamins or non at all). Vita-Lea is less than 50 cents a day so why not use the best?

In addition to learning about food storage and the use of a good supplement you might talk with any elderly person you can about how they got by in the last depression. Visit a nursing home or an assisted living organization or a veteran's home. The elderly would enjoy the company and most will be happy to share what they remember about times that most of us cannot yet imagine. A single idea could make a world of difference to you and your family in the near future. The time to prepare is now! Do not put it off. Something is better than nothing. If you take this seriously and prepare however seems best to you I feel certain that your life in the not-to-distant future will be better than it otherwise would have been. Don't be fearful. That is counterproductive. The top private experts (neither the ones you see on TV, of course, nor the ones who work for the government) say that at this late date nothing can be done to prevent the financial crisis. If they are not wrong I hope we can at least stall it a little longer. Those who have a personal relationship with God can always pray, for guidance and direction, which He is willing to give to those who sincerely ask! Those who founded this country knew this!

In the classic 1951 science fiction movie, "The Day the Earth Stood Still," the alien Klaatu, told Dr. Barnhardt that he would arrange a demonstration "the day after tomorrow" that would get the world's attention. He used his advanced technology to shut down all the non-essential electricity on the planet for half an hour. Would that such a demonstration could be arranged to get the world's attention to the financial crisis we will all soon be facing. Unfortunately, that which I have shared with you here could well be all the warning you will have. Do not take it lightly. Dum spiro spero*

God who gave us life gave us liberty. And can the
Liberties of a nation be thought secure when we have
Removed their only firm basis, a conviction in the minds
Of the people that these liberties are a gift from God?
- Thomas Jefferson

One of our "liberties" is the freedom to go into debt, at
Least until we are bankrupt. In March of 2006, The Federal
Reserve released it's "Z.1" publication revealing that by the
End of 2005 foreign investors held ELEVEN TRILLION
And 154 BILLION dollars worth of US financial assets.

You have to choose between trusting in the natural
Stability of gold and the natural stability of the honesty
And intelligence of the members of the government.
With due respect to these gentlemen, I advise you, as long
As the capitalist system lasts, to vote for gold.
- George Bernard Shaw

* The State motto of South Carolina. It means "While I breathe, I hope."

27. EPILOGUE: Space and Beyond

It was September of 2003 and the planet Mars, according to the newspapers, was the closest to the planet Earth that it had been in 59,600 years. My lunch hour was at 2 a.m. and instead of eating in the break room I went out to my car and had a sandwich and some hot tea. The classic radio station was off the air until 5 a.m. so I reclined the seat in my Chrysler and was looking at the stars and planets. I have always found the vastness of space fascinating although I have no personal desire to go to the moon or Mars. Just to know that the planet Jupiter has at least one of its many moons covered with moving ice and to imagine as do some of our scientists that there is a real possibility of life of some sort existing in the very deep ocean beneath that ice is quite remarkable. I was thinking of some of the NASA photos I had seen recently that had been taken from the Hubble Space Telescope and marveling at the stars I was observing and thinking of their great distances from each other. Suddenly I just started thanking and praising God for the beauty and the greatness of the galaxy and all of the stars and planets (over a hundred discovered outside our solar system so far) and all the beauty of His marvelous creation. Somewhere in the Bible it says that God dwells in the praises of His people. As I was praising Him, just as suddenly the Spirit of the Lord spoke to my spirit or inner mind and said, "There is much life in the Universe but it is very far away. Because of the age old problem of good versus evil most civilizations that have reached the atomic age have destroyed themselves. The nearest sentient life is over 500 light years. The nearest life technologically equivalent to earth is over 1,000 light years. Mankind will never reach them, but they, may, in the distant future (not in the lifetime of anyone now living) reach earth. They have become masters of space travel."

I was amazed, not so much at what I heard because it all seemed entirely plausible to me, but that I should be told something like this when I was not even an astronaut or connected in any way with our space program or even SETI (the Search for Extra- Terrestrial

Intelligence) for that matter. I was especially grateful to hear what I had been told because I knew that there were others like Isaac Asimov and Carl Sagan who, when they were alive, would have given almost anything to know what I now knew.

Over a thousand light years! In STAR TREK or STAR WARS that's just a few weeks or months or years but in reality it is an incredible distance. Our fastest space vehicle can go something like 60,000 miles per hour with a gravity boost from the moon or another planet but even if a star ship could travel a million miles per hour (making the moon a 15 minute trip and Mars less that a two day one) it would still take that ship going a million miles an hour well over half a million years to go a 1,000 light years! Time and distance have an entirely different framework when you are talking about the cosmos.

The Bible says that God made the world in 6 days, six units of time, where things were done in sequence, man being the most recent. Science agrees with the sequence and with man being the latest creation but the best that science can estimate the age of the earth to be is 4.7 billion years old. According to one translation of the Bible (and a little calculation) the earth is 4,712,727,000 years old. Even if rounded off that is far more accurate than just 4.7 billion years. How did I arrive at that figure? Well, one translation of the Bible says that to God a thousand years is but the blinking of an eye. Since God is omni-present and has no eyes in the human sense the reference must mean the blinking of a human eye.It takes .11 hundreds of a second for the human eye to blink.Six days is to "X" as .11 hundreds of a second is to a thousand years. The result, although the literalists will not accept it, is the much more accurate figure given above.

I noted with interest that no mention was made as to whether humans would be alive on Earth at that distant time when we "may" be visited. I also noted that everything I was told was in the present tense. If this distant civilization a 1,000 plus light years away was technologically similar to earth how could they at the same time have become "masters of space travel" when we haven't done any more than send a few small robots to a few other planets and moons in our own solar system? If it was yet to be how could I have been told that they "have become" masters of space travel? My guess is that from God's point of view, and as the Bible Code seems to point out, the present tense is all that ultimately exists. "Who ever heard of such a thing, a nation born in a day" was quoted by Isaiah thousands of what we call years before May 15, 1948, and yet it was written as if it were yesterday's news.

I include these words here, this fascinating information (to me at least), so that it will be recorded in some future data-base and will not come as a surprise to anyone alive at that time, so that it will not be a surprise any more than the major earthquake in "LACALIF" will be in the Hebrew Year 5770 (our 2010-11). Another thought occurs to me and that is that there must be a realistic propulsion system far beyond anything we have thought of as yet being practical, something that to us today would be akin to science fantasy. May we overcome our impulse towards evil and live long enough to discover it. Praise the Lord!

Printed in the United States
68549LVS00006B/18